MW00904677

the Power *of* Global Capital

NEW INTERNATIONAL RULES ~ NEW GLOBAL RISKS

Michael H. Hyman

THOMSON
™
SOUTH-WESTERN

Australia · Canada · Mexico · Singapore · Spain · United Kingdom · United States

The Power of Global Capital:
New International Rules—New Global Risks
Michael H. Hyman

Vice President/ Editorial Director
Jack Calhoun

Vice President/ Editor-in-Chief
Dave Shaut

Acquisition Editor
Steve Momper

Channel Manager, Retail
Chris McNamee

Channel Manager, Professional
Mark Linton

Production Manager
Tricia Matthews Boies

Production Editor
Elizabeth Lowry

Editorial Associate
Michael Jeffers

Manufacturing Coordinator
Charlene Taylor

Sr. Design Project Manager
Michelle Kunkler

Production Associate
Barbara Evans

Cover Designer
R. Alcorn

Cover Images
© Digital Vision

Compositor
Edgewater Editorial Services

Printer
Phoenix Book Technology
Hagerstown, MD

International Division List

ASIA (Including India):
Thomson Learning
60 Albert Street, #15-01
Albert Complex
Singapore 189969
Tel 65 336-6411
Fax 65 336-7411

LATIN AMERICA:
Thomson Learning
Seneca 53
Colonia Polanco
11560 Mexico, D.F. Mexico
Tel (525) 281-2906
Fax (525) 281-2656

UK/EUROPE/MIDDLE EAST/AFRICA:
Thomson Learning
Berkshire House
168-173 High Holborn
London WC1V 7AA
United Kingdom
Tel 44 (0)20 497-1422
Fax 44 (0)20 497-1426

AUSTRALIA/NEW ZEALAND:
Nelson
102 Dodds Street
South Melbourne
Victoria 3205
Australia
Tel 61 (0)3 9685-4111
Fax 61 (0)3 9685-4199

CANADA:
Nelson
1120 Birchmount Road
Toronto, Ontario
Canada M1K 5G4
Tel (416) 752-9100
Fax (416) 752-8102

SPAIN (includes Portugal):
Paraninfo
Calle Magallanes 25
28015 Madrid
España
Tel 34 (0)91 446-3350
Fax 34 (0)91 445-6218

For My Children
Aidan, Erin, and Benjamin

CONTENTS

ABOUT THE AUTHOR

Trained as a global economist at The London School of Economics, **Michael H. Hyman** is the founder of Global Financial Risk Solutions, a financial engineering company. He is also founder and past CEO of GH Asset Management (GHAM), a specialist global fixed interest asset management company with $1.2 billion of assets under management. GHAM's performance record as ranked by PIPER Performance Measurement Services was consistently in the top one percentile and rated number one in 1992, 1993, 1995, and 1996.

Mr. Hyman also founded a specialist software development company for financial services companies. He is self-taught in computer systems and information networks.

He was educated at the University of Miami, Florida, The London School of Economics, and London Business School. Mr. Hyman is a member of a number of professional organizations, including the Global Association of Risk Professionals (GARP), the Association of Investment Management and Research (AIMR), International Society of Financial Analysts (ISFA), the Young Presidents Organization (YPO), and the European Institutional Investor Institute.

Mr. Hyman has also published numerous articles in professional journals and is a frequent lecturer.

PREFACE

WHERE THIS BOOK STARTED

We have a much better understanding of the science of economics today than we did 20 years ago when I started my career in London. I wanted a global financial education—and not because I thought I would make more money. Instead, I believed my generation was too concerned with American financial issues and too little concerned with the global financial markets.

Since Americans are taught very little about global finance—multicurrency investment environments—I decided to head off to the financial frontier in London on a one-way $99 Laker Airways ticket. I arrived in the middle of Wimbledon fortnight in June 1981.

As an American living in London, I was privileged to receive an extraordinary education on the global capital markets, and to witness a sensational change from numerous domestic or sometimes regional economies and capital markets, to a single financial capital market that was global. I watched a critical evolution in the way fiscal and monetary decision-makers in many countries apply similar policies that cross most political barriers. Investment strategies, business strategies, and economic policies became more interdependent across the globe. More importantly, isolationism became unthinkable, an almost impossible policy for any nation to apply effectively.

Syndicated columnist and professor Thomas Sowell talks about law and order having an enormous impact on economic development:

> *"Law and order directly foster investment. Britain's pioneering role as the first industrial nation was greatly facilitated by its ability to raise large amounts of capital cheaply, under stable laws securing property. People are willing to invest their savings in long-term ventures, including those which build railroads, canals, and other infrastructure, at very low rates of return because (1) those returns were protected by property laws and (2) the stability of the currency meant that even modest rates of return would not be wiped out by inflation. By contrast, countries in which investments are jeopardized by extortion of officials and the confiscation ("nationalization") by governments find it difficult to attract needed capital, either from their own people or from foreign investors, except for projects having high and quick return."[1]*

In other words, the power of the global capital markets is enforcing international rules in the new global economy.

I was extremely fortunate to have worked for David Strecker, my first boss at Cigna International Investment Advisors. The Cigna Corporation, headquartered in Philadelphia, was created in 1982-83, when the Insurance Company of North America (INA), a property and casualty insurance company, merged with Connecticut General. Cigna International Investment Advisors served as the global investment operation for all Cigna assets held outside the United States. Our offices were at Finsbury Circus, one of the most beautiful spots in London. There I learned more in three months, starting as the lowest of the low trainees on the Cigna trading desk, than I had in four years of undergraduate business school and year of postgraduate economic studies. Among the people I learned from in 1983, were four portfolio managers, three fixed-income managers, and a lone equity manager.

Normally, property and casualty insurance companies invest their funds in liquid short-term investments, with the best investment vehicle being government bonds, because of the risk that an insurance claim drawing on the funds may arise at any moment. Conversely, life insurance companies, health insurance, and pension funds can invest in longer-term investments like equities because their insurance claims or retirement payouts are spread with some predictability over many years.

I was invited to begin by learning about government debt instruments along with the futures and options instruments ("derivative instruments") on these underlying cash securities. As a student, I had always thought that equity markets were "where it's at." However, I soon learned that the government bond markets were not only more interesting but a lot more fun. I learned about the government debt markets and was able to observe the flow of capital through domestic and international markets. While learning how to contend with foreign exchange and investment restrictions, it seemed to me that the only truly free capital markets at that time were the United States and the United Kingdom—the founding members of the notorious Anglo-Saxon capitalist system.

In the industrial world, the late 1970s and early 1980s were the days of double-digit inflation, high unemployment, and no economic growth, particularly in the United States, where the situation was termed "stagflation." I read books like *America's Competitive Edge* by Richard Bolling and John Bowles, which forecast economic and financial downfall unless the American people became more like the Japanese,[2] and *Paper Money,*[3] in which Adam Smith predicted that Saudi Arabian princes would control American lives because they controlled the supply and price of oil. The discipline of economics was studying the economics of inflation, while financial reading centered on how to account and invest in a high inflationary environment. Monetary assets like interest-bearing money market and bond market instruments were frowned upon for not protecting investors from the effects of inflation. And for light reading, I turned to a good Paul Erdman book like *The Crash of '79* or *The Last Days of America,*[4] which filled in missing pieces of the financial catastrophe jigsaw.

Pretty discouraging stuff for a guy who wanted a career in global finance, on the whole. What was I thinking?

The education I acquired along with the economic and financial events that occurred at the outset of my career made a huge impact on my thinking, and my investment philosophy. To a considerable extent, the experience in the early 1980s still shapes my risk-return profile and my investment horizons.

Along the way I studied global relationships and real interest rates. Real interest rates are the real return on savings, calculated by subtracting the rate of inflation from the normal interest rate. Managing sovereign debt instruments throughout the globe, with all the multicurrency capital markets risks that responsibility carries, has given me a unique insight into the global economy, where economic and financial convergence, the creation of wealth, and the emergence of a global middle class, have been among the many positive results. The Keynesian view that federal government should intervene to influence the direction of business cycles and a commitment to large central government have slowly given way to free-market forces.

The fall of the Iron Curtain created a huge marketplace for hundreds of millions of people. In other parts of the world, billions of consumers now have, or want, the right to choose how to manage their assets and provide a better future for their children. I believe a new economy has emerged—not the Internet economy that has been getting so much attention, but one that is all about free market forces, the right to choose on a global scale. The new international rules are about free, transparent capital markets, with a commitment to economic growth with low inflation.

The creation of wealth and of a global middle class are a product of the free-market system. The new economy means free movement of capital throughout the globe, which carries with it the implication of global capital markets financing the global economy. Financial and economic convergence is building to be a very powerful force that will cause large-scale structural change in the way of life and standards of living throughout the world.

The numerous economic and financial crises over the past 20 years have tested the global financial system and human resolves time after time. The system is much better for it. We tend to overlook the positive aspects of our significant accomplishments, but the global economic and financial systems are much stronger and more flexible today than ever before, paving the way to our new economy.

THE HISTORICAL PERSPECTIVE

We learn through mistakes we hope never to make again. The trend toward a global economy has been slowed by its string of human judgment errors over the past 20 years. Yet economic and financial relationships and interrelationships are much stronger, in spite of us.

The first economic and financial crisis I faced professionally was the Latin American debt crisis. At its outset in 1982, I did not understand the problem or its ramifications. Granted, at this point in the early 1980s, I was still a lowly trainee on Cigna's trading desk.

I remember trying to understand what was going on in Latin America. It seemed so complicated. But as I gained more experience in global capital markets, I began to comprehend the crisis and its implications, its causes and effects. Latin American countries, especially Brazil, Argentina, and Mexico, had borrowed huge sums of U.S. dollars from American banking institutions. These loans for long-term infrastructure projects were made in the 1970s, when real interest rates were low. Then three unrelated but self-fulfilling events took place:

1. Both nominal and real interest rates soared. The nominal rate is the face value, the published interest rate and yield on a bond. The real interest rate is found by deducting the inflation rate from the nominal interest rate. The real interest rate on foreign debt for Latin America increased from -10 percent from 1973 through 1978 to +8 percent from 1979 to 1982. Interest payments rose to unforeseen levels, making it virtually impossible for these countries to service their debt.

2. The world entered a recession in 1982, reducing growth in trade, and thus reducing the amounts of goods Latin American countries exported to industrial nations like the United States. This further compounded the difficulties they were having in servicing their interest payments.

3. Oil prices, which had risen in the early 1970s, followed declines in other commodity prices by falling in the early 1980s, complicating the already difficult terms of trade for commodity exporters.

In all these situations, the borrowers were not totally to blame. The moneylenders should have demonstrated more foresight about the risks these countries were undertaking.

During this time, the volatility (the percent change in price) in the government bond markets was enormous. (Volatility is defined as percent change in price.) The U.S. Federal Reserve Board raised the Federal Funds interest rate (the rate the Federal Reserve Bank charges commercial banks) from 5.5 percent in 1977 to 16.3 percent by 1981.[5] In October 1979, Federal Reserve Chairman Paul Volcker announced that the Fed would manage monetary policy by targeting money supply, not interest rates. Official interest rates soared in response to the increasing supply of money, adding more inflationary pressure. Consumer price inflation rose from 6.4 percent in 1977 to 13.5 percent in 1980.[6]

As real interest rates rose, the U.S. dollar rose as well, from a trade-weighted index level of 100 in 1980 to 142 by 1985,[7] adding even heavier burdens on Latin American countries trying to repay their dollar-denominated debts. A vicious circle set in. As terms of trade deteriorated, debt-to-export ratios rose, and Latin American economies slumped, causing the flight of capital from them into safe haven U.S. dollars. The result was the worst recession on the South American continent since the 1930s.

It was an incredible time, and a sad time, but I learned so much from it!

The Latin American debt crisis dragged on for nearly 10 years.[8] Some of the financial consequences are still felt today. Every aspect of this affair in our economic history had a significant impact on my own economic and financial thinking. In a later chapter, I will address this debt crisis further. I mention it now only to point up how it affected my understanding of the global debt markets, and the part it played in furthering global economic and financial convergence.

This point leads neatly to the following observation: The root of the problem was a dramatic shift in global real interest rates. There were numerous other events, related and unrelated, but the bottom line that ultimately caused the Latin American debt crisis to occur was a shift in value-for-money. When I say "value-for-money," I refer to the real savings rate, the real interest rate. Real value is what the investor receives from an investment in any interest-bearing instrument.

Every country, not just in Latin America, was uniquely affected by the global recession of the early 1980s. Amid all the anxiety, there were some crazy trading days. On January 28, 1985, a day I'll talk about in more detail shortly, the United Kingdom was being battered economically and the trade-weighted index for sterling had been in free fall throughout the month (a currency trade-weighted index measures the value of a currency in relation to its trading partners or another weighted average index). Sterling was considered a petrocurrency at that time because the U.K. had substantial tax receipts from North Sea oil. As the price of oil fell, the value of sterling fell with it.

That day I was working at Cigna International Investment Advisors directly with my boss, David Strecker. One of our investments was restricted to U.K. gilt-edge securities. The U.K. gilt market was the United Kingdom's government bond market, the highest quality investment in the U.K. In a market where market makers were called jobbers, the gilt jobbers wore top hat and tails on the floor of the London Stock Exchange. But our Cigna offices on the top floor of a building at Finsbury Circus were being redesigned and we had no heat. On January 28, 1985, as I struggled to save the portfolio, snow was actually falling through a hole in the roof onto my desk, where I was working not in top hat and tails like the people I had on the phones but in ski clothes. It was bloody freezing!

Where a currency is considered a petrocurrency, if the price of oil falls, tax revenues fall. Since the price of a barrel of oil is denominated in U.S. dollars, the U.K. authorities are exposed to currency risk when they convert their U.S. dollar tax revenues into U.K. sterling. For example, the price of a barrel of oil is $20. Say the exchange rate between the United Kingdom and the United States is $1.50 for every £1. When we convert the $20 barrel of oil into sterling, it is £13.33. If the exchange rate falls to $1.25 to the £1, then the sterling value rises to £16—but if the exchange rate rises to $1.75, then the sterling value falls to £11.42.

Clearly this kind of currency volatility can have a dramatic impact on the national revenues. When commodity prices fall, the desired effect, all things being equal, is to see the price of the currency fall in order to maintain level tax revenues.

In 1984, the global economic environment was awful. In the United Kingdom, oil prices fell throughout the year as the demand for oil dropped in response to stagnating economic growth globally, but in the United States, the dollar was rising because of the growth starting as a result of President Reagan's economic policies. With interest rates and real interest rates high, the U.S. dollar rose higher every month in 1984 and into 1985. For me, 1984 was a very difficult trading year—though not my worst, which was to come in 1994. But it was bad enough that I was quite anxious as we entered the New Year.

David Strecker had expected the Bank of England to raise interest rates early in the new year, so it came as no surprise when on January 11, 1985, interest rates (base rates) rose from 9.5 percent to 10.5 percent. The effect was minimal. We were not heavily invested in long-dated gilts, and sterling's value was nearing a bottom—or so we thought. But on January 14, a single day, interest rates skyrocketed by 2.5 percent, to 12 percent.

David left for meetings in Philadelphia just before the rise in base rates, because we thought we had a pretty clear view that perhaps the worst was over. Still, David wanted me to be careful.

No chance.

On January 28, sterling was in free fall again, and the price of those gilt-edged securities U.K. government bonds followed, because the fall in the value of sterling value, while good for oil revenues, was bad for inflation. As the currency devalued, the Bank of England would want to raise interest rates to fight off the inflationary pressures caused by the falling value of sterling. Calling the markets chaotic would be an understatement.

David, still in Philadelphia, and I talked to each other throughout the morning. He did not want me to preempt the next market move because he could see the possibility that gilt yields could rise one or two percentage points. Finally, at noon, the Bank of England raised interest rates by another 2 percent, to 14 percent. To add to the anxiety, the bank suspended trading in the gilt market for 45 minutes, an historic first.

David went nuts. We had to do some quick sums on what we thought was an appropriate yield for gilt-edged securities before the market reopened 45 minutes later. At first David suggested I do nothing until the market reopened, and then suddenly the telephone went dead. Great! I was truly on my own. There was not a telephone in the office that worked, except direct lines to our brokers.

I couldn't talk to my boss, and there was no market in U.K. gilt-edged bonds. Period. No prices. No liquidity. No way to judge the value of U.K. government debt. Basically, I had to decide whether 14 percent would be enough to maintain the value of sterling— enough to keep inflation in check and start heading it lower.

According to my sums, the market represented a screaming buy—sterling's value against the dollar was so low, nearly $1.10, and the U.K. government could expect a huge oil tax windfall. When the market reopened, I quickly bought long-dated maturities at the best price, just as I would instruct our brokers to pay the best available price for certain stocks. David was back on the telephone shortly after the market reopened, but I had already committed the best part of our cash reserves into the gilt market. He wanted to know if I had bought, sold. "What did you do?"

Before I could speak, he said, "I hope you didn't buy anything."

But in the next breath, after I told him how the market reopened, he said, "I'll kill you if you didn't buy anything."

After I explained, we shared a sigh of relief.

The U.S. dollar and U.K. sterling crisis would not end for another month but we had grabbed the best yields of that time. At the end of that particular telephone conversation, though there was actually snow accumulating on my desk, I felt it was a great day!

David Strecker was one of the great characters in my life. He was emotional, volatile, one of the best market traders and strategists I have ever met. Sadly, he died in 1998. I miss him.

The lessons I learned during the period I spent with him have stayed with me. Financial risks are often unknown or hidden deep beneath the surface of any financial transaction. The responsibility for a crisis rests with both lender and borrower, so it is not just for the borrower to resolve. Fiscal and economic structural reforms are also vital to attract and maintain investor confidence. Credibility is everything for fiscal and monetary policymakers. They cannot bluff their way out of economic problems or simply wish them away because that will only prolong or intensify the problems.

Just ask the Japanese, who since 1992 have been working hard to avoid the right decision for resolving their domestic debt crisis. They have been just hoping for the best, believing their financial and economic problems could not get worse, and then watching that happen.

Another important lesson is that government intervention in foreign exchange markets in an attempt to alter the direction of the price of a currency, will not change the ultimate direction or trend. Currency price movements reflect the underlying attractiveness of a country's investment environment. To reverse an adverse trend in the movement of currency prices policymakers must restructure whatever it is in their economy or financial system that is creating the currency weakness.

A variety of agreements among the G-7 governments have tried to influence the trend in currency price movements. Early on, in the Plaza Agreement on September 21, 1985, G-5 ministers agreed to work together to encourage "an orderly appreciation of the main non-dollar currencies against the dollar."[8] Then came the Louvre Accord on February 22, 1987, which attempted to stabilize exchange rates.[9] No matter how elegant the location of a meeting and the agreement produced there, central governments no longer have the financial buying power (unless they print money) to intervene to alter the trend of currency price movements. In a following chapter, I will discuss some of my later experiences with liquidity crises. The point I want to make here is that government intervention cannot be depended on to solve economic problems in the new economy.

I decided to leave Cigna International Investment Advisors in early July 1985 to start my own investment/money management firm. I felt I had to hurry to get myself set up, because London's "Big Bang" was due to take place in October 1986. "Big Bang" would deregulate London's capital market, reduce stockbroker commissions, and the London Stock Exchange, as a marketplace, would cease to exist. All transactions would take place over the telephone. I could no longer place an order with a broker to be executed on the floor of the Exchange. Also, foreign banking institutions were allowed to enter the market, owning and controlling British institutions. The times were exciting at the height of Prime Minister Margaret Thatcher's reign at Number 10, Downing Street.

A unique feature of the United Kingdom's investment management industry is that it was dominated by London merchant banks and Scottish investment houses. The prevailing philosophy was to invest in real rather than monetary assets. The reason was that inflation historically had plagued the U.K. economy through poor fiscal policy management. Investors like pension funds therefore invested 90 percent of their assets in equities rather than monetary assets like U.K. government bonds.

I thought I could see a need for a specialist/boutique global bond (fixed income) asset management firm in London. Since London was, as it remains, the center of the financial world, it made sense to set up there rather than return to the United States. U.K. pension funds were investing only 3 percent of their assets in fixed income instruments. I thought that had to change. In the United States and continental Europe, assets allocated to fixed income (monetary) instruments ranged from 40 to 60 percent, but invested only in domestic markets. Europe's regulations did not allow investment in nondomestic markets because European governments needed their pension fund investment pool to help finance annual fiscal deficits. I thought that would change, too.

In the United States, the question was always, why invest overseas? That was something else that would change. I also thought there would be a need to manage fixed income assets better, given the array of financial risks that accompany global investments. Fixed income investing was poor, and global fixed income was nonexistent. I wanted to change that as well.

As a specialist in a very narrow field within the investment management industry, I needed a diversity of clients as well as of investment products and services. As a businessman, I had to protect my business's revenue stream by diversifying clients by type and industry sector, find products with single currency return on investment or derived from a particular fixed interest market.

In other words, I did not want to be held hostage to any single interest rate cycle. I also had to offer my clients a global fixed income service, with the associated financial risks customized to individual client requirements. I was going to compete head-to-head with every major and minor investment bank, investment manager, and commercial bank—people and companies with historic pedigrees, long track records, and billions of dollars of assets under management. I was 26 years old, with no pedigree, and a foreigner in London.

Obviously, I had to offer performance and service at a much higher professional level than my competitors. I spent six months building my firm from back to front. I installed all the computer software systems needed to support, account, value, settle, and administer every permutation of global transaction I might encounter on behalf of my clients.

So I wrote my first software system, which became a business in itself. By 1994 "Portfolio Manager" would ultimately become PM4, the fourth generation system. I opened my doors for business in August 1986, without a single client, two months before "Big Bang." My money management firm would change its name and become GH Asset Management in January 1988.

Every day I was making 100 to 200 cold telephone calls, trying to find institutional clients. It worked. By 1993 I had over $1 billion of assets under management, representing 42 blue-chip clients from several countries with a variety of investment briefs. Our performance track record (except for 1994—I will tell you why it was such a bad year in a later chapter) was ranked in the top 1 percent over a 10-year period. The firm was ranked the number one global bond money manager in 1992, 1993, 1995, and 1996 by the Piper performance measurement service published by *Pensions & Investments* in the United States. This was a privileged time for me. I learned an enormous amount over 16 years, until the firm was sold in 1997. My investment philosophy was unique then, and I believe it still is today.

I viewed the global capital market as a single marketplace. When diversifying from a single currency to a multicurrency environment, I never believed in diversification for its own sake. I always sought to invest in the real value offered by each country. The government debt markets are the purest, most creditworthy investments, and their value determines value in every asset class throughout the world.

The new economic battleground, however, will be between two competing capitalist systems (1) market-oriented systems and (2) bank-oriented systems. Market-oriented systems are the Anglo-Saxon systems like the United Kingdom and the United States. Bank-oriented systems are also known as centralist capitalism, Rhineland system, or control capitalism. I talk about these two systems throughout the book.

The evolution of these two financial systems determines how capital is disbursed to business and entrepreneurs, through market-oriented channels such as the stock market or channeled through large banking institutions. These two capitalist systems define the way central government behaves fiscally and the way it intervenes in its own country. Are individuals well placed and enabled to participate in the markets? Or does central government know better than the individual and control the economy in a structured and interventionist way?

The process that created these two distinctly different capitalist systems began in 1719-1720 because of two interlinked events (1) the South Sea Bubble in England spurred the development of the stock market-oriented Anglo-Saxon model and (2) the Mississippi Bubble in France led to the bank-oriented continental European model.[10] These two financial and economic capitalist systems affect how financial institutions and the capital markets operate, and they affect corporate governance by the way information and resources are allocated to the marketplace. Each system affects how banks compete in each country and how government responds to financial and economic crises. In a nutshell, the underlying philosophy springs from the answer to a basic question: Who knows better, the individual or central government?

ENDNOTES

[1] Sowell, Thomas. 1994. *Race and Culture: A World View.* New York: Basic Books, pages 121-22.

[2] Bolling, Richard, and John Bowles. 1981. *America's Competitive Edge.* New York: McGraw-Hill.

[3] Smith, Adam. 1981. *Paper Money.* New York: Summit.

[4] Erdman, Paul. 1976. *The Crash of '79.* 1983. *The Last Days of America.* New York: Simon & Schuster.

[5] *International Finance Statistics.* 1997. Washington, D.C.: International Monetary Fund.

[6] Ibid.

[7] Source: DataStream.

[8] Barclay's Capital, *Global Currency Digest,* December 1997.

[9] Ibid.

[10] Allen, F., and D. Gale. 2000. *Comparing Financial Systems.* Cambridge, MA: MIT, page 29.

Chapter 1
INTRODUCTION

Over the past 20 years, market-driven forces have carved out new international rules for economic and financial behavior that affect everyone from political leaders to institutional investors to individuals. These new rules shaped by market forces cannot be politically dictated, as the reader will learn. They will affect our individual standards of living, our quality of life, and our ability to create wealth.

The new international rules will force political leaders to behave prudently in fiscal and monetary affairs, or global capital will not be attracted into their countries. An ability to compete for global capital is paramount. International as well as domestic investment affects every national society.

Assuming that investors and voters have a much better understanding of the science of economics today than they used to have, it is clear that the greatest threat to wealth and standards of living is inflation. Global investors have forced policy makers to recognize that they must manage inflationary pressures and expectations through inflation-targeting monetary policy accompanied by balancing fiscal budgets. This is not just a priority but an immediate necessity. Financial forces, the weight of huge amounts of global capital, have driven financial convergence throughout the industrial, developing, and emerging markets, causing a convergence in real interest rates and the real cost for money.

Each country today must compete globally to perpetuate the cycle for creating and improving the investment environment. One good way to compete is to reduce corporate and individual tax rates and enhance the ability of the private sector to invest with the entrepreneurial spirit necessary in today's modern global economy.

This book analyzes and offers an opinion about the new economic battleground, brought on by the free movement of capital and encouraged by the fall of the Soviet Union, where corporatist capitalism and Anglo-Saxon capitalism are battling it out. It will point up the difference between centrally controlled capitalism versus free-market capitalism. The reader will learn about the newest global financial risk—a return to post-World War II economic policies. The swing will require businesspeople and investors to concentrate on reducing those financial risks, which are not core to their business model or investment strategy.

For investors, both personal professional, and for all business decision makers, this book provides an understanding of the new rules governing and shaping the behavior of global investment flows. Readers learn about the risks affecting our global financial system, helping them to anticipate changes and potential financial difficulties, and craft solutions.

The reader will also learn about the macroeconomic and microeconomic indicators that may trigger financial and economic catastrophes. The new international rules—and the new global financial risks—are evolving every year. To prepare for and manage this global economic and financial change means to understand what is changing and why.

The book uses recent economic and financial events as lessons in economic and financial turmoil. The lessons demonstrate how the international financial rules may affect the European Monetary Union, the Japanese economic depression, the fall of Russia and its subsequent rise, the U.S. budget debate, and the aftermath of September 11th, which leads in turn to an examination of Islamic economies. We will also look at other events and policies affecting the global financial community in the new century.

Chapter 2
GLOBAL CAPITAL MARKETS

SOVEREIGN INDEBTEDNESS

The competition for global capital intensified as sovereign/government indebtedness proliferated in the 1970s and 1980s. At that time, governments were borrowing huge sums of money to finance fiscal excesses. Every year a government announces its fiscal budget. In the 1970s, 1980s, and early 1990s, the annual fiscal deficits rose substantially, so every government issued huge amounts of bonds to finance the annual budget deficit. The growth in global sovereign indebtedness during this period played a significant role in the way investment capital now flows throughout the world.

One of the key reasons for the Latin American debt crisis was the proliferation of debt issued by the United States government, which caused real interest rates to rise, crowding out domestic U.S. and foreign borrowers. The real cost of money rises and falls from the moves and changes in Federal funds interest rates. The real interest rate on Federal funds had risen from -4.0 percent in 1975 to +6.0 percent by 1983. The United States' annual federal deficit had also risen, from $40 billion in 1979-80 to $207 billion by 1983. In 1992 alone, it grew by $300 billion. The United States went from budget balance in 1970 to bloating deficits until 1996, when the United States started once again balancing its annual budget after total outstanding debt issued by the U.S. Treasury had reached $6.74 trillion.[1] U.S. government debt crowded out private sector borrowers, which caused the cost of money to rise as real interest rates rose. The U.S. dollar strengthened because investors rushed to buy high U.S. real interest rates, which offered better returns on investment than could be obtained in any other country. This led to capital flight from Latin American countries, among others.

The dollar weakened from 1970 until 1980 when it strengthened before weakening again in 1987. Real interest rates rose appreciably in 1979 and then dropped during the late 1980s. They were the driving force for appreciation of the dollar in 1980 and its weakness in the late 1980s.

While deficits were rising in the United States, the Europeans were expanding their welfare states through their own deficit spending. Outstanding government indebtedness there grew appreciably from 1980 until 1997. G-10[2] total government indebtedness rose from $1.8 trillion in 1984 to a whopping $7.9 trillion in 1997, seriously crowding out business investment. In the United States, government indebtedness grew far faster than gross domestic product, causing a further displacement of business investment capital.

When comparing industrial country indebtedness with emerging market external debts, it is no wonder that the world constantly encounters liquidity crises. Growth in the external national debt of emerging market countries as a percentage of their gross domestic product (GPD) was often more than 100 percent. Fortunately, since the early 1990s, emerging market countries have been reducing their total external indebtedness. What also happened as a result of the growth of external national debt for emerging market countries was the unfortunate timing for Latin American countries that borrowed U.S. dollars and invested them in what were intended to be long-term projects.

The need to attract foreign investors to help finance fiscal deficits also affected government balance sheets. These countries had also been incurring current account and trade deficits, which meant that greater proportions of their GDP were held overseas. The United States itself showed an incredible reversal in fortune as its net foreign assets fell from a $269 billion surplus in 1981 to a huge $781 billion liability by 1994—11 percent of its GDP.

One of the consequences of all the economic turmoil is that the global middle class taxpayers throughout the civilized world have a much greater understanding of the science of economics. We have made a number of structural changes leading to greater economic prosperity today. The globalization of the financial markets is partly due to the competition for global capital by sovereign borrowers. I would argue that, had it not been for our past difficulties, interest rate and yield convergence would probably not have occurred. As Joseph Stiglitz pointed out:

> *"The debt crisis of the 1980s shifted the focus to macroeconomics. Countries could not grow if governments did not provide a stable macroeconomic environment. Governments needed to hold their expenditures to their revenues and to limit the expansion of the money supply."*[3]

Around the world government fiscal and monetary policymaking has dramatically changed because of our past mistakes, creating a future for further global financial and economic convergence and a new economy.

GLOBAL CONVERGENCE

This section is not about globalization, but about global economic and financial convergence. Global economic and financial convergence is driven by investor appetite—the weight of capital. The weight of capital is the enormous pool of investment funds from mutual funds, pension funds, investment banks, institutional investor groups, insurance companies, and other types of pooled investment vehicles throughout the world. The International Monetary Fund (IMF) reported in 'International Capital Markets' (August 2001):

> *"Between 1990 and 1998, assets managed by mature market institutional investors more than doubled to over $30 trillion, about equal to world gross domestic product (GDP). Amid widespread capital account liberalization and increased reliance on securities markets, these investable funds became increasingly responsive to changing opportunities and risks in a widening set*

of regions and countries. Because global investment portfolios are large, pro-
portionally small portfolio adjustments can be associated with large and
volatile swings in capital flows. . . .[Portfolio] adjustments sometimes had a
significant impact on financial conditions in the recipient countries both when
they flowed in and when they flowed out. This underscores the powerful impact
that portfolio rebalancing by global investors can have on the volume, pricing,
and direction of international capital flows and on conditions in both domestic
and international markets."

Economic and financial convergence has created new international rules of financial and economic behavior. The weight of global capital dictates how these rules shape and govern the international capital markets and the way government officials govern their countries.

What are the rules? One is that central governments must no longer attempt to influence the business cycle, but must allow market forces to create and distribute wealth. This policy is necessary to create a new generation of entrepreneurs and greater financial and economic interrelationships than ever before.

The difficulty for the future of global economic convergence is striking the right balance between public and private finance. The rise of government indebtedness throughout the world could not continue forever. Eventually it would end—probably in tears, as it did in many countries. However, the cost of government is enormous today, and the lessons of the past should have taught us that we have to live within our means, publicly as well as privately.

Global economic and financial convergence is the result of the fall in the real cost of global capital, the competition for global capital, the creation of wealth, and the creation and expansion of a global middle class. Global convergence has been aided by a growing consensus among societies about the economic way of life they seek.

One of the more noticeable features of global financial convergence has been the fall in the real cost of capital. The competition for global capital has created an environment where each country must constantly and consistently improve its macroeconomy to ensure that it maintains investor confidence and attracts new investors to finance its programs.

The competition for capital intensified in 1987 when the United States became a net debtor. The ability to maintain a financial and economic competitive edge rests not only on the credibility of a country's macroeconomic policies, but also (and perhaps just as important) on real interest rates—the real cost of money. The benefit to the global economy is greater prudence in fiscal policy management along with anti-inflationary monetary policies.

We know the greatest threat to a country's standard of living and the creation of wealth is inflation. Policymakers do not have to be rocket scientists to work out the key policies necessary at any given time to keep inflation low. We are now enjoying the lowest real costs for capital in several decades. As confidence and credibility in macroeconomic policies grow, we see increases in foreign investment in emerging markets and cross-border transactions in bonds and equities. As the freedom of movement of capital increases and grows, so too does cross-boarder investment.

Whether a country is industrial, developing, or emerging, if it offers the global investment community a stable macroeconomic environment, it will be rewarded with lower real
interest rates, stimulating further economic growth. A 2001 article in *The Economist* stated:

> *"Foreign investment is 'globalization' in its most potent form. Economists and*
> *governments agree these days on the crucial importance of foreign direct*
> *investment. They see it both as global market's 'seal of approval' on a coun-*
> *try's policies and prospects, and as a force, especially in developing countries,*
> *for far-reaching economic change."*[4]

History will show that the reverse crowding-out effect (curtailment of public finance
in favor of private finance) will have had a greater and more positive impact on economic growth than the Keynesian-style policies governments used in the 1960s and 1970s that
attempted to control the pace of the business cycle. The key central conclusion of
Keynesian Economics is that there is no strong automatic tendency for the level of output
and employment in the economy to move toward the full employment level. This contrast
with the conclusion in Neoclassical Economics that adjustment in prices and interest rates
would tend to produce full employment in the economy. In summary, Keynes wanted government to intervene using budget deficits to stimulate economic growth and therefore
create more jobs.

Another very important aspect of global economic convergence is that it is not a zero
sum game. There does not have to be a loser for every winner. Everyone can be a winner.

In the 1970s, a private group called the Trilateral Commission was dedicated to the
view that U.S. relations with Western Europe and Japan provide the strategic core for both
global stability and progress. The thinking of the Trilateral Commission was to encourage
both closer and more cooperative relations between the United States, Europe, and Japan
and to investment in employing people in the developing countries. The theory was that
ultimately a middle-class society would emerge in those countries, and those people
would want the same middle-class amenities as people in industrial countries, creating
further consumer demand for goods and services from the industrial countries.

There is much discussion of the state of the global economy today in the public and
academic press. Some commentators suggest that today's economy was a result or by-
product of the fall of socialism and the demise of the Iron Curtain and of Soviet-styled
economic systems. Others suggest that the success of the Asian tiger countries made the
global economy successful. A third reason cited for the success of the global economy is
the technological advances in computers, telecommunications, and transportation.

All of these have had their effects, but I believe the biggest influence on the success
of our global economy today is the structural and market reforms that are leading the way
for private investment and smaller federal governments, leading ultimately to economic
growth characterized by low inflation. Advances in technology supporting global market
reforms helped reduced the cost of capital, which in turn facilitated the restructuring of
centrally planned economies and fueled the economic growth in Asia. The reformation of
the global capital markets has been itself a catalyst to ensure discipline in economics and
finance disciplines and reinforce policy decisions.

As standards of living rise, objectives and priorities in life change. Western society
wants to encourage better education, health services, and democratic development

throughout the world, because that will lead to a general improvement in global standards of living. The IMF predicts that developing countries will eventually control a radically greater share in world output than industrial countries. The baseline is 1984, when developing countries represented 34 percent of total world output, industrial countries 57 percent, and countries in transition 9 percent. By 2004, the proportions of global output are expected to be (1) developing countries 48 percent, (2) industrial countries 47 percent, and (3) countries in transition 5 percent.[5] That's what I call global economic convergence!

CREATION OF WEALTH

The creation of wealth throughout the world, as I have witnessed myself since the start of my career in 1982, represents a significant by-product of the new economy. Here I am referring not to all the new names on the *Forbes* richest people list, but to improvements in basic standards of living and creation of wealth in pension funds, mutual funds, and hedge funds (defined later in this chapter). Wealth is also being created by the use of derivative instruments linked by a 24-hour global marketplace. All of these activities within our global economy represent an awesome and powerful force—the weight of capital, "the market."

In my experiences in the global government debt markets, I observed larger and larger capital flows over time throughout those markets, particularly as capital began to move increasingly faster as competition for global capital and investors intensified. In fact, looking at the historic data, the greatest *real* wealth was created during the periods of falling inflation in the early 1990s and over the past five years. The rise in the value of world equity markets from $7.8 trillion in 1987 to $36.0 trillion by 1999—an enormous increase in valuation—occurred while government indebtedness was decreasing. Reverse crowding-out stimulated far greater business investment throughout the latter half of the 1990s.

As macroeconomies stabilized, there were large-scale shifts in the way households saved money, creating huge savings pools of pension and mutual funds. By 2030, 50 percent of the people in Germany will be over 65, as will be 45 percent of the people in Japan, 39 percent in the United Kingdom, and 38 percent in the United States.[6] One of the more interesting challenges that lie ahead for us, therefore, is provisioning for individual retirement. Many governments, among them Germany, have pay-as-you-go pension schemes. The government uses tax receipts to pay pensioners. These countries have no reserves set aside for future pension payments. It is hardly necessary to do the arithmetic to realize that when Germany has only 50 percent of its population (those aged 15 to 64) paying taxes, funding retirements will be a serious and major problem.

On the opposite side of the spectrum, Singapore forces its workers to save 40 percent of their salaries in a state fund. The pension fund industry will grow more rapidly in the future, as more governments follow this lead and require their citizens to provide for themselves in retirement rather than relying on the state.

The top 200 fund sponsors alone represent $3.1 trillion in assets.[7] It is estimated that in 2000 all pension fund assets in the top 15 world economies reached $12 trillion.[8] According to Watson Wyatt, the world's top 300 investment managers control $21.2 trillion.[9] A 1996 *Economist* article defined an institutional investor as:

". . . simply vast pools of money. Pension funds, mutual funds, and insurance companies control a huge chunk of most rich countries' retirement savings and other wealth. They are like trustees of the world's capital. By allocating it— shifting into and out of shares and bonds, countries and currencies—they move markets, hold governments to account, sire new companies and dispatch moribund ones. Understanding how they do this is essential to grasping the capitalist system." [10]

At the end of 1997, the U.S. banking system held $4.7 trillion of assets and the U.S. mutual fund industry held $4.5 trillion.[11] From 1970 to 1997, the number of U.S. mutual funds rose from 361 to almost 6,500 and the number of individual accounts rose from 11 million to 151 million. In 1985, the top ten U.S. institutional investors managed $969 billion. A decade later the top ten managed over $2.4 trillion.[12] The mutual fund sector grew at an annual rate of 20 percent from 1997 to 2201.[13] European mutual funds have only $1.5 trillion, although savings flows are picking up, becoming as large as those in the United States in 1997.[14] The steady flow into mutual funds and other institutional investors have driven equity markets to record levels and provided the finance for America's entrepreneurs. The total net private capital inflow to emerging markets has grown from $45.7 billion in 1990 to $274.8 billion in 1997, falling to $149.0 billion in 1998, $163.6 billion in 1999 rising to $216.4 billion in 2000.

The 1990s also saw the rise in private capital funds, called hedge funds or, in the words of Prime Minister Mahathir Mohamad of Malaysia, the "highwaymen of the global economy." The actual term "hedge fund" dates from the 1950s. It is defined as an absolute return vehicle, managed by entrepreneurial managers, which aims to achieve the highest return for a given level of risk. The value of hedge funds has risen from under $10 billion in 1990 to $650 billion by the end of 2001 and the number of hedge funds has grown from approximately 50 to 2,200. Inflows in 2001 were $8.4 billion in the first half and $6.9 billion in the third quarter of 2001, much of it after September 11th.

Hedge funds, which seem to make the headlines for all the wrong reasons, are a force to be reckoned with. Those hedge funds discussed in the media, like Long Term Capital, represent the minority, the macro hedge funds. All hedge funds use leverage for capital, but macro funds take positions in currencies, usually unhedged, based on the macroeconomic fundamentals of countries. When the economic fundamentals are inconsistent with the value of the currency, the funds take a bet on devaluation, usually selling the currency short.[15]

Derivative instruments are one of the more dangerous tools to aid wealth creation. The word "derivative" means something that is copied or adapted from something else, in this case a specific equity instrument or a stock market index. Derivative instruments are futures and options contracts. They can be based on interest rates, currency prices, government bonds, or all sorts of commodities from gold and oil to pork bellies and oranges. In today's marketplace, all types of institutions use derivative instruments, which are traded on an exchange or, if created by a specific investment bank, over the counter. Because of widespread acceptance and participation in these instruments, they have themselves become "commoditized." They can be created quickly in standard form by a given trading desk for a particular client, without extensive negotiation or complex documentation.[16]

The use of derivative instruments implies the use of margin or leverage, when a very small amount of money relative to the actual price of the instrument is required to be deposited with the exchange or the investment bank. The initial margin deposit exposes the investor to a risk that is no more than 1 or 2 percent of the nominal value of the derivative instrument.

A U.S. Treasury bond contract traded on the Chicago Board of Trade (CBOT) requires an initial margin deposit of $1,000 or $2,000 on a nominal $100,000 investment in U.S. Treasury bonds.

The nominal amounts of derivative instruments outstanding have rocketed and will continue to do so. The incredible increase in derivative instrument usage, rising from $729.9 billion in 1987 to $4.3 trillion in 2000, is based on the immense rise in interest rate and currency swaps, used mainly by institutions like banks to better manage their balance sheet assets and liabilities. These enormous sums of money add to the weight of global capital traded around the world. The weight of capital ("the market") governs the new international rules, and political policymakers must ensure that they keep the hand that feeds them (or their economies) happy. Herein lies the heart of the new economy.

THE GLOBAL ECONOMY

The global economy and its financial markets are very different places today than they were 20 years ago. Some might argue that all this change is bad because it has made us greedy. Not so, to my mind. On a macroeconomic level, all the changes taking place have overall made our lives better and more prosperous, demanding that individuals become more self-sufficient, not greedy, selfish, or self-centered.

Big federal governments cannot afford the costs of a modern society, particularly as life expectancies increase and populations grow. Federal deficit spending will ultimately force future generations to repay all that indebtedness. At some point, this will reduce their standards of living, because taxes will have to rise if the debt is to be retired. Monetary policymakers must be free of political shackles to ensure low inflation and economic stability.

We are creating a pretty good economic system for ourselves—one that provides not only the necessary safety nets, but, more important, private-sector shock absorbers to take the pressure off governments. Nothing ever stands still in life, though, and neither should the system we create for ourselves. However, we will enjoy greater global economic and financial interrelationships that will cross all cultural barriers.

Unfortunately, experts on this subject paint a gloomy picture of the difficulty we face in accomplishing this feat, which has not been done for thousands of years.

Without doubt, freedom is the surest path to prosperity. The more free a country's economy, the stronger its currency, because it attracts more foreign as well as domestic investment. The United States, for instance, has an expected inflow from foreign direct investment of $236.2 billion, representing 26.6 percent of the world's foreign capital inflows.[17] The British are second, with 9.3 percent of the world's inflows. This proves that the Anglo-Saxon economies offer the freest economies, unlike centralist capitalist systems, as I will demonstrate throughout the book.

The freedom of movement of capital throughout the world is here to stay. The private pools of capital will be the strongest force in our new economy.

ENDNOTES

[1] "Size and Structure of the World Bond Market: 1997: U.S. Dollar Nominal Value Outstanding." Global Securities Research & Economics Group, International Fixed Income Research, Merrill Lynch, Pierce, Fenner & Smith Inc.

[2] The Group of Ten Countries (G-10) are the United States, Canada, United Kingdom, Germany, France, Italy, Japan, Belgium, Sweden, and The Netherlands.

[3] Stiglitz, J. E. "The Agenda for Development in the Twenty-First Century." Annual World Bank Conference on Development Economics 1997, The World Bank, 1998.

[4] "The Cutting Edge." *The Economist,* February 14, 2001, page 80.

[5] "World Economic Outlook," October 1995, page 45. Washington, D.C.: International Monetary Fund.

[5] "Compelling Reasons to Save." *The Economist,* April 11, 1998, page 74.

[6] Source: *Pension and Investments,* January 26, 1998, page 20.

[7] Riley, B. "Mind the Pension Gap." *Financial Times,* May 20, 1998.

[8] Source: *Pensions & Investments,* July 7, 1997.

[9] "Compelling Reasons to Save." *The Economist,* April 11, 1998.

[10] Hale, D. "Our Mutual Revolution." *Financial Times,* April 22, 1998.

[11] "International Capital Markets." Box 5, *Trends in Fund Management.* Washington D.C.: IMF, November 1997, page 120.

[12] Hale, D. "Our Mutual Revolution." *Financial Times,* April 22, 1998.

[13] Ibid.

[14] Ibid.

[15] Banks, E. 1994. *Complex Derivatives.* Chicago: Probus Publishing, page 3.

[16] "The Cutting Edge." *The Economist,* February 14, 2001, page 80.

Chapter 3
FISCAL POLICYMAKING

After World War II new economic thinking began to consider the type and size of central governments. What is the right size for a central government—big? small? somewhere in between? It should have been an easy enough problem to solve.

The difficulties start, however, when special interest groups want spending for this program and that project. The members of special interest groups may want something, but as taxpayers they do not want their taxes raised to pay for expenditures on other people's special projects. That is why, to ensure they get elected, politicians promise the impossible—more spending but no new taxes.

When times get tough, leaders make a phone call to their friendly central bank manager and ask that the bank print more money—or, better yet, borrow hard currency from another country. Or issue more domestic debt. Ultimately, someone has to pay for any deficit, but not the politicians of the day—tomorrow, it will be someone else's problem. It seems a never-ending, self-perpetuating cycle. The bigger the government is, the bigger we need to be, and, of course, the bigger we must become. But to be bigger means controlling more and more of citizens' lives. Keynesian economics, whether it is called socialism or by any other label, means big federal government.

THE PAST

Fiscal policy and the size and role of central government have evolved dramatically over the past 20 years. How to achieve higher rates of economic growth, to increase the standard of living for every nation's citizens, is at the heart of the fiscal policy debate. Let me give you a brief summary of our immediate economic history to demonstrate the long distance we have traveled over a relatively short period of time.

Since 1980 there has been built a global consensus about the size and role of central government, part of the improvement in our understanding of the social science of economics that I mentioned earlier. In this chapter, I discuss how the new understanding led to the global consensus, and what that means for fiscal policymaking.

National self-determination, the decision of a nation about its social identity, is not the issue, but the way we financially manage our own federal government and ourselves has had to change in a big way, as has the financial management of other countries around the world. The debate is no longer about left or right, communism versus capitalism, but about right and wrong fiscal policies.

In the beginning, on the left side of the debate was Karl Marx, who predicted in the 19th century that capitalism would collapse from its own internal contradictions, especially the tendency to exploit the working classes. Marxism led to what came to be called communism in the Soviet Union, China, and Eastern Europe. The economic system of communism was one in which the means of production, most capital and land, were state-owned and national economies were centrally planned.[1]

On the opposite side of the ring, wearing the blue trunks, are the classical economic thinkers, led by Adam Smith. In 1776 he argued that workers and producers, interested only in helping themselves and their families, were the basis for the success of the economy. The public interest would be best promoted by individuals pursuing their own self-interest.[2]

My studies of many economic scholars from the past showed me how the circumstances of their time had a huge impact on their economic thinking. Their beliefs reflected a different era—the Great Depression in the 1930s and the difficulties facing the global economic system after World War II. Keynesian economics was born during this period.

For those readers whose memory of Economics 101 has faded, Keynesian economics was the body of thought developed by John Maynard Keynes, culminating in the publication of his *The General Theory of Employment, Interest and Money* in 1936. Its central theme was that a capitalist system does not automatically tend toward full-employment equilibrium. According to Keynes, the use and expansion of fiscal or monetary policies could raise aggregate demand and could cure the resulting "underemployment equilibrium."[3] In essence, Keynes believed that an economy's output and employment did not automatically return or move to full employment. Therefore, Keynes advocated active government policy could be effective in managing the economy—deficit spending. Underemployment equilibrium is a fancy description for the unemployed that should be employed. The use of fiscal policy to help the underemployed meant increasing public expenditure and ultimately the fiscal deficit. Easing monetary policy meant printing money.

I do not think Keynes ever contemplated that the fiscal or monetary stimulus would last in some cases for a decade or more. However, Keynes did offer fiscal policymakers an alternative to the classical thinking of Adam Smith and the socialist thinking of Marx. Keynes insisted that appropriate fiscal policies were required to deal with extended periods of unemployment. Because prices and wages within the economy were inflexible, he said, the central government had to adopt fiscal policies to smooth out the market clearing process and ensure that supply and demand are equalized.

Keynes's theories led industrial governments to intervene in the business cycle in an effort to protect labor markets. The creation of the welfare state in the United States in the 1960s was based on Keynesian thinking. As fiscal policies expanded and budget deficits rose, government became bloated. During the 1970s European governments attempted to protect and maintain employment levels by protecting industry from market forces. Federal governments employed measures that subsidized employers to keep staff on their payrolls. For instance, instead of creating policies to make the labor market more flexible, European governments introduced measures to reduce working hours rather than increase unemployment lines. Central governments intervened to protect industries like steel, shipbuilding, aerospace, airlines, and automobiles. They also established counter-cyclical public sector employment programs.

Fiscal policymakers raised taxes and incurred huge fiscal deficits to afford their policies. Central government got bigger and bigger, perpetuating itself at its newly swollen size. By the end of the 1970s, the crowding-out effect had become an obvious problem, a phenomenon I observed firsthand, especially when I was starting my career in London. The proportion of taxes received as a percentage of gross domestic product (GDP) increased throughout the 1970s and 1980s (Table 3.1).

Table 3.1: Taxes Received to GDP (as a percentage)[4]

	1974	1976	1978	1980	1982	1984	1986	1988
France	10.3	13.6	17.0	21.6	27.7	33.3	36.4	38.5
Germany	n/a	n/a	n/a	21.8	24.8	26.0	27.1	27.3
Italy	2.1	3.5	5.5	8.5	14.3	18.1	21.7	25.0
Japan	5.5	7.0	8.0	9.7	10.7	11.1	11.7	13.3
Netherlands	24.5	31.1	35.6	40.6	46.3	48.0	49.0	48.6
Sweden	7.8	11.7	14.6	16.7	21.4	26.0	30.4	36.3
United Kingdom	7.5	11.0	13.0	19.3	25.0	26.8	28.6	31.5
United States	7.3	7.8	9.5	12.2	14.9	14.7	15.8	17.3

Table 3.1: Taxes Received to GDP (as a percentage), *Cont'd*

	1990	1992	1994	1996	1997	1998	1999	2000
France	40.5	42.9	44.3	42.0	43.0	n/a	n/a	n/a
Germany	28.8	34.5	37.8	32.0	32.0	32.0	n/a	n/a
Italy	31.0	37.4	35.4	39.4	33.0	31.0	35.0	34.0
Japan	14.4	22.0	n/a	n/a	n/a	n/a	n/a	n/a
Netherlands	47.0	51.8	52.7	28.0	29.0	29.0	30.0	30.0
Sweden	44.2	47.4	43.3	34.0	36.0	38.0	38.0	40.0
United Kingdom	36.8	40.0	41.3	37.0	38.0	40.0	40.0	n/a
United States	18.9	19.7	21.5	24.0	20.0	20.0	21.0	22.0

This table shows the increase in tax revenues received by fiscal authorities as greater proportions of their GDP are consumed by taxation. The United States, for example, saw a rise in tax revenues from 7.3 percent of its GDP in 1974 to 24 percent by 1996, though the percentage fell back to 20 percent in 2000. This table also demonstrates the crowding-out of business and private monies from the private sector to central government.

A number of interesting conclusions can be drawn from Table 3.1. First, those countries that financed welfare state programs by accruing deficits are being penalized for past fiscal laxity as the tax burden has risen sharply to pay off past deficit spending. A real challenge for these countries will be paying down their outstanding debts in a deflationary or low inflationary economic environment. In the past, countries with high budget deficits relied on inflation (believe it or not) to devalue their indebtedness (and that of future generations of deficit spenders). Table 3.1 also shows that the prudence of those who kept the burden of taxation on society steady are better equipped to face any fiscal challenges today or national emergencies tomorrow—an issue that has surfaced since September 11, 2001.

Another interesting statistic is that annual interest payments as a proportion of GDP trebled throughout the 1980s and early 1990s. This trend is particularly evident with countries that have used deficit spending to finance their welfare states. And please do not forget the statistics from Chapter 2, which showed the amount of government bonds outstanding as a percentage of GDP rising in line with interest payments. Some of these countries have over-leveraged themselves—borrowed too much money—for the next several generations. When tax burdens are high as the penalty for a country having a mountain of outstanding debt, the ability of policymakers to reduce taxes relative to other countries becomes difficult. Creating an environment to compete and to offer attractive financial packages to international companies becomes an almost insurmountable task for government officials.

Of course, miracles can happen. In a recent book on Keynesian economics, Will Hutton[5] tries to revive Keynesian ideas for Britain and Europe. He sees the state as the employer of last resort in order to smooth the economic cycle and argues that a return to full employment must include active management policies based on demand and redistribution of income through the tax system. He wants higher taxes to pay for greater public spending.

What I find scary about this kind of thinking was anticipated in *The European*[6] (a good weekly newspaper that went out of business in 1998):

> *"Europe is central to Hutton's Keynesian model. One of his central points is that Keynesian demand management policies, coupled with social-democratic industrial organization and employment practices, can work—provided the global financial markets do not interfere with them."*

Is Hutton kidding? No industrial country can keep out the global capital markets, even if it wanted to. I do not know of any *trying* to keep global capital out. Even North Korea has to find money from somewhere. Keynesian policy, or the abuse of Keynesian ideas, has done enough damage. Perhaps it is time to find another way. In the meantime, from the perspective of being globally competitive, those countries with low debt-to-GDP levels will be able to reduce their tax burdens and offer more competitive packages and economic prospects for the future.

A few years ago, the headline on the front page of the *International Herald Tribune* (March 16, 1999) read:

> *"Sweden Pays the Price of High Taxes."*

Sweden cannot attract executives nor keep those it has because of the tax burden from fiscal excesses of past years. Sweden is only one of many countries that will have difficulty doing business in the new economy. And the competitive gap between low- and high-debtor countries will widen.

As I examined interest payable in relation to GDP, I could feel myself cringe at the Swedish number in the 1990s—which has led to the country's difficulties today. During a severe economic recession from 1991 to 1993, the Swedish government had to incur greater indebtedness as their GDP shrank and interest payments soared to 7.7 percent of GDP. That is a huge amount. Clearly, the cost of funding in real terms has outstripped many countries' real economic GDP growth rate. This is a very important point. When a government issues debt—government bonds, for example—with a coupon payment of 8 percent per annum, and the annual inflation rate is rising at 3 percent, the real rate of return is 5 percent—5 percentage points above the inflation rate. That means that if an economy's GDP is growing at an annual rate of 4 percent with an inflation rate of 3 percent, real economic growth is rising by only 1 percent.

This relationship between government debt, real yields, and an economy's real economic growth rate is very important to me. Why? Because if a government is offering me, an investor, a risk-free investment of 5 percent over inflation when the economy is only earning 1 percent, monetary assets are offering me a better value than the real economy. This was the position the Swedes were creating for themselves. On the other hand, countries that have observed fiscal prudence are able to help themselves further by funding their debt at much lower real interest rates.

It is interesting to see the effect Prime Minister John Major's policies had on the United Kingdom during its recession in 1991 and 1992. Interest payable rose from 3 percent of GDP in 1993 to 4.8 percent by 1996. At the same time, taxes were increased to the point where their share to GDP grew from 28.6 percent in 1986 (the heart of Mrs. Thatcher's years) to 41.3 percent in 1994. Italy has an uphill struggle to overcome its annual interest payments, which rose to 14.4 percent of GDP in 1996. With taxes as a percentage of GDP nearing 40 percent (see Table 3.1), the future for the Italian people will be difficult, as they try to repay outstanding debt while their tax burden is increasing.

Increases in the size and scale of central government can also be seen through the trebling of the proportion of central government expenditures relative to GDP over the past 15 years. The bottom line is that central governments have been getting bigger and bigger, representing a huge contribution to the GDP. This trend cannot continue forever. The larger the role federal governments played in their contribution to GDP, the more difficult and the greater the cost to reverse this trend. Removing the fiscal stimulus coupled with debt repayments during periods of budget surplus could be an enormous economic contracting force until the reverse crowding-out effect begins to stimulate the private sector. A reverse crowding-out effect occurs when a decrease in government expenditures increases private investment. As we saw in Table 3.1, growing proportions of the wealth of the industrial countries wealth is being tied up by central government. The risk of excessive central public sector borrowing is also perpetuated by the rising cost of money when the central government crowds out the private sector. For example, if a country's public debt were 100 percent of GDP, a one percentage point increase in the interest rate on public debt is equivalent to 1 percent of GDP primary fiscal slippage[7]—an additional 1 percent of GDP must be used on additional interest expense.

Using fiscal deficits to finance economic growth and influence the state of the business cycle is very risky for future generations. The active use of fiscal policy either to stabilize difficulties or to influence the business cycle has declined substantially since the 1980s. Economic theorists have defined economic growth as an ability to explain observed patterns in long-term trends in output across countries, while the business cycle instead is affected by the factors that cause output to fluctuate around long-term trends.[8] Fiscal policy expansion, causing further budget deficits that increase the structural deficit, has declined considerably over the past five years. The size and scope of indebtedness has forced governments on both left and right to consolidate their fiscal policies and budget positions.

The International Monetary Fund (IMF) suggests that the turnaround in fiscal policies is due to several factors. First, experience suggests that active fiscal policymaking has not only failed to stabilize economic activity but in fact has itself been destabilizing. Budget deficits and total outstanding debt have been ratcheting higher. Politicians have not reduced spending; nor have they raised taxes enough to prevent debts from rising. Second, increased awareness of the distorting effects of high tax rates and the advantages for private sector decision-making of a stable tax structure have forced politicians to think twice about raising taxes in pursuit of fiscal stabilization.[9]

Flexibility—being prepared for a rainy day—is one of the keys to fiscal policymaking, as we learned from the events of September 11, 2001. Fiscal policy must be prepared for new financial realities, because neither voters nor global investors will tolerate politicians introducing new spending programs simply from a desire for historic reverence.

Our job is to keep the pressure on political leaders to ensure that our future is not sold short. The sustainability of expansionary fiscal policy is difficult to predict. An effort must be made to protect future generations while reducing the high levels of outstanding debt-to-GDP. The financial and economic costs of September 11th are a case in point. The United States was able to respond to the crisis because of the sound fiscal position it had taken over the previous five years. Without the annual fiscal surplus and the amount of total debt-to-GDP paid down, it is unlikely that fiscal policy makers would have been able to respond effectively to the events of September 11th. The lesson: During periods of normality, pay down debt so the country will have more flexibility in times of crisis.

Interest payments as a proportion of annual federal expenditure has been rising dramatically in the U.S., which means that a greater proportion of our tax dollars is being used to pay interest and coupon payments on government debt securities. The true test for any politician is when unforeseen events, opportunities, and difficulties present themselves. The real problem is the short memory of the electorate, who forget the success of previous policies. The electorate cares about today, and its tax burden tomorrow. Its members could have cared less about President George Bush's success during the Gulf War. It's the economy, stupid! He raised taxes for the benefit of future generations, he compromised with his opponents, and the voters threw him out of office.

The German electorate has quickly forgotten the tremendous opportunity of German reunification in 1989 and, more important, the fact that it was able to absorb another economy even at the wrong price and still achieve European Monetary Union convergence criteria objectives in 1997. This was an amazing feat—but unemployment is at 11 percent. It's the economy, stupid! The German economic machine rose to the occasion to achieve reunification. Fiscal and monetary policies were coordinated (most of the time) and the country was able to respond to the economic and financial costs of reunification. Yet, on October 17, 1998 the German voters dismissed Chancellor Helmut Kohl, after more than a decade of service and achievement.

This is one reason, I believe, that politicians will find it more difficult to make correct economic decisions—as market forces and the electorate want instantaneous positive results from policy. Politicians manage a portfolio of fiscal policy investments, both long-term and short-term. Like other portfolio managers, they have their good investments and their bad ones. But voters measure their policy successes at every election.

Having been manager of a global sovereign-debt portfolio, I understand their predicament. The one thing I have learned about the fiscal and monetary policy machinery is that politicians know no more than I do. Even if they are privy to vital information earlier than I would be, they will want me—their potential investor—to know and understand their policies as soon as possible. This is transparency. They must behave just as I do when I present my investment strategies, philosophies, and processes to potential investors, demonstrating how an investment portfolio will get from A to return-on-investment B. But in the new economy, when markets will reflect and respond more swiftly, even instantly, to all available information, fiscal policymakers will pay heavily for poor results. The financial power of the new international marketplace rules.

If my investment strategies do not work and I under perform, I can expect to be fired. Similarly, the politician can expect to be voted out of office. If I deliver five wonderful years of portfolio performance and one bad year, I expect to lose clients. Similarly, politicians can expect to lose votes.

Fiscal transparency also refers to the ability to review the results instantly, mine and the politicians. It's a reality. Get used to it!

Look at Italy. As of March 2002, Prime Minister Silvio Berlusconi's coalition represented the 56th postwar Italian government. That's an average of a new government almost every year. The weakness resulting from years of coalition governments can be seen in the national accounts. Fiscal policy has nowhere to go, because Italian politicians of all stripes created such a huge debt mountain for themselves. They used future generations of income to finance their economic achievements today. Italians now use 25 percent of their total federal budget on interest payments.

When I look at the figures for the United States, though the picture is a bit better, my blood pressure still rises. Sixteen percent—16 cents of every dollar—of my federal tax payment each year is used to pay interest on debt securities from a previous generation! I do not want my children to be in this situation. Though the United States has one of the smallest federal governments of all our trading partners, which is good, we must work harder to ensure the best return for every penny of tax revenue. The United States has no national healthcare system and is spending $250 billion, but interest payments primarily the result of previous budget deficits, averaged 7 percent of federal spending in the late 1960s and 1970s. But due to the large budget deficits that began in the 1980s that share quickly doubled to 15 percent of federal government spending in 1989. When the federal budget went into surplus (I hope nobody blinked when it happened), interest payments were dropping until September 11, 2001 to approximately 11 percent of federal spending—soon to rise again.

Fiscal policies have always reflected the social climate of a particular period. Today is no different. The pattern of federal expenditure in the United States reflects the needs of society, but times are changing and the future will require that individuals be more self-sufficient rather than relying on big federal government. The debate in the United States over budget deficit spending has been a leading issue since I was able to vote. It seemed to intensify in the 1980s during the George Bush administration as the harsh realities of the previous 10 years of high deficit spending caught up with the electorate. The Reagan administration's policy of supply-side economics (a term coined when President Reagan came into power in 1981) forced the U.S. economy into its deepest recession as tight credit caused interest rates to rise to 20 percent in the effort to defeat inflationary forces. At the same time, fiscal policymakers cut taxes, causing the budget deficit to balloon. Inflation was indeed tamed by monetary policy from 13 percent in 1980 to 3.2 percent in 1983.

Although they were perhaps ill timed, supply-side economic policies certainly proved, along with Prime Minister's Thatcher's policies in the United Kingdom, that government was too big. The supply-side thinking of the 1980s paved the way for the Clinton administration's economic experiment in 1993. Clinton wanted to resolve the unemployment problem in the United States and reduce the budget deficit by both raising taxes and reducing public expenditure. The gamble would create a reverse crowding-out effect, reducing real interest rates and stimulating job growth through private investment.

As I said in Chapter 2, in the 1970s and 1980s increased government expenditure and budget deficits caused a decrease in private investment—the crowding-out effect. The public sector was winning over the private sector in the fight over a limited supply of funds.

Reverse crowding-out occurs when the public sector reduces its expenditure, balances its annual fiscal budget, private investment is back in the game. In 1993 the unemployment rate was 7 percent and the fiscal deficit represented 4.9 percent of GDP. Let there be no doubt that the economic recovery was well under way in the Bush administration then, which allowed the Clinton administration to gamble on reducing federal expenditure, raising taxes, and balancing the annual budget. Because the gamble worked, it helped herald the new global economy of smaller central governments and steady non-inflationary growth while reducing indebtedness. I will discuss later how the capital markets, specifically the government bond market, can serve as a check and balance on policymakers today and into the future, saving taxpayers billions of dollars a year.

Professor Joseph Stiglitz nicely summarized the economic impact of deficit reduction policies on economic growth in his 1997 textbook, *Economics*. Stiglitz argues:

> *"Deficit reduction is supposed to make room for more private investment, and thus stimulate economic growth. Consider the consequences of reducing a $150 billion deficit to zero. The lower deficit will reduce interest rates, increase investment, cut down foreign borrowing, and perhaps lower domestic savings."*

He concludes by quantifying the reverse crowding-out effect:

> *". . . reducing the deficit by $150 billion increases investment by $75 billion,"* which equates to an increase in economic *"output by 0.1 percent. This may seem like a small number, but accumulated over a large number of years, it can make a large difference."*[10]

The United States has proven that a policy of reducing the fiscal deficit can stimulate economic growth and create jobs.

The best action we can take for future generations is to pay off our debts. Reducing annual interest payments and total outstanding debt will create more prosperity than cutting taxes and increasing expenditure. Once debt has been reduced, tax and expenditure policies can be reviewed. As debt is paid down, the reverse crowding-out effect will allow greater amounts of private capital to be injected and invested in the U.S. economy. Reducing outstanding debt and annual interest payments perpetuates budget surpluses, providing greater opportunity to extend the life span of fiscal responsibility.

Central governments rarely spend or invest money wisely, certainly not as carefully as we individuals try to look after ourselves.

CHANGE—LIVING WITHIN OUR MEANS

Macroeconomic policymakers must be credible. Fiscal policy must be clear, concise, and understandable, and policymakers have to deliver what they promise. Capital markets will not be fooled, because actions speak louder than words.

Government debt markets react to fiscal policy the way stock markets react to corporate earnings. During periods of uncertainty, government yields rise and prices fall. The credibility of a country's fiscal policy and the policymakers themselves is a major factor in fund managers decisions about asset allocations to countries and the extent of risk within these countries throughout the period to bond maturity. The credibility of elected officials who must follow through with unpopular fiscal policies during periods of severe social unrest is a major issue. Not all political leaders can stand up to the stress. However, the longer economic and financial reforms take to implement, the more dramatic their later impact.

Reforming the fiscal policymaking process and reducing the size of central government are essential to attract investment from both home and abroad. Providing a prudent fiscal policy for future generations must therefore be a priority today. Life does not, and never will, sit still. Continuing improvement in fiscal policymaking will be rewarded, but investors in government bonds will punish any perceived negative deviations in policy.

The competition to improve national fiscal position is fierce today. The emergence of Eastern and Central European countries whose fiscal positions are improving and are vastly better than their Western European counterparts will ensure vigorous and lively competition for investors throughout Europe.

In a large majority of investment situations, a manager determining how much of a government bond portfolio to invest in a given country is likely to give preference to those countries where there is clear direction in fiscal policy. Another important factor is the transparency of the economic and financial system. Certainly, transparency gave me a greater sense of control over investment positions.

A good example takes me back 15 years to when we invested in the Australian government bond market. Australia released economic statistics, such as the consumer price inflation index, quarterly, not monthly as did the United States and other industrial countries. This lack of transparency in economic and financial statistics did not generate a great deal of confidence. Australia was a very difficult country in which to invest. Moreover, the logistics of actually investing in Australia were extremely difficult. At one stage, I went ballistic when our custodian bank in Australia lost the certificates representing our investments "down under."

A custodian bank actually effects the transaction, which means the bank transfers the required cash to buy the bonds and gets in return the physical government bond certificate. The United Kingdom and the United States release these kinds of statistics weekly and monthly, and settlement of government debt securities by computer happens the next business day. I might believe—as indeed I did—that Australian government debt offered the best value in the world, but because I was unable to monitor the Australian government's policy progress (the lack of transparency) and was also unable to monitor the investment (problems with the custodian bank), I chose to limit my exposure.

The Conservative Party in the United Kingdom, led by Margaret Thatcher, swept into power in 1979. When Mrs. Thatcher became Prime Minister of Great Britain and before her first budget announcement in 1979, she said:

> *"Our general approach was well known. Firm control of the money supply was necessary to bring down inflation. Cuts in public expenditure and borrowing were needed to lift the burden on the wealth-creating private sector. Lower income tax, combined with a shift from taxation on earnings to taxation on spending, would increase incentives."[11]*

Her government's fiscal policy—reducing the size of central government, reducing taxes, and tighter monetary policies—was targeted at reducing inflation by controlling the supply of money.

When fiscal policymakers stray beyond the understanding of either the electorate or the government bond market, they are punished by the markets first and the voters second. Two good examples are the successors to President Reagan and Prime Minister Thatcher (1) President George H. Bush raised taxes and (2) Prime Minister John Major not only raised taxes, he allowed the budget deficit to soar—the ultimate sin—and thereby created a boom-bust economic cycle.

Fiscal policy convergence was also exhibited by the developing countries. The International Monetary Fund's May 1993 *World Economic Outlook* states that:

> *"There is considerable evidence that macroeconomic stability and the removal of structural distortions boost growth by improving the incentives to save and invest, as well as the efficiency of investment. As more countries implement stabilization and structural reform policies, the medium-term prospects for the developing world appear brighter than they have been for some time."[12]*

As an institutional investor, I know the key to fiscal policy is affordability, credibility, and ultimately its ability to achieve stated policy objectives. I would never pass judgment on how societies spend their national budgets. Each nation has its own unique social needs and desired standards of living. I do, however, pass judgment on a country's national *accounts*. We could adopt the view of Samuel Brittan, who in 1997 remarked in the *Financial Times:*

> *"The state is not very good at promoting either happiness or economic growth, both of which it should leave to citizens to pursue in their own way."[13]*

Yet European fiscal policymakers are struggling to strike the right balance between market forces and social safety nets. This is one of the reasons I do not think the European Monetary Union can work over the longer term, because each European country has the unique characteristics, and they are reflected in its fiscal policymaking.

The key to keeping investors attracted to a particular country is greater fiscal transparency—the more the better, there is never enough. Fiscal transparency is absolutely necessary, no matter what type of policy is implemented. Transparency will ensure that whatever the fiscal policy, there will always be a price and a market for that government's debt securities. Transparency in all government operations "is necessary for sound government finances, good governance, and overall fiscal integrity," as an IMF interim committee declared in September 1996.[14]

One of the better definitions for fiscal transparency in fact comes from the IMF:

". . . an openness toward the public at large about government structure and functions, fiscal policy intentions, public sector accounts and projections."[15]

The demands of institutional investors on the emerging and developing nations to create an open and transparent system are not only inevitable, but also absolutely necessary. Many industrial countries need to heed the advice they are giving to their emerging and developing neighbors. Transparency is a precondition for sound economic policies. A transparent financial accounting system makes it possible for the market to (1) determine what a government has, or has not, actually accomplished and (2) compare budgeted and actual fiscal results. Fiscal transparency can also help make the people of a country more confident in its government.[16]

Nontransparent fiscal policies tend to be destabilizing. They create investor uncertainty. In government operations, transparency is critical in not only the budget process but also in tax policy and administration and debt financing. A model of transparency occurs every year on the second Tuesday of March at 3:30 p.m. This is when Chancellor of the Exchequer of the United Kingdom stands up in Parliament and announces the government's annual budget. Conversely, there is nothing more unnerving than having a position in Russian government bonds, as I did, and reading the front page of the *Financial Times* on June 11, 1998:

"Russia Borrows $200 Million in Secret. . . . Short-term loans from western banks seek to ease pressure on Kremlin to borrow through domestic debt market."

This secret deal took place only days after Russia had raised $1.25 billion with a Eurobond issued on June 3. If I, as an investor, realize I do not have all the facts and figures—let alone finding out later about *secret* credit lines—my confidence in that market drops. I then choose to invest in other emerging countries where there is much greater fiscal transparency.

At its 50th meeting, April 16, 1998, the interim committee of the IMF Board of Governors adopted the Code of Good Practices on Fiscal Transparency—Declaration on Principles. The Code is based on four general principles:

1. Clarity of roles and responsibilities, defining clear boundaries between public and private sectors.

2. Public availability of information.

3. Open budget preparation, executing, and reporting.

4. Independent assurances of integrity, which requires external audits and statistical independence from the political process.

In the mid-1980s, almost two decades ago, general elections around the world had huge economic implications arising from dramatic fiscal policy shifts. Political parties competing from the left or right meant the difference between big and small government, socialism and free-market fiscal policies. Since then there has been a convergence of thought on how fiscal policy could be effectively balanced with a competitive tax structure.

Market forces and competition among the industrial and emerging countries will drive fiscal policymakers to offer an attractive fiscal environment. For example, Italian borrowers may be used to competing with the British, Dutch, Spanish, and Japanese borrowers but now have to compete head-to-head with their eastern and central European neighbors.

Eastern and central European countries are emerging from the end of the cold war much as Germany and Japan rose from World War II. Many countries from Eastern Europe have been rapidly restructuring their economies, offering an exciting and attractive investment environment. The move from centrally planned to market economies has forced these fiscal policymakers to redefine the role of central government. Those countries that have been disciplined have been rewarded with lower real interest rates, lower inflation, faster growth, and continuing progress towards further fiscal reform. Poland, the Czech Republic, Hungary, and Slovenia and continuing progress towards further fiscal reform has been offered spots within the European Union, which is discussed in Chapter 9.

I discovered an interesting piece of data within a footnote about the cost of capital for countries that fail to live up to their fiscal reforms:

> *"Although real interest rates at a particular time depend on inflation outcomes that are not yet known, it is estimated that real interest rates in advanced countries such as the Czech Republic and Hungary range from 2 to 3 percent, with real interest rates in less advanced countries such as Russia and the Ukraine expected to range from 10 to 20 percent."*[17]

The lesson: There is a tremendous price to be paid for fiscal laxity.

The IMF reported recently that most transition countries have made substantial progress toward achieving fiscal balance. Of the 24 transition countries, 16 are projected to have annual government deficits of 3 percent or less in 1998, compared with 14 countries in 1997 and only 8 as recently as 1992.[18] Table 3.2 shows the financial convergence in these countries of general government balances in relation to GDP.

The countries of Eastern and Central Europe have learned very quickly that they must reduce their budget deficits as they become more competitive with the major economies.

The trend of general government revenue relative to GDP has dropped appreciably as well. This was very difficult in the early years of slow domestic growth in these countries, but it now gives many of them the ability to drive their revenues lower as a percentage of GDP than the major advanced countries. In fact, these changes have already reduced the role of central government in these transitional economies.

The new international rules govern fiscal policymaking. The new global economy is about market forces. It is about economic and financial convergence in the understanding of fiscal policymaking. It is about the belief that governments must live within their means. Many countries believe they have struck the right balance between the social policies the electorate wants and what a country can afford. The new international rules are the checks and balances that prevent betrayal of fiscal reform.

Table 3.2: Countries in Transition: General Government Balances (as a percentage of GDP)[19]

	1992	1994	1995	1996	1997
Albania	-20.0	-7.0	-6.9	-10.7	-12.0
Armenia	-37.6	-16.4	-11.1	-9.3	-6.7
Azerbaijan	3.5	-11.4	-4.3	-2.6	-2.8
Belarus	-2.8	-2.6	-1.9	-1.6	-1.2
Bulgaria	-5.2	-5.8	-6.4	-13.4	-2.6
Croatia	-4.1	1.5	-0.9	-0.5	-1.4
Czech Republic	-2.1	-1.2	-1.8	-1.2	-2.1
Estonia	-0.3	1.3	-1.2	-1.5	2.4
Georgia	-34.5	-16.5	-5.3	-4.5	-5.0
Hungary	-6.9	-8.3	-7.1	-3.1	-4.6
Kazhakstan	-7.3	-7.1	-2.2	-3.0	-3.7
Kyrgyzstan	-17.6	-7.7	-13.5	-6.3	-5.7
Latvia	-0.8	-4.0	-3.3	-1.3	1.4
Lithuania	0.5	-4.8	-4.5	-4.6	-1.9
Macedonia	-9.6	-3.2	-1.3	-0.4	-0.3
Moldova	-23.9	-9.1	-5.8	-6.6	-6.8
Mongolia	-6.0	-10.3	-6.4	-9.0	-9.0
Poland	-8.0	-2.0	-2.7	-2.5	-1.7
Romania	-4.6	-1.8	-2.6	-3.9	-4.5
Russia	-18.4	-10.4	-5.8	-9.5	-7.5
Slovak Republic	-11.9	-1.3	0.3	-1.3	-4.9
Slovenia	0.2	-0.2	0.0	0.3	-1.2
Tajikistan	-31.2	-10.5	-11.2	-5.8	-3.4
Turkmenistan	13.3	-1.4	-1.6	-0.8	0.0
Ukraine	-24.0	-8.7	-4.9	-3.2	-5.6
Uzbekistan	-12.2	-6.1	-4.1	-7.3	-2.8
Major advanced economies (24)	-3.8	-3.5	-3.3	-2.8	-1.5

Greater faith in the policy, and the policymakers, will also have a significant effect on an investor's asset-allocation decisions, both the size of a country's allocation and the amount of duration risk at any given time. Fiscal credibility is essential—particularly when governments want to issue debt securities with 30-year maturities.

There are two types of distinctly different institutional investors who invest in any government debt market (1) domestic institutional investors and (2) foreign investors. The two groups may take totally contrasting views on the value of a particular government debt market. As domestic capital markets, particularly government debt markets, open themselves to foreign investors, they begin to rely more and more on foreign investment. Table 3.3 shows the huge increase in the interest of investors from all regions of the world in U.S. government debt.

The reliance upon foreign investors has forced U.S. fiscal policymakers to clean up their act—how they govern and spent taxpayer monies. In 1996, foreign investors purchased a total of $371 billion in all three categories listed in Table 3.3. The reality of the new economy is that our fiscal policymakers avoid angering foreign investors and keep them happy, because we may need their money again.

PROTECTING OUR PUBLIC FINANCES

Innumerable aspects of fiscal policymaking have changed over the past 20 years, but the history of fiscal behavior gives policymakers today, and perhaps for years to come, very little room to maneuver in terms of discretionary fiscal policies. Until the total outstanding government debt to GDP ratio falls substantially, policymakers have their hands tied by the new international rules. The global capital markets force a different approach to fiscal policymaking on the politicians. It will no longer be a domestic affair, a solely domestic concern. International competition for global capital will cause policymakers to think twice before they return to fiscal deficit spending. This does not mean that society cannot see its own unique desires and objectives reflected in its nation's annual budget. However, the safekeeping of the national accounts will have to be managed with an eye on foreign investment flows and the rising competition for capital from emerging countries. (A discussion on the budget deficit post September 11 is discussed in Chapter 12.)

Prior to leaving the subject of fiscal policy, I want to make absolutely clear that fiscal policy convergence is not about the way we spend our money. Global fiscal convergence concerns how we manage our financial affairs and our national accounts. Each country has its own approach to fiscal policy and its own anxieties about the future. In a visit to the Ukraine, the President of Portugal, Jorge Sampaio, based on his country's experiences over the past 30 years, offered the Ukrainian people advice on how to catch up with Western countries.

The Portuguese story is an example to the eastern and central European countries of fiscal reform. The *Financial Times* reported:

"Portugal toppled an authoritarian regime, emerged peacefully from revolutionary turmoil, privatized a state-dominated economy, made parliamentary democracy work, joined the European Union, almost caught up to Western European living standards and qualified for economic and monetary union."[20]

In 1992, I would have given wonderful odds that Portugal would never meet the Maastricht Treaty convergence criteria for entry into European Monetary Union for the second wave membership in 2002, let alone become a charter member in 1997. Even though Portugal has had a successful transition, they need to continue efforts toward further fiscal reforms. The new global economy will force Portugal to reform further and, despite President Sampaio's selling reform policies to his eastern and central European neighbors, the Portuguese are ambivalent toward the former Soviet Bloc for two very good reasons. First, "the market economies under construction in Eastern Europe compete with Portugal for foreign investment. Most offer a lower paid but better educated workforce, production capacity much closer to big north European markets, and a higher level of technology in some industrial sectors."[22] The second Portuguese concern is the day the

Table 3.3: Net Foreign Purchases of U.S. Bonds (in millions of U.S. dollars)[21]

	Continent	Country	Marketable Treasury Bonds & Notes	Bonds of U.S. Government Corp. & Federal Agencies	Corporate Bonds
1972			3,316		1,881
1973			305		1,961
1974			-472		1,039
1975			1,995		766
1976			8,096		1,202
1977			22,843	2,712	1,617
1978			4,710	1,273	1,024
1979			2,863	545	733
1980			4,898	2,557	2,829
1981			15,054	1,566	3,467
1982			17,319	-358	1,809
1983			5,427	-15	918
1984			21,499	1,175	11,721
1985			29,208	4,340	39,792
1986			19,388	6,976	43,672
1987			25,587	5,047	22,492
1988			48,832	6,740	21,224
1989			54,203	15,094	17,296
1990			17,918	6,267	9,672
1991			19,865	10,244	16,915
1992			39,288	18,291	20,789
1993			23,552	35,428	30,572
1994			78,801	21,680	37,992
1995			134,115	28,729	57,853
1996 *(of which)*			244,725	48,960	77,978
	Europe *(of which)*		118,345	18,803	56,194
		Germany	17,647	1,650	3,514
		France	2,624	243	4,931
		Italy	1,960	-84	-78
		United Kingdom	65,381	10,942	43,702
		Spain	18,414	7	462
	Asia *(of which)*		98,001	14,596	9,806
		Japan	41,390	7,595	6,099
		Singapore	7,802	1,341	1,095
		China	14,453	2,756	257
		Taiwan	4,608	-1,129	8
		Hong Kong	14,366	915	1,737
1997			184,171	49,853	84,358
1998			49,039	56,802	121,930
1999			-9,953	92,200	160,392
2000			-53,790	152,841	182,403

European Union's aid, amounting to over 3 percent of Portugal's gross national product, flows from Southern Europe and Ireland to East European countries joining the European Union.[23] If I were Portuguese, I would start worrying about the day when the aid from the EU stops because, at some stage, the fiscal policymakers are going to have to find 3 percent of GDP in annual spending from somewhere. Finding the fiscal revenue during the recent economic slowdown is very difficult, with GDP economic growth at 0.50 percent in 2002 with little more in 2003.

Ukraine has a very interesting set of fiscal problems and issues to address. The Ukrainians are funding themselves with an annual budget deficit representing 35 percent of the total expenditure in 1998. They have funded 57 percent of the total debt with short-term domestic Treasury Bills, and financed the balance by hard-currency loans. The Ukrainians will be facing a very similar future to what the Latin American countries encountered in the 1980s. Fiscal irresponsibility causes a huge amount of pain for an economy. The Ukrainian problems are more complicated, but there is a strong probability of a future liquidity crisis ending up as a debt crisis when hard-currency loans become difficult to repay. They will also have the added difficulty of selling their domestic treasury bills—the only solution is to print money. The Ukrainians started the new century in a very difficult position, with $3.2 billion to pay on its debts and only $1 billion of it in hard currency reserves. In 2002, the Ukrainian debt service amounted to $1.2 billion and is expected to rise to $1.6 billion in 2003. In addition, the Ukrainians will have to work extremely hard to overcome their tarnished reputation—the U.S. Treasury defined Ukraine as a country of primary money-laundering concern as well as alleged of illegal arms sales. The Ukrainian government is in a desperate position causing them to take desperate measures. Ultimately, the Ukrainians will discover and develop their own form of a market economy.

The Dutch discovered the part-time employment economy in Europe as a way to restructure their economy fiscally. They were able to reduce their total outstanding indebtedness and achieve low unemployment rates leading to European Monetary Union. They made extraordinary progress towards fiscal reform, not sacrificing their traditional quality of life, rather than a policy of growth at any cost. As the annual fiscal budget shrank, the structural unemployment rate was rising 2.5 percent per annum in 1982. They were able to adjust their labor force, in which part time employment accounted for 38.1 percent of all employment in the Netherlands. In the United Kingdom, part time employment constituted 24.6 percent of all employment, and in Germany it was 16.3 percent. In the new Dutch system, "individuals could no longer count on so much generosity from the state if they lost their jobs."[24] In an *International Herald Tribune* article, Ruud Lubbers, former Prime Minister of the Netherlands, described the new Dutch way as "not aiming to maximize gross national product per capita, rather, we are seeking to attain a high quality of life, a just, participating and sustainable society that is cohesive."[25]

Over the past 10 years, one of the highest country allocations has been a Dutch government bond. My confidence in the policymakers was such that I would invest in 30-year zero-coupon Dutch government securities. I also had a great deal of confidence in the new Dutch system. The Dutch policymakers achieved a flexible, cost-efficient labor market while shrinking the size of their federal government and reducing their outstanding debt-to-GDP ratio. At the same time, the Dutch have managed to achieve a 4.7 percent unemployment rate, which compares favorably with the United Kingdom, unlike Germany's 11.5 percent and France's 12.2 percent.

The Dutch offered investors a stable combination of fiscal and monetary policies. Fiscal policies do not have to be a version of American policies to be successful. Each society should be able to spend its national budget as it sees fit. However, the state of the national accounts is the concern of foreigners when they have monies invested in the domestic government debt markets. That's particularly true when financial and economic crises occur and foreign governments, along with organizations such as the International Monetary Fund, are called in to help solve the economic or financial crisis.

The days of fearing extremist economic policies (excluding the German Green Party), which increase public expenditures that send government bond yields soaring, are slowly fading into history. Interestingly, one of the last political parties to turn away from social-ist ideology and embrace the new international rules was the British Labor Party. The new Prime Minister for Great Britain, Tony Blair, the head of the first Labor government in 18 years, spoke to the French National Assembly, led by socialist Prime Minister Lionel Jospin, about the new Labor party and the type of government he planned to lead. The new British Labor government believes "we must maintain strong, prudent discipline over financial and monetary policy, within financial systems that are open and transparent. There is no right or left politics in economic management today. There is good and bad."[26]

I remember when British general elections created more anxiety for me than any other European general election because of the extreme consequences of a Labor party victory. The potential inflationary impact of socialist economic policies of the Labor party would send the U.K. government debt market, gilt-edged securities prices lower, causing bond yields to rise 1 or 2 percent (100 to 200 basis points).[27] Those days have certainly changed.

In our new global economy will see fiscal policy and central government as a com-plement to free-market economies, rather than as a substitute or in conflict with each other. One of the responsibilities of central government in the future will be to create the institutional infrastructure, which markets require to work effectively.[28]

During 2000 and 2001 the debate over fiscal policymaking have been directed at pol-icy that will create greater economic growth in an effort to revive economic growth. However, governments, even the best of them, are unable to do anything substantive to revive an economy from a recession. The best policy that has the most immediate affect is monetary policy, to be discussed in the next chapter. The two reasons fiscal policy is not as instantly effective are that (1) financial stimulus takes time to filter into the economy and (2) government is not capable to find the right way to efficiently execute that finan-cial stimulus. Monetary policy has an immediate affect as interest rates across the board lower bowering costs that can be used by business and individuals.

Indeed, fiscal policy can be used in combination with monetary policy such as the cleaning up of the savings and loan debacle in the United States. The Federal Reserve reduced interest rates aggressively over the short term while Congress used taxpayer monies to write-off the bad loans. In the past, fiscal policy was initially used to fight an economic recession. This quickly turns to a policy to boost economic growth into the future. This, then, causes government indebted to bloat resulting in inflation, higher inter-est rates, and higher taxes.

I believe that fiscal prudence, maintaining a balanced budget, using the past budget surpluses to pay down outstanding debts as a national asset to be treasured. Therefore, any fiscal measures used today to fight off the effects of economic growth slowing in early 2001 along with the aftermath of September 11, 2001 should be short and sweet. Once the economic objective is achieved, to get back to a balanced budget as soon as possible. America's finest hour would be to use the budget surplus in the short term to shore up our military, recover financially from September 11, allow the natural selection from capitalism's creative destruction to restructure the U.S. economy post-technology bubble, and to let the Enron bankruptcy run its course. By fiscal year 2005 we should be back to a balanced budget policy. That would be a truly magnificent accomplishment for the United States.

The way in which many capitalist countries respond to economic recessions is a function of the type of capitalist system that they have adopted, as discussed earlier.

ANGLO-SAXON VERSUS CENTRALIST CAPITALISM

According to my reading, the term capitalism first appeared in 1630 and is defined by the *Oxford English Dictionary* as "an economic system in which the production and distribution of goods depend on invested private capital and profit-making." However, there are two distinct schools of thought on how capitalism should actually operate (1) the Anglo-Saxon system and (2) the Centralist Capitalism. The Anglo-Saxon system is used by the United States and United Kingdom. The Centralist system has been adopted by the Japanese and German economies.

The difference between the two is significant. In *Stock Market Capitalism: Welfare Capitalism Japan and Germany versus the Anglo-Saxons* (2000), Ronald Dore describes the difference and contrast as shareholder sovereignty for the Anglo-Saxons versus employee sovereignty for centralist systems. From shareholder-favoring to employee-favoring firms, from genuine capitalism to pseudo-capitalism. "They all mean the same thing. The transformation of firms run primarily for the benefit of their employees into firms run primarily, even exclusively, for the benefit of their shareholders. And for the whole economy—it means an economy centered on the stock market as a measure of corporate success and on the stock market index as a measure of national well-being, as opposed to an economy which has other, better, more pluralistic criteria of human welfare for measuring progress towards the good society."

History has a great deal to do with the development of these two systems. As I mentioned earlier, economic policy is a function and a sign of the times. Germany and Japan post-World War II wanted to protect their employment rates, and therefore tried to control their business cycles. Centralist Capitalism in essence believes that central government knows what is best for the overall economy and therefore will interfere and prioritize industry, exports, and imports. Whereas Anglo-Saxons allow market forces and the individual to prevail and decide what is best for their economies—managed capitalism versus free-market capitalism.

These two systems will be discussed throughout this book and will have a huge impact on and define our new global economy. An extremely timely summary of the differences between these two economic systems was summarized in a *Financial Times* editorial (January 26, 2002) entitled "The Best US Export" in response to an adjacent article by Richard Waters which discusses the amount of time required by U.S. companies to recover from their period of corporate destruction. This editorial describes the differences between controlled capitalism, continental Europe, and the Anglo-Saxon variety, the United States. Please also note the debate behind this editorial for the discussion on the future of the European Monetary Union, in a later chapter.

"Joseph Schumpeter would have found this week's US corporate news far from surprising. 'Capitalism . . . is by nature a form or method of economic change and not only never is, but never can be stationary,' he asserted in 1942. . . . rarely has one week better illustrated this thesis.

Creative destruction is alive and well in the US. The Enron affair might not show 'the genius of capitalism' there as, Paul O'Neill, the Treasury secretary, rather clumsily put it. But it is impossible to think of a European Amazon or, for that matter, large bankruptcies or a corporate restructuring in Europe that has occurred without serious political stink.

This difference has allowed the US to be more successful over time: not in all respects, but in the most important measures of economic performance and prosperity. It has been more innovative: Germany once a rival but recently slipped behind. US employment growth has been nearly 0.8 percentage points higher a year on average since the mid-1980s. Profitability has consistently been higher. And its capitalism has generated many more corporate success stories. For every European company such as Vivendi, there are many Microsofts, Intels, or Wal-Marts.

Naturally, the categorization of the US as a dynamic economy compared with sclerotic Europe is a gross oversimplification. Many industries in the US, such as farming and steel, seek protection from competition and politicians are inclined to grant it. In Europe, industries such as mobile telephony display the full power of creative destruction. A strong performance by Nokia this week confirmed it dominance of the mobile handset market, while Ericsson yesterday posted the largest loss in Swedish corporate history. It announced a furthermore from handset production to building mobile networks.

These exceptions aside, the challenge for European policy-makers is to structure the European economy so it can emulate the dynamism of the US. This is an import worth having.

The European capital market is often seen as a place to start. But simply recreating US-style finance in Europe is unlikely to provide the required magic. The UK has long shared its capital market structure with the US but its economic performance over many decades has been distinctly European.

The answer lies deeper, in the culture and outlook of individuals on either side of the Atlantic. In Europe there is a tendency to view the world as a zero-sum game: someone's gain must be another person's loss. Hence the struggle to maintain the status quo. In the US, individuals are more willing to adapt: to embrace change; to find the next market; or to seek a new opportunity. It is that attitude that European politicians must strive to achieve with public policy.

No one disputes that this will be difficult. Too much creative destruction and entrepreneurs would not be able to secure advantage from their innovations.

*They would not bother to enter the market. But European regulations currently
err on the side of protecting incumbents."*

This editorial goes to the heart of the debate for the future of fiscal policy making into
the next millennium for every country throughout the world affecting everything down to
individual and corporate taxation rates.

ENDNOTES

[1] Samuelson, P., and W. D. Nordhaus. 1985. *Economics.* New York: McGraw-Hill Inc.,
page 902.
[2] Stiglitz, J. E. 1977. *Economics.* New York: W.W. Norton & Co., page 150.
[3] Samuelson, op. cit., page 908.
[4] Source: *International Financial Statistics Yearbook 1997.* Washington, D.C.:
International Monetary Fund.
[5] Hutton, Will. 1999. *The Stakeholder Society.* Washington, D.C.: Polity Press.
[6] Lightfoot, Warwick. "Timely But Flawed Plea for a Keynesian Revival." *The
European,* December 7-13, 1998, page 21.
[7] Casselli, F., A. Giovannini, and T. Lane. "Fiscal Discipline and the Cost of Public Debt
Service: Some Estimates for OECD Countries." IMF Working Paper, April 1998.
Washington, D.C.: International Monetary Fund.
[8] "The Business Cycle, International Linkages, and Exchange Rates." *World Economic
Outlook,* May 1998, page 58. Washington, D.C.: International Monetary Fund.
[9] Ibid., page 72.
[10] Ibid., page 913.
[11] Thatacher, M. 1993. *The Downing Street Years.* London: Harper Collins Publishers,
pages 41-42.
[12] "Convergence and Divergence in Developing Countries." *World Economic Outlook,*
May 1993, page 43. Washington, D.C.: International Monetary Fund.
[13] Brittan, S. "Money Only Helps A Little." *Financial Times,* December 18, 1997, page 10.
[14] "Transparency in Government Operations." *World Economic Outlook,* May 1998, page
121. Washington, D.C.: International Monetary Fund.
[15] Ibid.
[16] Ibid.
[17] "Progress with Fiscal Reform in Countries in Transition." *World Economic Outlook,*
May 1998, page 102. Washington, D.C.: International Monetary Fund.
[18] Ibid., page 98.
[19] Source: IMF Staff Estimates.
[20] Wise, P. "Portugal Takes on Mentor Role to Eastern Europe's Economies." *Financial
Times,* April 23, 1998.
[21] Source: U.S. Department of Treasury. *Treasury Bulletin.* "International Capital
Markets," November 1997. Washington, D.C.: International Monetary Fund.
[22] Ibid.
[23] Ibid.

[24] Lubbers, R. "In Seeking a 'Third Way,' the Dutch Model is Worth a Look." *The International Herald Tribune,* September 16, 1997.
[25] Ibid.
[26] Speech by the British Prime Minister, The Right Honorable Tony Blair, to the French National Assembly, March 24, 1998. Press Notes, 10 Downing Street, London.
[27] A basis point is equivalent to a 0.01 percentage.
[28] Stiglitz, J. E. "An Agenda for Development in the Twenty-first Century." Keynote Address, The Annual World Bank Conference on Development Economics 1997, The World Bank, Washington, D.C., and page 22.

Chapter 4
MONETARY POLICYMAKING

Monetary policy is a check and balance on the fiscal policymaking process. Until debt-to-GDP levels drop, fiscal policymaking will be constrained and policymakers will have greater responsibility for steering domestic economic growth. Most central banks are generally responsible for monetary policy.However, most are not independent from political interference. In the new global economy, central banks will become more independent and will have more responsibility for the economic success or failure of their respective economies. Central banks "have the rudiments of a real power base in society's demand for greater financial security, greater stability in the value of money, and in the widespread distrust of politicians. They have placed themselves in a position to play a growing role in wider policy construction in the European Union."[1]

Lawrence Summers, undersecretary for economic policy during the Clinton administration, then Treasury Secretary and now President of Harvard University said:

"Monetary policy is destiny. The prospect for peace and prosperity for the rest of this century and beyond depends as much on monetary policies as on any other factor."[2]

A November 14, 1998 *Economist* article, "The Central Banker As God," predicted:

". . . 1998 may be remembered as the year in which the power of central bankers reached its zenith. They should enjoy their moment of glory! It will not last."

I think it *will* last in the new global economy and central banking will evolve significantly over the next few years.

As a society we have a number of economic and financial issues to solve. In terms of our economic way of life, what is inflation? Should price stability be the key focus of monetary policy? In a word, yes. Should our financial system operate secretly or transparently? Should central banks be lenders of last resort and, if so, who gets bailed out? When banks are bailed out, the people running the banks, those who cause the financial trouble, are known as a "moral hazard." They are the reason for financial mistakes, the mistakes that cause systematic risks to the financial system. The central bank or government of the day is required, or feels obliged, to bail out the bank from its financial troubles.

HISTORY

For the sake of clarity, following is a brief review of our recent history of monetary policymaking. A review of our monetary history is necessary to permit me to tie it in with the present and to talk about the future. Besides, you will learn a few trivia facts.

Central banks were created to help governments finance wars, or resulted from abuse of the domestic financial system.

The Swedish Riksbank, formed in 1668, was the first *central* bank.

The first *public,* the Bank of Amsterdam, bank was created in 1609 to address the growing financial needs of merchants in Amsterdam. Prior to the creation of the Bank of Amsterdam, the Dutch had 14 mints throughout the country, making 341 silver coins and 505 gold coins. The Dutch Parliament established the bank to sort out the problem of their domestic currency and to create a clearing system for its merchants' accounts.[3] The Bank of Amsterdam folded in 1819, after it lent heavily to the Dutch East India Company, which suffered huge losses during a war with England in 1790.

Every central bank has its unique story and origin. A few more stories? My pleasure.

The Bank of England was created to finance wars. The "Old Lady" came into being to finance the nine-years' war with France which began in 1688. The bank's charter was sealed on July 27, 1694. By the end of the Napoleonic Wars in 1815, the British Government had amassed a national debt of 850 million Sterling.[4]

One of the more colorful stories deals with the debt involving Barings Bank. No, not the mid-1990s version, but the one that took place in 1890. After Barings Bank lent too much money to Argentina, the Bank of England organized a bailout for Barings among "city" institutions and gold borrowed from France and Russia.[5] *The Economist* commented at that time:

> *"A dangerous precedent might have been set if bad management can count on being saved."*[6]

Sound familiar?

I do not intend to rehash the gold standard or Bretton Woods, but I do want to raise another interesting point from the history books. In 1844, the English Parliament passed the Bank Charter Act, limiting the supply of money and bank notes tied to the Bank of England's gold reserves. The British Parliament of that time understood the link between money supply and price inflation.[7]

Interestingly, central banks started springing up all over Europe during this period. Spain created its central bank in 1782 to finance its participation in the American Revolutionary War of Independence.[8] The French created the Banque de France in 1800 to finance Napoleon's wartime needs. By the end of the nineteenth century, Europe claimed the formation of 15 central banks.[9]

The United States Federal Reserve System dates from 1913. Only because the constitution forbade the creation of paper money by individual states and at the federal level.[10] Former Chairman of the Federal Reserve Board, Paul Volcker, remarked,

> *"We sometimes forget that central banking, as we know it today, is, in fact, largely an invention of the past hundred years or so. Only a few central banks can trace their ancestry back to the early nineteenth century or before. It is a*

sobering fact that the prominence of central banks in this century has coincided with a general tendency towards more inflation, not less. By and large, if the overriding objective is price stability, we did better with the nineteenth century gold standard and passive central banks, with currency boards or even with 'free banking.' The truly unique power of a central bank, after all, is the power to create money, and ultimately the power to create is the power to destroy."[11]

As a student, I learned about the Federal Reserve Banking System in the United States, but never about the development of central banks and monetary policymaking in any other country. When I began work in London, I soon learned about the global monetary system and other domestic central banking institutions and their importance. Central banks and the bankers were always mysterious to me. Their coming into existence and evolution into the present form, which did not occur until the 1950s and 1960s, were shrouded in mystery. More recently, central banks resemble each other. The new European Central Bank, along with the central banks in Eastern and Central Europe, resemble the German Bundesbank in structure and style. Of all the official public organizations throughout the world, global central banking undoubtedly will evolve unlike any institutional structures from our past. Central banks will ultimately become the check and balance against elected politicians. Our central bank will become our economic and financial Supreme Court.

So who are these mysterious all-powerful institutions? A central bank is a bank from which other banks can borrow. But it is more than a banker's bank. It is also responsible for stabilizing the level of economic activity by controlling the money supply, the availability of credit, and for regulating the banking system to ensure its financial health.[12]

Central banks are responsible for monetary policy, the policies that affect the supply of money and credit and the terms on which credit is available to borrowers.[13]

The history of central banking has been short but lively. Inflation, the scourge of any economy, has become a modern economic battle between central governments, central banks and market forces. The ability to print money, the power of life, has tempted politicians and central bankers alike since the beginning of this century.

When preparing to write this chapter, I had to go back to the history books. The last time I had studied the history of monetary policymaking was during post-graduate studies at the London School of Economics when the required reading, *A Monetary History of the United States 1867-1960* by Milton Friedman and Anna Schwartz, kept me awake at night. Since the publication of Friedman and Schwartz in 1963, we have come a long way in our understanding of monetary policymaking. In many ways, because of constant abuses to our monetary systems in the past (printing money), we have started to develop a common understanding to prevent these abuses in the future. Independent central banks, with a strong constitution that focuses on fighting inflation and controlling the money supply, are of great importance. In each case in history, political interference with and lax control of the supply of money has caused great economic hardship.

The German hyperinflation after World War I is an excellent example. The demands for German reparations forced the German authorities, under the Versailles Treaty, to repay war debts in gold and prewar marks. The German currency devalued, the cost of repaying debts rose, and unemployment rose. German authorities expanded the money supply—printed money—to solve the problem, which, in fact, perpetuated it.

In more recent times, there have been three major inflation peaks (1) 1973-74, (2) 1979-80, and (3) 1989-90. In each case, changes in exchange rate regimes, supply shocks, and macroeconomic policies played a role in the creation of inflationary pressures. The 1973-74 and 1979-80 inflation peaks saw steep increases in commodity prices, particularly oil. However, the lessons, according to the International Monetary Fund, are "that the inflation response to such shocks depends on policies and also on the behavior of wages."[14] No kidding! In more specific terms, first "it is important to limit the monetary accommodation of adverse supply shocks, since the inflation that is permitted tends to get built into inflation expectations, to become persistent, and to raise the subsequent disinflation." Second, "flexibility in labor markets—the ability of both wages and structures of employment to adjust in response to shocks—plays a crucial role in determining the output and inflation costs of such shocks."[15]

One of the historic legacies from colonial times are currency boards. One of the ways to control the supply of money is through the use of a currency board.

CURRENCY BOARDS

A currency board is a monetary arrangement that allows authorities to issue domestic currency only in exchange for a specified foreign currency at a fixed rate, and which sharply limits or eliminates the discretion of authorities to create money by extending credits.[16]

Currency Boards are portrayed as the ultimate fix for emerging countries in their battle to reform economically. On the contrary, they are not the ultimate fix, but the ultimate commitment to build credibility, to fight inflation, to bring down interest rates, and for resumption of investment and economic growth. A currency board must be accompanied by tight financial policies such as structural reforms, privatization, fiscal consolidation toward a balanced budget, and, perhaps more importantly, the prohibition to monetize fiscal deficits—the inability to print money to finance a government's annual fiscal budget deficit.[17]

A currency board represents an unequivocal commitment to supply or redeem, without limit, monetary liabilities at a fixed exchange rate. Under this system, a currency board replaces a central bank and cannot extend credit to government, the banking system, or anyone else. Under these conditions, short-term interest rates are purely market determined, linked to interest rates in the country to whose currency the domestic currency is anchored, and completely independent of the will of the monetary authorities.[18]

A currency board must have sufficient hard currency reserves in order to convert the domestic currency into the hard currency. Domestic interest rates will rise in relation to the hard currency interest rate in an effort to attract buyers for their domestic currency. Conversely, domestic interest rates will fall relative to the hard currency interest rate in an effort to attract sellers of the domestic currency. The movement in domestic interest rates ensures that an appropriate amount of hard currency reserves is always available, which also pegs the exchange rate for the domestic currency with the hard currency.

Under a currency board arrangement, the central bank stands ready to exchange unlimited amounts of domestic currency liabilities for the designated pegged hard currency. The currency board is legally required to have sufficient hard currency foreign exchange reserves measured in terms of the designated pegged currency, to meet designated domestic liabilities.[19] As I said earlier, a currency board is the ultimate economic sacrifice, because monetary policy, economic and financial competitiveness, has been delegated to the hard currency, pegged currency country. So why would any country delegate its economic authority to another country? Credibility.

I am approaching the subject of currency boards from a monetary policymaking point of view, and not from the fact that the currency's exchange rate is fixed—pegged against the foreign currency. I will talk about currencies and my philosophy regarding currency risk in a later chapter.

According to the International Monetary Fund, a currency board could be attractive to three groups of countries (1) small open economies with limited central banking experience and incipient financial markets, (2) countries wanting to belong to a broader trade or currency area, and (3) countries trying to enhance the credibility of exchange-rate-based disinflation policies.[20] "A currency board arrangement may be seen as a special case of a rules-based monetary system. . . . It is a system based on rules rather than discretion that serves to establish credibility and avoids losses resulting from decisions that can sometimes be undertaken within a myopic time scale."[21]

Historically, colonizing powers with dependent territories—the British with Mauritius in 1849, the French colonies, and the United States with the Philippines—used currency boards. Otherwise currency boards were not used other than for trade reasons. Recently there has been a rise in the use of currency boards:

- *Hong Kong (1983).* Continues today.
- *Argentina (1991).* Continues today.
- *Estonia (1992).* Still in existence in 2003. However, the current account deficit was rapidly becoming a concern as it reached 11.1 percent of GDP in 2002 and was expected to decline to 9.4 percent by the end of 2003. The good news is that inflation is now expected to fall to 3.3 percent in 2003.
- *Lithuania (1994).* So far a real success story. There was a current account surplus up to 2002, which may slip into deficit in 2003. Inflation is hovering around 0.5 percent with total debt-to-GDP falling from nearly 30 percent in 2000 to 24 percent in 2003.
- *Bosnia (1997).* Still in existence in 2003. In the February 2003 issue of the *Monetary Bulletin,* the governor of the central bank of Bosnia-Herzegovina, Peter Nicholl, stated ". . . the currency board arrangement is a very successful principle of the monetary policy which resulted in a low inflation and stable currency in the B-H, which are very important for economic growth and investment."
- *Bulgaria (1997).* Still in existence in 2003.
- *Indonesia and Russia.* After controversial discussion in 1998 regarding implementation, a currency board never materialized.

So why the recent rise in the use of currency boards? A currency board builds credibility, reduces inflation, allows interest rates to fall, and creates an environment for the resumption of economic growth. A political commitment to a currency board is the ultimate sacrifice for a politician because it commits him to restrictive and often oppressive economic policies. There is little doubt that a currency board regime can help achieve dramatic reductions in inflation rates. With the transparency of the fixed exchange rate as a nominal anchor, the domestic currency exchange rate is fixed to the foreign hard currency, and the loss of monetary flexibility enhances the anti-inflation credibility of policymakers.

Currency boards also impose fiscal discipline because printing money cannot finance central government expenditures.[22] The average inflation rate under a currency board arrangement is about four percentage points lower than other types of pegged exchange rate policies.[23] The object of the exercise is to radically restructure all the facets of the economic and financial system, creating competitive, low inflationary economic growth.

Currency boards are the ultimate policy in an effort to create a credible economic and financial environment. Credibility is everything. It is fiscal and monetary policymaking, it is a transparent and open financial system, and, most importantly to investors, a currency board represents a credible policy for the future investment environment.

My two favored currency board arrangements during the 1990s were Bulgaria and Argentina. Bulgaria has gone through a remarkable period of structural change and success under its currency board arrangement. Prior to the introduction of a currency board in 1997, Bulgaria was an economic and financial mess. When the Soviet Union collapsed, so too did Bulgaria's economic future—more than 80 percent of its trade was with the former U.S.S.R. and its satellites. Real economic growth collapsed by -7.3 percent in 1992, -1.5 percent in 1993, followed by minimal economic growth in 1994 and 1995. However, further economic collapse in 1996 (-10.9 percent) and 1997 (-5.7 percent) forced authorities into action. The exchange rate, the Lev, followed the economy down, and the average exchange rate of 23.3 Lev for every $US fell to 1,712.7 in 1997. Inflation rose from 82 percent in 1992 to 1,083 percent by 1997.

The introduction of the currency board arrangement fixed the Lev to the German Deutche Mark and, as of January 1999, the Lev was subsequently fixed or anchored to the European Euro. The economic objective for Bulgarian leadership, headed by Ivan Kostov and a center-right coalition government, is to catch up with Central European economies and achieve qualification for membership in the European Union by 2007. I believe this is a commitment that Bulgaria may be able to achieve. Bulgaria has reduced its trade dependency on Russia and former Soviet Bloc countries from more than 80 percent to 8 percent, replacing them with Italy, Germany, and Greece. Economic growth is climbing, albeit slower than expected by forecasters, but rising nonetheless. As of December 1998, consumer price inflation has fallen to a year-on-year rate of 1.0 percent, coupled with a healthier banking system with capital adequacy ratios rising to an estimated 31 percent. In addition, a cautious lending practice by the Bulgarian banks has improved. The IMF has provided Bulgaria with a three-year $860 million loan agreement to support its balance of payments deficits, and the World Bank and other institutions are providing more than $1 billion in medium-term infrastructure project finance. In addition, during the Russian and Asian economic crises along with the war in Kosovo, the Bulgarians have provisioned a 2 percent budget cushion in the event the economy did not perform as expected. State company privatizations are running behind schedule. The government has taken advantage of its currency board arrangement with remarkable success. As Bulgaria prepares to enter the European Union, two difficult choices were made in early 2002 by the government of

Prime Minister Saxe-Coburg (1) to reduce their fiscal deficit and (2) to slow their current account deficit. An interesting point in time and challenges lay ahead for the Bulgarians as they prepare for entry into the European Union in 2007.

In a report by the Bulgarian National Bank entitled "Shadowing the Euro: Bulgaria's Monetary Policy Five years On" by Martin Zaimov and Kalin Hristov, (November 2002), they summarize the past five years:

> *"That [the] currency board ensured price and financial stability the Bulgarian economy needed as a precondition for stable and sustainable economic growth. In the post 1997 period, Bulgaria achieved the lowest and most stable inflation rates since the beginning of the economic reform, combined with the highest and most stable output growth. The fiscal policy was oriented toward low budget deficit. This policy had in practice afforded the government greater flexibility by increasing its disposable income due to reduced interest payments and growing tax base as a result of high economic growth. The fixed exchange rate had a positive effect on the volume of foreign trade. Persisted current account deficit, created mainly by import of investment goods, was financed by stable inflows of foreign direct investment. Reformed and modernized banking system provided solid ground for robust economic growth."*

Argentina had one of the most successful currency board arrangements. Unfortunately the currency board blew apart in 2001. As described by the Central Bank of Argentine Republic in their fourth quarter 2001 *Bulletin of Monetary and Financial Affairs:*

> *"... from the end of 1997 through to the present various situations developed with a potentially significant impact on the performance of the sector, beginning with a major international financial crisis and ending with a severe weakening of the domestic political framework. Specifically, the steady decline in economic activity levels—in a recession that has already extended over three and a half years—a severely worsening fiscal situation, rapidly growing public debt and the responses generated in the political sphere have all been responsible for a crisis . . . ."*

The *Bulletin* further chronicles events that

> *"... led to a strong mistrust by economic agents and a flight from domestic assets—particularly public debt and bank deposits. The latter phenomenon in particular led the Government to impose severe restrictions on the withdrawal of cash from the banking system and controls on capital movements, which until that time had enjoyed unrestricted mobility. By the end of the period a major political debate was in progress on the ability of the exchange rate mechanisms adopted to facilitate macroeconomic equilibrium in the medium term, given the existing situation."*

The final episode of this debacle was reported by the *Bulletin:*

> *"Social unrest caused by the prevailing economic situation, which had led to rising unemployment and the events that were unfolding, including those relating to*

the restrictions imposed on the local financial system, resulted in the resignation of the country's President on December 20, further aggravating the political crisis that had been developing over the last two years. At the end of the period the president designated to replace the outgoing chief executive announced the suspension of payments on the national government's foreign debt."

By mid-2002, an abstract of an *Economist* article (August 10, 2002), 'Finance and Economics: Argentina's Bottomless Pit; Economics Focus':

"The economic crisis that struck Argentina last year has deepened into one of the worst and most intractable such calamities in living memory. Economists have not been slow to offer accounts of what went wrong, but there is as yet no settled version. That makes it difficult to recommend solutions. Meanwhile things keep getting worse. The economy is shrinking, inflation is surging, and the country's banking system is in ruins. Some economists believe—and this is all too plausible—that hyperinflation may have to finish its demolition work before rebuilding can begin. Lately, support has been growing for dollarisation—that is, for the formal adoption of the dollar as the country's currency. Another possibility would be to leave a partial freeze on deposits in place—with arrangements to secure its removal over time—in order to stop the mismatch between deposits and loans causing a run on the banks."

By October 2002, Karen Krebsbach wrote for *US Banker,* "Crying got Argentina" reported that:

"Argentina remains mired in its worst recession and banking crisis in history, a kind of economic twilight zone reminiscent of the financial and social chaos that characterized the American Great Depression. With more than half of Argentines in poverty, unemployment stuck at 30 percent, and a currency slide of 70 percent, few can recall when this nation of 37 million was the wealthiest in Latin America. The fiscal death knell for Argentina, now in its fourth year of intractable recession, was sounded in December, when the government defaulted on its $155 billion public debt, triggering domestic political instability and a financial meltdown that has spread to nearby Brazil, Uruguay, and Paraguay. Four presidents later, J.P. Morgan Securities was warning of the 'total collapse of credibility in the banking sector,' and citizens were protecting government banking curbs—collectively referred to as the corralito—which left funds virtually untouchable. The IMF fears that a new plan to lift the corralito will trigger a flood of withdrawals and spark inflation."

More recently, the Argentine economy is turning around, with construction activity rising by 63 percent in January 2003, the first since 1998. Economic growth is expected to actually rise by 1.4 percent in 2003, the first time since 1998, with the current account balance of 9 percent of GDP by 2003. The Argentines have met their IMF targets—but what a way to end a currency board arrangement. Argentina is a case study of how not to move from a currency board arrangement to a floating exchange mechanism.

The main benefit and the reason for introducing currency boards in this chapter is that they represent a tremendous commitment by emerging nations to participate in the new global economy and abide by the new international rules. Currency boards also help create an atmosphere where interest rate and yield convergence with industrial countries is inevitable. The emergence over the past 10 years and subsequent commitments to currency board arrangements is additional evidence to support our greater understanding of the science of economics—the need for low and stable inflation rates and open transparent markets. As President Clinton remarked to Russian President Boris Yeltsin during the Summit meeting in Moscow on September 2, 1998, Russia, along with everyone else in the world, including the United States, must play by the rules of the international markets.

I do not want to spend too much time on specific currency board arrangements. I will talk in later chapters about why they may work in one country but create more chaos and problems for others. The fact is that currency board arrangements are being used throughout the globe and, no doubt, will continue to spring up as emerging and developing nations strive for economic and financial convergence on a par with the industrialized nations. To play by the international rules is not an American conspiracy. Although global reality is harsher for some than others, the rules are the same for everyone.

POLITICS

We need to know how central banks may evolve into our future and the role they will play in our new global economy. Central bank independence is fast becoming a political hot potato (since the day Vice President Dan Quayle misspelled "potato," I am petrified whenever I come across this word). A great deal of study and research has occurred over the years on this subject. Increasing the independence of a country's central bank can help to achieve and maintain low inflation. The principal reason is that a central bank, endowed with the mandate to pursue price stability, may thereby be better insulated from political pressure for lower interest rates or monetary funding of fiscal deficits.[24]

Greater independence of the central bank should not come at the expense of reduced accountability. Independence is meant to ensure that the operation of monetary policy is not affected by short-term political considerations. Central bank independence, however, is only an ingredient to ensure a low inflationary environment. In countries where the central banks are considered the most independent in the world, such as Germany and Switzerland, the public's aversion to inflation is intense and ingrained into their economic and financial systems.

There are two distinctions in central bank independence, introduced by Guy Debelle and Stanley Fischer in 1994[25] (1) goal independence and (2) instrument independence. *Goal independence* allows the central bank to choose the ultimate goal of monetary policy, rather than its being determined by the government of the day, or legislated by the constitution. *Instrument independence* lets the central bank pursue its aims (self-imposed or legislated) in a manner that the central bank authorities require to meet their goals.[26]

I cannot think of a central bank that is goal independent. Goals are either set by government or legislated in a constitution. If achieving price stability is a goal, then central banks must be instrument independent. The commitment to a low inflationary environment has led to a rise in the use of currency board arrangements, as discussed in the previous section, and a rise in independent central banks. The German Bundesbank is the most successful and considered to be the model for central bank independence.

Throughout Europe and emerging European countries, the central banks are modeled on the German constitutional laws governing German central banks. The "Bundesbank Act" and its duties govern the German Bundesbank and objectives are defined as follows:

> *"The Deutsche Bundesbank shall regulate the amount of money in circulation and of credit supplied to the economy, using monetary powers conferred on it by this Act, with the aim of safeguarding the currency."*[27]

Safeguarding the currency means keeping its value, purchasing power, stable. For the German central bank to perform its task without political pressure, the legislature accorded the Bundesbank a high degree of independence. Under the Bundesbank Act, the central bank policymakers are required to follow and support the general economic policy of the federal government "without prejudice to the performance of their duties."[28] In exercising their powers, the Bundesbank is independent of instructions from the federal cabinet and to any ongoing parliamentary control.[29] So how does the Bundesbank achieve the stability of the Deutschemark?

To maintain the value of its money, the Bundesbank ensures that not too much money is in circulation. The German authorities believe that controlling the supply of money stock is an essential condition to achieving price stability. The Bundesbank's monetary target is expressed in terms of the money stock M3. Germany money stock M3 comprises currency and deposits of non-banks with domestic credit institutions in the form of sight deposits, time deposits for fewer than four years, and savings deposits with three months' notice to withdraw funds. Central bankers throughout the world would love the Germans' independence. What a surprise! As I suggested at the outset of this chapter, central banks, along with their monetary policies, will become more important and economically more influential. The new global economy is forcing politicians to allow greater central bank independence with the single objective of their monetary policymaking being "price stability." Following are a few examples to prove my point.

In Scandinavia, the oldest central bank, the Swedish Riksbank (established in 1668), conducts monetary policy with price stability as the overriding objective. This amounts to keeping the average rate of price increases—inflation—at a low and stable level. More specifically, the rate of inflation is to be limited to 2 percent with a permissible margin of one percentage point up or down. This is what the Riksbank means by "safeguarding the value of money."[30]

But central bank independence continues to evolve. Even the oldest central bank's independence is undergoing transformation. In November 1998, the Swedish government introduced a bill in parliament that strengthens the Riksbank's independence. The Swedish parliament will "hand sole responsibility for monetary policy to a committee of senior bank officials," according to the *Financial Times* (November 25, 1998). Under the bill:

> *". . . the existing eight-member governing board, comprised mainly of laymen elected by parliament and responsible for setting Sweden's monetary policy framework, would be abolished. A new board, also appointed by parliament, would have no influence over monetary policy. Its only function would be to appoint a directorate of seven Riksbank officials to exercise monetary policy independence."*[31]

The constitutional changes to Swedish Riksbank will move Sweden closer to the new European Central Bank and help prepare Sweden for European Monetary Union, if so desired.

As mentioned earlier, the Riksbank has a 2 percent inflation target with a +/-1 percent margin. Although the Swedish Parliament decided in November 1997 not to participate in European Monetary Union, more recently it has announced a referendum on Swedish participation in European Monetary Union to be held in September 2003.

The Bank of Finland became independent in 1917 and, according to its constitution, it "operates under the guarantee and care of Parliament," with the primary objective being to maintain price stability.[32]

The Finns however, decided to join European Monetary Union at a Finnish Markka conversion exchange rate of FIM 5.94573, with the European Central Bank now controlling monetary policy and the Markka being exchanged for Euros in 2002. (The EMU is discussed in a later chapter.)

The New European Central Bank has adopted a Bundesbank-styled constitution and objectives, which came into force on January 1, 1999, with the introduction of a single currency for 11 European countries, called the Euro.

In Eastern and Central Europe, the newest central banks have also embraced constitutions and objectives similar to the German Bundesbank. With the exception of Belarus and Turkmenistan, central banks in all 15 Eastern European nations have broad de facto autonomy to pursue price stability.[33] The more successful central banks in Eastern and Central Europe quickly enacted the necessary legislation to create German Bundesbank-like constitutions to gain market credibility and play by the new international rules. For example, the Bank of Hungary was created by the Act on the National Bank of Hungary in 1991. It states that the central bank is independent of the government and reports to the parliament on its activities with the goal of maintaining the value of the national currency, called the Forint.[34]

In the Act creating the Czech National Bank, dated December 17, 1991, Article II states:

> *"The primary objective of the Czech National Bank is to ensure the stability of the Czech national currency."*

Article III obliges the Bank to report to Parliament at least twice a year.[35]

The National Bank of Slovakia, established on January 1, 1993, is also an independent institution whose primary function is to ensure the stability of the Slovak currency.[36]

The Croatian Central Bank is also responsible to Parliament, with its main objective being the maintenance of exchange rate stability as well as price stability.[37]

All four of these countries are preparing for entry into the European Union with economic and financial convergence continuing at a rapid pace.

Two of the Baltic countries have adopted currency board arrangements. Article VII from the Law for the Bank of Lithuania states the principal objective "shall be to achieve stability of the currency of the Republic of Lithuania."[38] In Estonia, the mission of the Bank of Estonia "safeguards the national and international confidence in the stability and integrity of Estonia's currency and monetary system."[39]

The point of these examples is that each country uses its own words to state the same mission and objective—get inflation down and keep it there! In our new global economy, maintaining a low inflationary, productive environment is absolutely essential to being competitive in a global marketplace. If not, the global markets take action. I am not referring to the short-term, high profile, headline-making financial traders, but the long-term investors who invest huge sums of money as part of a long-term diversification strategy.

In other countries around the world, the stability of the value or purchasing power of one's currency should be the primary focus of a central bank. The primary objective of inflation-fighting has been occurring in Mexico, Brazil, Hong Kong, New Zealand, and South Africa. In addition, there has been a long list of recent changes to central bank legislation, giving greater independence to central banks in an effort to curb inflationary pressures. Most legislation over the past few years has updated or revised legislation enacted over 50 years ago. The list includes Belgium, France, Greece, Italy, Mexico, Pakistan, Peru, Philippines, South Africa, Uganda, and Venezuela. Undoubtedly many more will come.[40] If all of these countries are seeking to maintain the purchasing power of their domestic currencies, why is there inflation and movements in currency prices?

The simple reason is that monetary policy alone is not going to solve all inflation problems within an economy, no matter how brilliant the governor of the central bank. Fiscal and monetary policies must work hand-in-hand, and the public must motivate policymakers and truly believe that a low-inflationary environment is essential to its well-being. There must exist a cultural and social aversion to inflation—period.

But the final point on central bank independence is *credibility*—the ability to make the right decisions to achieve primary objectives in monetary policymaking.

Central bank independence, along with the social support it receives, is one of the first ingredients I look for when investing internationally. I have to protect the absolute and relative value of my investments. If I ignore this type of detail, the overseas investment will devalue by inflation in that foreign government bond market. Not only would I fail to achieve the return on investment, I could actually lose a great deal of money. Therefore, central bank independence and its credibility are the backbone of monetary policymaking, and are absolutely vital in my decision-making process.

A number of quantitative models have attempted to simulate and quantify central bank independence. In a study by Alex Cukierman, the model uses four interesting characteristics or variables, which are assigned a rating or code. The first variable concerns the appointment, dismissal and term of office of the chief executive officer of the central bank (usually the governor). The second variable concerns the resolution of conflicts between the executive branch and the central bank, and the degree of participation of the central bank in the formulation of monetary policy and in the budgeting process. The third represents final objectives of the central bank as stated in its charter. The fourth variable states legal restrictions on the central banks. Such restrictions take the form of various limitations on the volume, maturity, rates and width of direct advances, and of securitized lending from the central bank to the public sector.[41]

I believe central bank independence will proliferate. Without the independence, I will be hesitant to invest in that country. There are plenty of other investment opportunities that satisfy my investment criteria. Therefore, I do not have to accept the risks of political interference in monetary policy. In the new global economy, as shown in the previous chapter, fiscal policy will be restrictive, because the annual fiscal budget must balance and we must repay and, hopefully, pay down our national debts. Monetary policymaking will become, if it is not already, the rudder for global economic growth. Domestic government bond yields will instantly reflect the belief in low inflationary policies. With less focus on fiscal policy, because of the restrictive nature of future policy, the markets will focus more on monetary policy.

MONETARY POLICYMAKING

The International Monetary Fund argued in December 1997 said:

> *". . . that during the past 25 years monetary practice in most countries has increasingly been characterized by the attempt to achieve credibility of purpose while expanding the freedom of monetary authorities in controlling policy instruments. Thus the world has gradually moved toward monetary frameworks in which, through appropriate institutional devises, a better trade-off between credibility of goals and flexibility of instruments could be achieved."*[42]

What is monetary policy supposed to achieve? By definition, monetary policy affects the supply of credit and the terms on which credit is available to borrowers.[43] As I mentioned earlier, many central banks are turning to "price stability" as their prime and sole objective. Chairman of the Board of Governors of the U.S. Federal Reserve Bank, Alan Greenspan, offered a definition for *price stability*:

> *"Changes in the average price level are small enough and gradual enough that they do not materially enter business and household decisions."*[44]

However, price stability is not always the sole objective. Many central banks have a broader range of objectives. The United States Federal Reserve Bank and the Federal Open Market Committee should seek "to promote effectively the goals of maximum employment, stable prices, and moderate long term interest rates." The Federal Reserve embraces the interdependence of these objectives that emphasize price stability as the means toward achieving maximum sustainable growth in both production and employment.[45]

The Bank of Japan is mandated to conduct monetary policy to support the national economic objectives, which may include potential economic growth, full employment, low inflation, or a sustainable balance of payments. During the 1960s, for example, the objective of the Japanese government was to eliminate external imbalances (the current account deficit), which the Bank of Japan's monetary policies pursued.[46]

In the new global economy, monetary policy will take on a greater role, particularly in the emerging and developing economies, which must ensure that price stability policies are in place and stay in place. Maintaining and containing inflationary pressures are essential for our global economic future.

So, what is the definition of inflation? "The rate of increase of the general level of prices."[47]

What inflation rate do we follow? Consumer prices, producer prices, asset prices, wholesale prices, employment costs, commodity prices? Or do we follow currency prices? Each country, region, province, county, and individual has its own unique inflation rate. Think about it. If you do not smoke cigarettes or a tobacco product, why care about rising tobacco prices? Tobacco represents 0.9 percent of the United States' consumer price index. If you ride a bicycle and never have to buy gas for an automobile, then a rise in either the price or taxes on a gallon of gas will not affect your wallet. In France, for example, one of the interesting facts of life is the use of nuclear energy to create electricity for their train system. This means that train ticket prices do not rise when oil prices rise as in other countries that use oil-powered train systems.

The creation of an index to measure inflation is easier said than done. Should an inflation rate look at all aspects of an economy or at specific details of inflationary pressures? I do not believe that we can create an inflation index, which will represent all things to all people, but we do need to examine all the aspects of inflationary pressures, which exist in various shapes and forms. When is the inflation measure revised to reflect our changing economy and evolving standards of living? Should it be every year or every 10 years?

I am not preparing a lecture on inflation. I studied economics, but I am no economist. But if monetary institutions such as central banks focus their objectives on fighting inflation and fiscal policies are annually adjusted for the inflation rate, then we need to have a general understanding of inflation measurements. As a global investor seeking to invest in real value and in monetary assets such as government bonds, I need to understand and rely on the information and statistics being compiled and released, which is another aspect of transparency. If central banks are targeting inflation, then an appropriate benchmark needs to be defined. According to a report from Michael Boskin, "Toward a More Accurate Measure of the Cost of Living," presented to the United States Senate Finance Committee in December 1996, a 1 percent annual deviation either way in the calculation of the consumer price index represents $600 billion over a 10-year period from 1997 to 2006. That is why the calculation is so important. A 1 percent effect would be comprised within the national budget and have a 40 percent effect through tax increases and 60 percent in the form of budget entitlements, which is the inflation adjustment I referred to earlier. Needless to say, any negative recalculation of budget entitlements is a political hot potato.

In recent years, numerous studies re-examined the measurement issues surrounding the consumer price index. Until I had read these various reports, I had no idea of the difficulties in gaining an honest assessment of inflationary pressures. The Boskin Commission reported that the current consumer price index in the United States might overstate inflation by between 0.8 and 1.6 percentage points annually. The conclusion most reasonable was an overstatement of 1.1 percentage points per year. Many of the arguments presented by the Boskin Report are not new, such as the frequency with which the actual components of the consumer price index are weighted. In the United States the consumer price index is re-weighted every 10 years. On the other hand, the United Kingdom re-weights its retail price index every year.

An annual re-weighting of the components represented within a consumer price index is clearly preferable. But staying with the Boskin Report, there were several other interesting aspects, which, no doubt in an Internet society, will pose even greater problems for a reliable inflation calculation. I suppose, with the advent of a global consumer society, someday we may have a global consumer price index.

To provide a better understanding of what is involved in calculating the United States' consumer price index, the Boskin Report gives us some background:

> *"The technical issues related to the consumer price index are extremely complicated. The consumer price index is provided by classifying 207 strata of con-*

sumption items in 44 geographic areas, resulting in 9,108 components in the
consumer price index. Aside from the sheer size of the consumer price index,
the methodology also can be a source of problems. The consumer price index is
an index composed of a fixed weight market basket of goods and services." (See
Table 4.1.)

Table 4.1: United States Consumer Price Index (Components and their
weights and January 2003 annual inflation rate.)[48]

Item	Weight %	Jan 2003 %
All items:	100.0	0.4
Food	15.583	0.2
Housing	40.854	0.7
Apparel	4.220	-2.8
Transportation	17.293	0.8
Medical care	5.961	0.4
Recreation	5.943	0.4
Education & communication*	5.798	0.5
Tobacco	0.992	0.0
Personal care	3.356	0.3

*Communication includes personal computers and peripheral equipment.

Re-weighting the U.S. index only every 10 years does not allow for product and service substitution effect—substituting a higher price with a lower price good or service.
Also, a newer issue is outlet substitution effect, which encompasses the discount outlets
now available throughout the United States. The more difficult aspect of measuring inflation is quality improvement—the price of the good may rise, but the life of the product
increases.

In the United Kingdom, the inflation data issued is also very complicated because the
British include mortgage payments in their figures. Why? A majority of Brits own their
homes. The oddity of including mortgage payments appears when interest rates rise, with
most mortgage rates being floating rates based on the price of short-term interest rates
rather than long-term 30-year yield in the United States. When short-term interest rates
rise in the United Kingdom to combat inflationary pressures, the mortgage payment rises,
thus raising the inflation rate. Another interesting aspect of the British calculation is its
comparison to the European consumer price index. If the United Kingdom joins the single currency (the Euro), it will have to adopt the European statistical calculation conven-
tions. A study of the United Kingdom's RPIX (retail price index excluding mortgage
interest rates) compared with the HICP (harmonized indices of consumer prices) indicates
that the United Kingdom's version of the HICP is running around 0.9 percentage points
lower than the RPIX version. A positive aspect of the British statistic is its re-weighting
of the index each year to reflect changes in consumer spending. However, British officials
agree that substitution, along with quality improvements, is lacking in their measure.

The German central bank, the Bundesbank, conducted a similar study and placed an
upward bias in their inflation rate measure of 0.75 percentage points. The upward bias in

their consumer price index is why the Bundesbank has targeted inflation for 2 percent because it probably is as close as possible to achieving price stability.

With all good intentions, I do not think that a truly perfect "all things to all people" consumer price index will be discovered. Central bankers along with global investors must continue to look at a wealth of statistical data reflecting various forms of inflationary pressures. However, I recently discovered a paper by Deutsche Bank that introduced a broader index encompassing many aspects of the overall inflation picture (Table 4.2).

Table 4.2: Broad Price Index[49]

Index	Weights %
Consumer prices	67
New house prices	9
Existing home prices	7
Producer price index (finished goods)	5
Producer price index (crude prices)	3
Producer price index (intermediate prices)	4
S&P 500	5

The Deutsche Bank idea provides for weighting of what the United States may actually be feeling by way of inflationary pressures, which better reflects the behavior of prices throughout the U.S. economy. Achieving price stability is the ultimate objective. Discovering the best way to measure it remains hotly debated. But the fact is that inflation-targeting is gaining momentum with central bankers. However, the use of money supply targeting is also used and seen to be an integral assessment in the direction of inflation.

Measuring the supply of money in the economy may seem to be out of date.However, I can assure you that money supply figures are keenly watched and followed by me. Even though money supply may not be deemed the best measuring stick for inflation, I still watch the weekly and monthly money supply and credit figures available in every country that I invest.

Money supply and bank credit figures are important. Although at times, money supply numbers may send out false signals over shorter periods of time, there is no question in my mind that too much money in any type of economy is inflationary.

Prior to discussing the different policies needed to achieve the objectives, I want first to talk about inflation-targeting and, secondly, money supply targets. Independence and the transparency of monetary policy can be greatly improved by the use of a stated benchmark target to gauge the success and failure of a central bank's monetary policies.

INFLATION TARGETING

The opening paragraph of "Inflation Targeting as a Framework for Monetary Policy," published by the IMF, called inflation:

> ". . . bad news. Besides distorting prices, it erodes savings, discourages investment, stimulates capital flight (into foreign assets, precious metals, or unproductive real estate), inhibits growth, makes economic planning a nightmare, and, in its extreme form, evokes social and political unrest."[50]

Inflation-targeting is a monetary policy framework under which policy decisions are guided by expected future inflation relative to an announced inflation target.[51] While most central banks express a desire for low inflation, the distinct feature of inflation-targeting countries is that the inflation rate is the overriding objective of monetary policy.[52] There cannot be a conflict of interest, such as an unemployment target, an economic growth target, money supply target, nor an exchange rate policy. The inflation target dictates monetary policy.

A framework of "rules" tends to serve central banks, along with political decision-makers and the public at large, better than "discretion." The markets better understand a set of rules governing when a central bank should raise or lower interest rates. The absolute rules-based system fixes the value of a currency to the value of gold, which removes all judgment from central bank monetary policymaking. A rule can be based on a nominal GDP objective, a money supply target, an exchange rate objective, or it can be based on a price level or inflation objective. The other difficulty with monetary policy-making is that interest rate changes take time to affect the economy. Therefore, monetary policy is not necessarily a fine-tuning mechanism for the economy. Fiscal policy is discretion, but monetary policy must be based on discipline. The Chancellor of the Exchequer from 1984 to 1989, Nigel Lawson, suggests:

"A direct price-level objective has the great advantage of simplicity. Indeed if it had been followed in most of the post-war period we almost certainly would have benefited."

He also argues that:

". . . a price level rule works best when there is some authority removed from day-to-day political pressures, such as an independent central bank, which is free to choose its own method, but which is held strictly to account for the results achieved in terms of price stability."[53]

Inflation-targeting is necessary for the credibility of a central bank's monetary policy. When credibility is questioned, the reinforcement of an inflation-targeting policy is required. A common feature of those countries that are adopting inflation target as a sole objective for monetary policymaking is their relatively poor inflation records over the past 30 years. There are two good arguments for inflation targeting. The first is more recent and the second more historic. Over the past 10 years there has been a strong re-emphasis on price stability as the primary goal for monetary policy. Second, in the early part of this century, one of the most influential economists was Irving Fisher. He believed that:

". . . one method of mitigating [the evils of a variable monetary standard] is the increase in knowledge as to respective price levels."[54]

I will talk more about Irving Fisher in Chapters 5 and 6.

In Chapter 1, I discussed our greater understanding of the science of economics and also how a common understanding is driving the convergence of policymaking objectives—such as inflation-targeting, around the world. The accountability aspects of inflation-targeting are also helpful. The inflation target provides an anchor for inflationary expectations and a yardstick or benchmark to judge the success or failure of monetary policy.

The most significant difference between fiscal and monetary policymaking is the need for central bankers to understand and interpret economic and market forces, which may create inflationary or deflationary forces. In my view, central bankers must be market savvy, irrespective of the mission, objectives, and targets used. The reason is that any monetary policy action must preempt inflationary pressures, inflation targets—actual inflation falling or rising above the inflation target—or output targets or whether money supply growth is used as the target. In the case of inflation targets, "preemptive strikes" are absolutely necessary in an effort to avoid any build-up or any sort of inflationary pressures underneath the surface of an economy.

In developing countries, as in the industrial world, a move has increased toward price stability and, therefore, inflation targeting. An International Monetary Fund Working Paper states: "The Scope for Inflation Targeting in Developing Countries," identified two major prerequisites for adopting an inflation target. The first is a desire for independence of monetary policy from fiscal dominance (sounds like a married couple). The second is the absence of any desire for a particular level in the currency's exchange rate or any other nominal anchor. In the new global economy, the achievement of price stability will be as competitive as an arms race, and forms part of the new international rules governing the economic behavior of nations. Once again, I need to roll out a good example as the best way to prove that a greater and common understanding for the science of economics will reshape our global financial markets and our economic way of life.

Early in 1998, the Czech National Bank decided on a change in monetary policy to enhance credibility and reduce inflation. Therefore, targeting inflation was required as the Czech Republic prepared for entry into the European Union. The Czechs announced two inflation targets. The first was for 1998 with the inflation target set for 5.5 to 6.5 percent. The second, for the year 2000, was set for achieving 3.5 to 5.5 percent net inflation. That was quite a commitment for a country that had consumer price inflation of 20.8 percent in 1993, falling to 8.5 percent in 1997.

In Chapter 3, I talked about the competition which emerging Eastern and Central European countries presented to the industrialized countries of the European Economic Community. The competition for economic and financial stability is another aspect to that competition. The introduction of the new monetary policy inflation target in the Czech Republic was intended "to enrich the credibility of the currency and to ensure its stability already at the very beginning of economic transformation." Also, "the considerable independence that the central bank was given at that time corresponds to contemporary world trends. . . . current economic experience provides evidence that monetary policy can significantly influence prices, only, rather than employment and/or economic growth in the long run." In its conclusion, the Czech National Bank admits, ". . . achieving both inflation targets [1998 and 2000] will be a demanding task. However, the Czech National Bank designed the disinflation path carefully, taking into consideration some limiting factors. Specifically, the inevitable convergence of domestic and foreign price levels . . . ."[55] The Czech Republic is quickly becoming integrated into Western Europe, competing for its capital and economic market share.

The Czech National Bank has achieved its inflation objectives, albeit with the help of slowing global economic growth. In its October 1998 "Inflation Report," the Czech National Bank reported that:

". . . the year-on-year net inflation index dropped from 6.5 percent in June to 4.3 percent in September."

and

". . . forecasts show that at the end of 1998 net inflation will be substantially below the lower limit of the inflation target [5.5 percent]."

The CNB expected inflation at below 4 percent by the end of 1998. They have also stated at the end of the introduction to their report:

". . . that the medium-term target set for the end of 2000—namely the interval of 3.5-5.5 percent—can be realistically achieved."[56]

The Czech Republic offers an excellent example of inflation-targeting, coupled with disciplined monetary policy, and demonstrating flexibility in fiscal policymaking. Achieving the inflation target caused the economy to slow and the budget deficit to rise by more than 22 percent in 1999 due to lower tax revenues. However, since 2000 the Czech currency, the Koruna, has appreciated by 20 percent in real value. (Real currency appreciation is defined and discussed in Chapter 9.) Economic growth is recovering, although the federal budget deficit and current account deficit continue to grow.

The good news is that inflation is barely visible as the Czech's prepare for entry into the European Union although they will be hard pressed to achieve their Maastricht Treaty budget deficit criteria of 3 percent per annum before entry in 2006.

The other good news is that the monetary policy is working as inflation is expected to remain below 2 percent well into 2004, but unless the fiscal deficit and current account deficit are reigned in, inflationary pressures will build.

South Africa is also a country looking toward inflation-targeting. A J. P. Morgan report entitled "Inflation Targeting in South Africa" (January 22, 1999) stated the reasons inflation-targeting was desirable. First, it would make the South African Reserve Bank more transparent and, second, it could make wage negotiations easier as unions would be better able to predict the future inflation rate. However, the inflation target is a range of 1 to 5 percent , which is not a proper target. The government does not back the target. It does not have a time horizon or deadline for achieving the target goal. And it is a very wide target goal, which does not project transparency as a policy in itself.[57]

However, since 1999, South Africa has enjoyed moderate economic growth, a falling inflation rate, with a slight hiccup from 2001—6.5 percent—to 12.4 percent in 2002. Although the good news is that expectations are for a fall in inflation to 5.6 percent by 2004. The exchange rate has stabilized from Rand 12 per U.S. dollar in 2001 to an average Rand exchange rate of 8.6 per U.S. dollar in 2002.

In November 1998, The Bank of Hungary introduced its first "Quarterly Report on Inflation" stating that the:

". . . objective of the Quarterly is to regularly provide the public with a view on the current and expected path of inflation and also about how the central bank evaluates the macroeconomic environment which determines inflation. By doing so, it is hoped that a much wider public than before will be aware of the objectives of monetary policy and the central bank's measures will be easier to follow and understand."[58]

As mentioned earlier in this chapter, the Hungarians are negotiating and preparing for membership into the European Union and ultimately becoming a member of the single currency.

The focus on inflation fighting is picking up and will become part of the global competition for global capital in the new global economy.

In the United States, a Joint Economic Committee of the U.S. Congress released a study in April 1997 entitled "Establishing Federal Reserve Inflation Goals." In the introduction, the study states:

> ". . . recently several members of Congress have endorsed the concept of price stability as the principal policy objective for Federal Reserve Monetary Policy."

The rationale for adopting the goal of price stability was listed in the study as (1) price stability enables money to perform its various functions, (2) price stability enables the price system to work better, (3) price stability promotes transparency, accountability, and credibility, and (4) price stability enhances fiscal discipline.

The study also lists three benefits once the rate of inflation falls (1) price stability lowers interest rates, (2) price stability works to stabilize financial markets and interest-sensitive sectors of the economy, and, most importantly, (3) low inflation promotes growth. The study concludes that the time is opportune to adjust targets for price stability.

Of course, some argue against inflation-targeting. They prefer a more robust target, which includes output, exchange rates, and employment. History has proven that targeting all these variables, trying to keep every segment of the economy and society happy, has led to global debt crisis, crowding out private capital flows. Clearly, I disagree with a convoluted approach. Keep monetary policy focused on one thing—inflation!

MONETARY TARGETING

The use of monetary targets, the growth in the supply of money to an economy, is worth discussion. The German Bundesbank has been setting an annual monetary target since 1974, and its inflation record is unmatched. What does the German Bundesbank know that we do not?

Tim Congdon and Brian Reading at Lombard Street Research in London argue that:

> ". . . monetary targeting controls monetary things, not real things. It puts limits on the growth of money income, not real income."[59]

Their message is that:

> ". . . the fashion for targeting inflation itself, rather than the monetary causes of inflation, can only result in depression."[60]

I hate to keep quoting him, but Nigel Lawson summarized the money supply argument well:

> "In virtually all modern economies, the central bank operates through its control of short-term interest rates. But the relationship between interest rates and the money supply is as uncertain as is the relationship of the quantity of money, however controlled and defined, to either the price level or to nominal GDP. A

money supply target, in a country where financial institutions and practices have been fairly stable, can be a very useful aid to policy, as for instances in Germany. But it can never be on automatic pilot. Judgment is always required; in selecting the monetary role, in deciding how to enforce it, and in assessing when short-term departures in either direction are acceptable."[61]

Money supply targets have been downgraded as a primary benchmark when managing monetary policy, but it does not lessen its importance as one of many indicators any professional must be aware of. Money supply statistics are very important to me as an advance indicator for future inflationary pressures. I watch everything—money supply, the velocity of money, commodity prices, producer prices, consumer prices, and so on.

No matter the precise definition for a central bank target and objective, the individuals running central banks today do not have a crystal ball to predict the future of inflation. There is no substitute for market judgment. Inflation is a disease that takes no time to enter an economic system, but like any other "virus," if treated early, the treatment, albeit stressful, can be successful. However, that is nothing in comparison to its being left unchecked and allowed to fester. An article, "On Target," (*The Economist,* September 6, 1997) summed up the argument for central bank targeting:

"Whatever its target, a central bank's credibility is still the most important ingredient in monetary policy."

CREDIBILITY

The issue of central bank credibility in our global economy can be portrayed as nothing more than belief in one's monetary system. However presented (in terms of objective, constitution targets, and so on), if a society does not believe in its monetary system, words will not keep it together. International investors will go elsewhere until a central bank's monetary policy serves its country best by maintaining price stability to protect the real value of its currency. Without credibility, the central bank will not survive as a productive institution, which is the reason many countries turn to currency board arrangements to achieve credibility. Ultimately, credibility and reputation are all a central bank really possesses. It cannot raise taxes. It can print money and earn interest on the money it issues, called seigniorage, but that is it. The weight of responsibility for central bankers is enormous, with greater responsibilities to come as the global economy develops. Credibility is a combination of many attributes such as independence, transparency, track record, and personalities. At the end of the day, deeds speak louder than words.

The German Bundesbank is the most credible central bank in the world. Professor Rudi Dornbush states in a June 1998 article in the *Financial Times* on the fiftieth anniversary of the introduction of monetary reform, that the Germans have achieved their:

" . . . economic miracle built on free market economics and in five decades of uncompromising pursuit of price stability. No other central bank has sustained price stability like the Bundesbank."[62]

Professor Dornbush offers three central points for its success over the past 50 years (1) "A commitment to price stability, not necessarily day to day, but clearly a trend," (2) "the easily verifiable targeting of monetary aggregates as the key commitment to price stability," and (3) "reiterating to the German public the Bank's promise of 'price stability,' but not necessarily of full employment, high growth, and quick prosperity."[63]

Every country around the world is trying to find or define a version of credibility on behalf of its central bank along with its monetary policies. Arguments and deliberations about how central bank monetary policies are arrived at, by a group or committee of individuals, should be made available to the public. If the group's or the individuals' commitment to anti-inflation policies is not strong or not in support of the central bank governor, then, irrespective of the rules of engagement, credibility goes down the drain. Political influence is difficult to avoid, and political interference is certain death for achieving the best monetary policy mix.

As I prepared to write this section, I could not help but notice how many articles Alan Greenspan has been receiving lately. The pressure on Mr. Greenspan in March 2002 to reduce interest rates was extremely intense. But this pressure is part of the job. Giving way to political or public pressure is always the easy choice, but it is not so easy for a central bank governor to stand up for what is right against a tide of public opinion. Credibility in monetary policymaking is everything for investor confidence. It will loom even more crucial as part of the new international rules in our new global economy.

SAFETY NETS

In the United States from 1980 through 1992, more than 4,500 federally insured depository institutions with approximately $650 billion in assets failed.[64] The figure paled in comparison to what happened in Asia, Russia, and Latin America in 1997 and 1998, a subject I will return to in Chapter 11.

My first experience with a bank failure came in the summer of 1984—Continental Illinois Bank of Chicago, with $41 billion in assets. I can remember the rumors and stories flying around the market that the bank was in trouble with its loan portfolio, causing foreign and domestic depositors to withdraw their funds. The United States government became alarmed and decided to guarantee all deposits held at the bank. In effect, the government, with a wave of its hand, nationalized the bank. During the Continental Illinois debacle, I learned a few things. One of the more interesting was something called a TED spread.

A TED spread is the interest rate difference between U.S. Treasury bill yields and the Eurodollar deposit interest rate (the most creditworthy banking institutions deposit interest rate for three months). The U.S. Treasury bill is the most creditworthy, safest investment in the world. An investor may put his funds into U.S. Treasury bills and receive the yield it offers, a lower interest rate than available on a bank deposit. Or the investor may deposit funds with a banking institution and receive an interest rate offered by the bank. The difference between the credit risk of a bank going bankrupt and the United States government (governments can raise taxes or print money to repay their debts) is the difference between the yield on a U.S. Treasury bill and a Eurodollar deposit.

At the beginning of 1984, the U.S. Treasury bill yield was 9 percent and a three-month CD yield was 9.69 percent. (I could not find the exact Eurodollar interest rate, nor do I want to introduce the T-bill futures contract or the Eurodollar futures contract at this time, so I used the three-month certificate of deposit yields for this argument. It still lets me prove my point.)[65] The spread between the two deposit interest rates was 0.69 percent—the TED spread. This spread relationship fell to approximately 0.45 percent in February 1984, but rose to 0.72 percent in April, 1984, rising further to 1.28 percent in May, and remaining at this level until August. The TED spread fell to 0.57 percent by November 1984. During this six-month period, commercial banks, on average, had to pay 0.75 percent higher than normal versus the U.S. government to attract the necessary capital to fund their banking operations.

The interest spread and its movement is also the way to visualize a flight to quality. Depositors were investing their funds in U.S. Treasury bills instead of keeping their money on deposit with commercial banking institutions because of their safety fears—a flight to quality.

The governance, supervision, and maintenance of our domestic banking system, let alone the international banking system, is a vital responsibility which normally resides with the central banks. Over the last three decades, we have had to endure a Latin American debt crisis in the late 1970s, the United States savings and loan debt crisis, European and Scandinavian bank crises in the late 1980s, and more recently in Japan, Asia, Russia, and Latin America.

Professor Jacob Frenkel, Governor of the Bank of Israel, presented his thoughts to a seminar in Washington, D.C. in January 1997:

> *"Sound banking requires effective regulation and effective supervision leading to the strict maintenance of capital adequacy ratios. These regulations should also facilitate governance and market discipline through improved information and better transparency. But, more generally, sound banking cannot be a static concept because globalization itself is dynamic. And if globalization is a dynamic concept, so are the innovations in the capital markets. And if financial instruments and practices are evolving, so must the regulatory and the supervisory capacity be dynamic."*[66]

Dynamic supervision of our financial system is essential in the new global economy. There are two absolute sides to the argument about safety nets. First, no bank (its owners and managers) or its depositors should ever suffer losses. Conversely, absolutely "no bailouts" for banks and their depositors.[67] I firmly believe that the owners, managers, and professional investors must be held responsible for their actions. The small depositor and unprofessional investor need to be protected, to a degree, from bad management, also known as "moral hazard." I do not believe in blanket coverage protection for a banking system. Professional managers need to be held more accountable in all facets of life. With the use of more leverage—the use of more rather than less borrowed money—in the global capital markets, professional managers must be held responsible for their investment decisions.

An excellent example is the collapse of a hedge fund in Greenwich, Connecticut, called Long Term Capital Management, in September 1998. This firm had a management pedigree, which included Nobel Laureates and ex-Federal Reserve Bank Governors. It had a capital base, actual cash in their bank account, so to speak, of approximately $3.5 billion. From what I have read, at one point in 1998 they had investment positions in excess of $200 billion. If this fund lost more than 2 percent of its invested value ($200 billion), these managers and investors would lose all of their capital ($3.5 billion). According to newspaper reports, Long Term Capital Management had run up losses of approximately $100 billion. I believe that when it all goes wrong, as it did for Long Term Capital Management in September 1998, the investors, shareholders, management and their creditors should pick up the tab—not the government. I have very strong views about risk taking in the global capital markets—from credit risks to the leveraging of capital and borrowing money. However, I do not leverage, and I do not believe in excessive leveraging as a tool. If I can't afford it, I don't own it.

When should a central bank intervene, or draw the line, and allow a financial institution to fail? Ambiguity is probably the key word in this case. An IMF Working Paper on "Transparency and Ambiguity in Central Bank Safety Net Operations" stated:

> *"Arguments for ambiguity in central bank operations build on the basic arguments for discretion, and rest on the need for flexibility for a central bank in order to sustain its credibility over time. Such arguments rest on the view that a cook book approach to problems in financial markets is likely to be inefficient and that the circumstances associated with a particular situation and the assessment of the relative costs and benefits of action will always have to be decided upon case by case."*

I agree. That was easy.

The cases of Long Term Capital Management and Continental Illinois Bank are two in which the central bank authorities posed a risk to the financial system of the United States, irrespective of who is to blame. But in the future, if we are going to have a robust, dynamic, and secure financial system, monitoring creditors and leveraged positions is essential. I do not care if the fund is called a hedge fund, commercial bank, mutual fund, investment bank, pension fund, or local government (such as Orange County California). The problem is leveraging and, if not controlled soon, we may face a tax rise to pay for it, such as the savings and loan debacle and the local residents of Orange County. Leveraging must be more accountable to the system as a whole, preferably and naturally through the central bank.

The Lloyd's Insurance Market offered an unlimited ability to underwrite insurance risks through their "Names." These individuals may pledge their entire net worth, but in fact have to pledge only a small amount of money to the insurance market. It failed because of the size and scope of huge financial losses in the 1980s and 1990s that they had to underwrite.

We, the taxpayers, cannot afford to underwrite blank check writing in the new global economy. Whatever we decide, we had better start doing it quickly, because the leveraging that I confronted in 1994 (to be discussed in a later chapter) and unwinding in 1998 is huge. I learned from the global government bond market collapse in 1994, and yet it continues.

New Zealand has created an interesting new banking supervision system worth mentioning. An article entitled "Banking Soundness and the Role of the Market" by Donald Brash, Governor of New Zealand Central Bank, outlined New Zealand's new approach. It stated:

> *"The authorities decided to place greater reliance on market disciplines through public disclosure by banks, increasing the accountability of bank directors and management, and reducing the extent of prudential regulation."*

Their thinking is that public disclosure will force banking management to behave prudently; versus a set of rules, which require and regulate the way banks may behave. The rules in New Zealand came into force on January 1, 1996. They deserve much credit for their successful efforts. The New Zealand approach may not work best for every country. I hope central banks will lead the way—educating, supervising, and governing our financial markets with monetary policies that enhance our everyday economic lives.

When the terrorist hit the World Trade Center on September 11, 2001, the central banks took quick and decisive action, reducing interest rates and providing as much liquidity to the marketplace that was necessary to ensure that the global financial system would continue to operate. The central banking community fulfilled their role to the fullest as their task to avert a loss in confidence, prevent panic, particularly in the midst of a settlements problem at the Bank of New York, the custodian bank and bookkeeper of more than half of all government bonds traded throughout the world each day. In fact, the *Financial Times* reported in a wonderful synopsis "Cool Nerves at the Central Banks" on how the Federal Reserve and European Central Bank behaved after the day of the attack— September 11th. Deutsche Bank, a German bank, acted as the main clearing bank for U.S. transactions allowing more than $500 billion of market transactions to pass through their system in the days that followed, picking up the void left by the Bank of New York.

One of the interesting lessons that is pointed out in the *Financial Times* article is the fact that when the U.S. stock and bond markets re-opened from their suspension (September 11 to September 17), cutting interest rates by 0.50 percent before the opening bell in New York, the stock market fell very sharply. Not because of investors fear for the financial system but for their fear of what congress might do with fiscal policy. Congress had approved a $40 billion package for spending on defense and security—what could the market expect as it turned its attention to more economic packages for the U.S. economy?

The slide in the stock market sent a signal to congress that they should let the markets sort them selves out rather than have central government attempt intervention, with the usual lack of success. What would happen to the budget surplus? A budget deficit would reverse the process of more money in the hands of the private sector versus the public sector, causing inflation to rise. Uncertainty in policy making sends the markets in one direction, downward. Fears about it all dissipated later in the week and as we now know the U.S. economy has been rebounding ever since.

CONCLUSION

The world is a very different place from the 1950s. My point, however, is that after the past two decades the new international rules require international central banks to deliver price stability. The inflation roller coaster ride since the 1950s has given way to a desired culture for price stability, although I feel very strongly that the inflation roller coaster had nothing to do with the exogenous shocks to our economy, such as the oil price rises in the 1970s. It had more to do with real interest rates being too low, lagging behind the inflation roller coaster. Monetary policy was reacting to, rather than in control of, inflationary pressures. But that had to change.

If we want to live in a prosperous new global economy, living with low inflationary economic growth requires vigilance and preemptive monetary policymaking to keep inflation in check. Inflation in the OECD countries is at 40-year lows. If the inflation statistics do represent an overshoot in the annual inflation rate of 0.5 to 1.5 percent per annum in the industrial countries, then with the average inflation rate in the range of 1.5 to 2.0 percent per annum, I think we have achieved price stability.

Achieving price stability was the easy part. Maintaining a low inflationary economy will be much more difficult. Price stability will create more political conflict between monetary and fiscal policymakers and authorities than when the inflation rate was high and out of control. Vigilance is required to keep the government authorities in check.

ENDNOTES

[1] Deane, M., and R. Pringle. 1994. *The Central Banks*. New York: Penguin Group.

[2] Ibid., page 32.

[3] Ibid., page 34.

[4] Ibid., page 39.

[5] Ibid., page 40.

[6] Ibid., page 40.

[7] Ibid., page 41.

[8] Ibid., page 42.

[9] Ibid., page 43.

[10] Ibid., page 48.

[11] Ibid. Forword by Paul Volcker, July 1994, pages vii and viii.

[12] Stiglitz, J. E. *Economics*. 1997. New York: W. N. Norton & Co., page 728.

[13] Ibid., page A14.

[14] "The Rise and Fall of Inflation—Lessons from Postwar Experience." *World Economic Outlook*, October 1996, page 101. Washington, D.C.: International Monetary Fund.

[15] Ibid., page 103.

[16] IMF Survey, February 24, 1997, page 54. Washington, D.C.: International Monetary Fund.

[17] "The Magic of Currency Boards." Focus Eastern Europe, Emerging Markets, December 1996, Deutsche Morgan Grenfell.

[18] "Currency Boards," Box 5. *World Economic Outlook*, October 1997, page 84. Washington, D.C.: International Monetary Fund.

[19] "Making Currency Boards Operational Requires Wide Array of Technical Preparations." IMF Survey, January 26, 1998, page 29. Washington, D.C.: International Monetary Fund.

[20] Ibid., page 27.

[21] Enoch, C., and J. T. Balino. "Currency Board Arrangements Issues and Experiences," August 1997, page 1. Washington, D.C.: International Monetary Fund.

[22] Perry, G. E. "Currency Boards and Extreme Shocks How Much Pain How Much Gain?" The World Bank, 1997, page 1.

[23] "Currency Boards the Ultimate Fix?" IMF Working Paper, January 1998, page 3. Washington, D.C.: International Monetary Fund.

[24] "Central Bank Independence and Inflation," Box 11. *World Economic Outlook*, October 1996. Washington, D.C.: International Monetary Fund.

[25] Ibid., Footnote 1.

[26] Ibid.

[27] Source: Deutsche Bundesbank.

[28] Ibid.

[29] Ibid.

[30] Sveriges Riksbank.

[31] "Sweden Expected to Boost Central Bank Independence." *Financial Times,* November 25, 1998.

[32] Bank of Finland.

[33] "Central Banks in Transition Economies Pursue Market-Based Reforms." IMF Survey, February 9, 1998, page 44. Washington, D.C.: International Monetary Fund.

[34] Bank of Hungary.

[35] Czech National Bank.

[36] National Bank of Slovakia.

[37] Croatian National Bank.

[38] The Bank of Lithuania.

[39] The Bank of Estonia.

[40] Cotterelli, C., and C. Giannini. "Credibility without Rules? Monetary Frameworks in the Post-Bretton Woods Era." December 1997, pages 18 and 19. Washington, D.C.: International Monetary Fund.

[41] Cukierman, A. 1992. *Central Bank Strategy, Credibility and Independence.* Cambridge, MA: MIT, page 372.

[42] Ibid., page 2.

[43] Stiglitz, op. cit., page A14.

[44] "Price Stability," Box 3. *World Economic Outlook,* May 1993, page 24. Washington, D.C.: International Monetary Fund.

[45] Ibid., page 25.

[46] Ibid., pages 25-26.

[47] Stiglitz, op. cit., page A14.

[48] Source: J. P. Morgan.

[49] "Market Issues." Deutsche Bank, May 25, 1998, pages 13 and 14.

[50] Debelle, G., P. Masson, M. Savastano, and S. Sharma. "Inflation Targeting as a Framework for Monetary Policy." 1998, page 1. Washington, D.C.: International Monetary Fund.

[51] "Inflation Targeting: Theory and Policy Implications." IMF Working Paper, June 1996, page iii. Washington, D.C.: International Monetary Fund.

[52] "Inflation Targeting in Practice." IMF Working Paper, March 1994, page 4. Washington, D.C.: International Monetary Fund.

[53] Lawson, N. 1992. *The View From No. 11.* London, U. K.: Bantam Press, pages 418 and 419.

[54] "Targeting Inflation." A conference on Central Banks on the use of inflation targets organized by the Bank of England, edited by Andrew Haldane, March 9-10, 1995, page v. (Fisher, I. 1992. *The Purchasing Power of Money.* New York: Macmillan.)

[55] "Inflation Report." Czech National Bank, April 1998, pages 1 and 2.

[56] "Inflation Report." Czech National Bank, October 1998, pages 1 and 2.

[57] "Inflation Targeting in South Africa." Global Data Watch, January 22, 1999, page 55.

[58] "Quarterly Report for Inflation." National Bank of Hungary, November 1998.

[59] Harris, A. "A Lament for Targeting of Money Supply." *The Times,* September 3, 1997.

[60] Ibid.

[61] Lawson, op. cit., page 417.

[62] Dornbush, R. "In Praise of Hard Money." *Financial Times,* June 18, 1998.

[63] Ibid.

[64] Barth, J. R., and R. D. Brumbaugh, Jr. "The Role of the Deposit Insurance: Financial System Stability and Moral Hazard," "Current Legal Issues Affecting Central Banks." Washington, D.C.: International Monetary Fund, 1997, volume 4, page 393.

[65] Source: United States Federal Reserve Bank Economic Data.

[66] Frankel, J. A. "Capital Mobility and its Impact on Operations of a Central Bank," "Banking Soundness and Monetary Policy." Washington, D.C.: International Monetary Fund, 1997.

[67] "Transparency and Ambiguity in Central Bank Safety Net Operations." IMF Working Paper, October 1997. Washington, D.C.: International Monetary Fund.

Chapter 5
REAL INTEREST RATES

In the preceding chapter I defined real interest rates as nominal or money interest rate minus the inflation rate equals the real interest rate. Now let's look at an explanation of its importance.

I have given many presentations on the subject of real interest rates, which forms part of my analysis and are an integral part of my investment philosophy and strategy. I believe that the real interest rate is the fundamental form and the most basic way to value the cost of capital, both domestically and internationally. Real interest rates provide me with a way to start, approach, and think about investment strategies.

When I started building the computer software systems for my money management business, I focused on the real interest rate and real yield relationships. They became particularly interesting as I created hedging strategies for the system and became more aware of the various underlying financial risks in the global capital markets. When I hedge against the financial risks of an adverse currency price movement, I think about real interest rates analysis. The next chapter I discuss these strategies.

The economist who most influenced my understanding of real interest rates and, ultimately, global capital market movements was Irving Fisher, Yale University economics professor (1867-1947). Professor Fisher's *The Theory of Interest,* published in 1930, has remained a handy desk reference since my LSE days. Here are a few definitions, which I hope will better explain the thinking on real interest rates and aspects of his work.

Irving Fisher's analysis begins with the definitions for *income* and *capital*. He describes three successive stages of a person's income (1) enjoyment or psychic income, (2) real income, and (3) money income.

Enjoyment income is psychological and cannot be directly measured in any way. Fisher approximates its measure through real income. Real income generates our ability to buy physical "things" or "events," which give us enjoyment. As examples, he says real income provides us with the psychological enjoyment of the shelter of a house, the music of a victrola or radio (a victrola is a record player; I suspect my children will have to be taught what a record player was), as well as wearing clothes or eating food, reading a newspaper, and all the other innumerable events which contribute to our enjoyment. Fisher calls it our "bread and butter." The only way to measure our enjoyment is by the amount of money paid to receive them.

Real income, the next stage in Fisher's analysis, is measured through our cost of living. The total cost of living, in the sense of money payments, is a negative item—out of pocket expenses for shelter, food, and so on.

The third stage, *money income,* therefore consists of money received by a person for meeting their costs of living.

Another way to look at the three stages of income is that money income is commonly called income. Enjoyment income is the most fundamental, but cannot be measured. Therefore, for accounting purposes, real income, as measured by the cost of living, is the easiest and most practical measure.

The important point I want to make is that we need to convert our money income into real things, which may or may not give us pleasure. Let's face it, who enjoys paying bills? The money we save, Fisher points out, from our money income, is not turned immediately into real income to purchase things but is being saved to be converted into real things at a later time.

In summary, a person's annual income must be used to buy real things, and the money that is saved must be used to purchase real things in the future. We measure the income and spending aspects of our lives through our cost of living. Fisher offers an example:

> *". . . when a man lends $100 this year in order to obtain $105 next year, he is really sacrificing not $100 in literal money but one hundred dollars in goods such as food, clothing, shelter, or pleasure trips, in order to obtain next year not $105 in literal money but one hundred and five dollars worth of other goods."[1]*

This is an example of the purchasing power of money.

The rate of interest is a percentage premium on present goods over future goods of the same kind. Fisher goes on to define the difference between the interest that is expressed in terms of money and the interest expressed in other goods. There is an interest rate expressed in terms of our money, which we can read in the newspapers each day. But, in reality, no goods or services in today's market see prices rise equally, consistently, and constantly against one another. As I suggested in Chapter 3, each person theoretically has his own measurable cost of living and inherent inflation rate or consumer price index affecting that individual's cost of living. Therefore, every good and service we require to keep us happy today, and more importantly in the future, has its own inflation rate and impact and therefore its own real interest rate.

Speaking for myself, I realize that in 15 years housing costs will probably rise at a different inflation rate than my children's college education. If you have children who will attend college in 15 years or so, T. Rowe Price's Web site (*www.trowprice.com*) has a calculator for education costs. The sums of money to be saved to meet that cost objective are daunting. Therefore, the amount of money we need to save today for a home or college education tomorrow may vary dramatically. To ascertain the amount of money required in the future, go back and determine the real interest rate or real yield. You'll arrive at the sum of money needed to achieve that requirement.

For example, say oranges are rising in price by 10 percent per annum and the price of apples remains the same over the same period of time. Assume that money interest rates are 10 percent. If I lend the money I was going to use to buy oranges to another person, and that persons repays the principal amount of money—the orange money—plus 10 percent interest on that sum of money, then I can buy an orange a year later with the money I receive. However, if I lend the money I am planning to use to buy an apple in one year's time, I am able to buy an apple and save the 10 percent interest received from the loan. In very simple terms, this is how I exploit different real interest rates throughout the global capital markets. This is the logic that I apply when seeking to add real value to a portfolio of monetary assets. This simple analysis is very useful in other asset class categories.

This point also affects every investment decision in every aspect of life. For instance, if I am a 35-year-old saving for retirement in a pension fund (assuming retirement age of 65), I must save and ensure that I receive enough of a return on my investment to enable me to purchase the goods and services that I will require in 30 years. If, for example, I invest my savings into U.S. Treasury bills and assume that the real interest rate on U.S. Treasury bills is 0 percent over the next 30 years, and inflation or the cost of living rises by 5 percent per annum for that period, the money that I receive at age 65 will enable me to purchase 48 percent of the goods and services that I enjoyed at age 35. And as time moves on, my purchasing power will continue to diminish as my cost of living rises after retirement. The money I invested for retirement was safe, invested in the most credit-worthy instrument available, but I did not invest that money appropriately to capture the rising cost of living.

One of the difficulties of comparing global real interest rates in the 1980s was that the only truly free markets were the United States and The United Kingdom. Any regulation, tax or laws, which restrict the freedom of movement of capital, will void my valuation process. As the freedom of movement of capital expanded throughout the globe in the 1990s, I have found and used real interest rates, real yields, as a starting point to value the global fixed income marketplace. More specifically, when diversifying from a single currency environment, such as U.S. dollars, to a multi-currency environment, the first decision in the asset allocation process is to seek adding real value to that single currency fixed-income return on investment. I will look at and value those countries which offer better real value today and into tomorrow to add value to the single currency, in this case U.S. dollars.

In recent years there have been a number of interesting studies on the subject of real interest rates. Actuaries, who are experts in probability theory, spend their time working out and ensuring that pension funds and insurance policies achieve the necessary real return on investment to ensure that the required real liability is met at some future date. I am not in any way comparing monetary assets with real assets—such as equity assets. The importance of real interest rates is never more evident than during asset allocation decisions, which are supposed to ensure that the purchasing power of the investor is protected. Real assets have consistently outperformed monetary assets. I believe this will continue into the future. Barclays' Bank examines the relationship between equities and U.K. gilt-edged bonds (U.K. government bonds) and, since 1956, has published one of the oldest ongoing annual studies. As an example, Barclays' February 2002 and 2003 editions of the Equity-Gilt studies demonstrate the importance of real interest rates (also the importance of the apples and oranges example). Table 5.1 shows the results of these studies:[2]

Table 5.1: Real Investment Returns by Asset Class (% per annum)

United Kingdom

Asset Class	2002	10 Years	20 Years	50 Years	103 Years*
Equities	-24.5	3.9	8.2	7.0	5.0
Gilts	6.7	7.2	6.6	1.2	1.2
Corporate bonds	6.6	8.6	N/A	N/A	N/A
Index-linked	5.1	5.1	3.5	N/A	N/A
Cash	1.1	3.4	4.6	1.8	1.0

United States

Asset Class	2002	10 Years	20 Years	50 Years	77 Years
Equities	-23.0	6.2	8.7	7.0	6.8
Bonds	13.9	6.8	7.6	2.5	2.3
Cash	-0.7	1.3	2.4	1.3	0.7

*Entire sample since 1899.
Source: Barclay's Capital Gilt-Equity Study, February 2002 (U.K.), February 2003 (U.S.).

A number of interesting conclusions can be drawn from Table 5.1. First, look how real interest and real yields have risen in the past 10 to 20 years. They have been rising as inflation has been rising from the first half of the 20th century to the second half. Second, relative to equity investments and in absolute terms, look how monetary assets such as bonds and cash have risen in real terms. I believe this is not a phenomenon but a reality resulting from global competition for capital. Remember all those charts and tables in earlier chapters and the rise in global indebtedness? Higher real monetary returns on investment are the direct consequence for the rise in real interest rates and the subsequent returns on investment. Table 5.1 gives a good picture of the significance and impact real interest rates have on investment decisions. Similar studies were conducted over differing periods of time. Compare Table 5.2,[3] to Table 5.3.[4] The results are not surprising but are interesting to see.

Table 5.2: Real Returns, International Comparisons

United Kingdom 1946-1997	Germany 1952-1997	Netherlands 1947-1997	France 1951-1997	Japan 1970-1997
*Equities**				
7.0	7.3	8.0	7.8	5.6
*Bonds**				
0.3	4.0	1.5	2.1	3.6

Table 5.3: Real Equity and Bond Returns*
(geometric means, % per annum)

United Kingdom	United States	Germany	Netherlands	France	Japan
			1970-1997		
Equities					
8.0	7.6	5.6	10.0	7.6	5.6
Bonds					
3.6	3.2	4.0	4.0	2.9	3.6

*Geometric averages, local currencies.

GLOBAL REAL INTEREST RATES

According to an International Monetary Fund Staff Studies Report:[5]

> *"The global real interest rate is arguably the most important price in world financial markets."*

When I read this comment, I wondered why, if it's so important, is it ignored or given so little attention. In our new economy, the real price of capital will become *more* important. Costs of living will converge throughout the globe, believe it or not. Think about it. For instance, look at what is happening in Europe where 300 million people will have a common cost of living index. I expect the European Union will ultimately rise to 500 million people within a few years as eastern and central European countries join the E.U.

Real interest rate convergence will create a common cost of living standard throughout the world. I am not suggesting that everyone's standard of living is going to rise and converge, but the cost of living certainly will converge. Global finance will no longer be a single currency, domestic market. It will become a global affair, a global single capital market, and a global real interest rate. In the new economy, we will be global savers and global investors.

When I look at real interest rates or real yields in different countries, there are several characteristics that I consider very important. I will look at each country's real interest rate and government bond real yield in absolute terms, and then in relative terms to other countries. The next step is to look at the direction of the real interest rate or real yield. The last factor is the quality of the real interest rate, the policy and the policymakers behind the direction, relative and absolute value.

The relative value of the real interest rate is reached by comparing the real interest rates or real bond yields available for investment in each country's government bond market. I am not comparing the nominal or money interest rate or yield from one country to another, but the real yield. There may be three countries with nominal interest rates of 10 percent, but their inflation rates may be 3, 5, and 7 percent. Therefore, the real yields on the three investments are 7, 5, and 3 percent respectively. Looking at real interest rates and their relative value is a good place to start when investing in a global fixed income environment.

Going back to the example, on the face of relative real value, the 7 percent real yield country looks best as an investment (10 percent nominal yield minus the 3 percent inflation rate). The 7 percent real yield is offering substantial value. However, this is the time to look at the other real interest-rate characteristics, which require much more homework and human judgment. The direction of real interest rates will require human judgment because what might look attractive today could be disastrous in a few months. For example, a country having a low inflation rate and high real interest rate today may not tomorrow. This particular country may have a high unemployment rate with a high annual budget deficit, social pressures on the government to lower interest rates, increase central government spending, and a non-independent central bank that starts to print money. If this were the 7 percent real interest rate country, this is not a government debt market that would be attractive to me. The real interest rate in this country could fall from 7 percent today to zero or a negative real interest rate in a few months. The optimal direction is a falling inflation rate accompanied by a reduction in nominal interest rates.

The last aspect, which again requires human judgment, is to determine the quality of the policy and policymaking and, at times, to a large extent, the individuals who stand behind all aspects of fiscal and monetary policymaking. If, for example, fiscal and monetary policymakers are determined and committed to prudent fiscal policy and promote the freedom of movement of capital while maintaining low inflationary economic growth, these aspects will comfort investors. This promotes an economic environment that protects the investor's purchasing power. If, on the other hand, as in an earlier example, a government's reversing course on fiscal and monetary policy at the first sign of social difficulty (a policy which may pose difficulties for its people over the short term but is beneficial for the economy over the longer term) does not bode well for investor confidence. More importantly, most investors, such as myself, have long memories. The cost in real interest rates on the cost of capital, as demonstrated in earlier chapters, could be enormous, prolonging economic difficulties.

I do not care to create an econometric model; I do not think I am capable, nor do I subscribe to or believe in black boxes, crystal balls, Santa Claus, or the tooth fairy. Observing real interest-rate relationships over the past 16 years throughout the global capital markets has been extremely useful, and I have learned from many mistakes. Professor Fisher warned me of the most important lesson, one taught almost 80 years ago, by writing:

> *"The fact that interest expressed in money is high, say 15 percent, might considerably indicate merely that general prices are expected to rise (i.e., money depreciation) at the rate of 10 percent, and that the rate of interest expressed in terms of goods is not high, but only 5 percent."*[6]

The lesson here is that there are always reasons why interest rates are high—they are never high because government authorities want to give money away. Understanding this fundamental concept is critical. In other words, you do not get something for nothing.

During times of crisis and high stress, I would quickly sketch a real interest rate chart to reinforce investment decisions. I broke down the world into four tiers of real interest-rate categories, which would compete for global capital. The four tiers in the 1980s became five tiers in the 1990s. As a result of the global debt crises of 1997 and 1998, along with the launch of the European Monetary Union, five tiers of competing real interest rates will most likely become three. The differences from Tier One to Tier Four are credibility, transparency, a commitment to low inflationary growth and, perhaps most importantly, central bank independence. Tier One countries, the most creditworthy, require the lowest real interest rate. These categories and the qualitative assignment of one tier versus another are based on my professional judgment. Table 5.4 is an example of the many countries and the real interest-rate tiers that I kept track of in the 1980s, and Table 5.5 is an example for the 1990s.

Table 5.4: Four Categories of Countries
(Tiered by the level of sustainable real yields over an interest rate cycle in the 1980s)

Tier 1	Tier 2	Tier 3	Tier 4
United States	United Kingdom	Belgium	Argentina
Japan	France	Spain	Mexico
West Germany	Austria	Italy	Brazil
Switzerland	Canada	Australia	Other least
	Netherlands	New Zealand	developed
	Denmark	Ireland	countries
		Finland	
		Sweden	
		Portugal	

Table 5.5: Five Categories of Countries
(Tiered by the level of sustainable real yields over an interest rate cycle in the 1990s)

Tier 1	Tier 2	Tier 3	Tier 4	Tier 5
United States	Japan	Czech Republic	Argentina	Russia
Switzerland	Italy	Poland	Mexico	Bulgaria
Germany	Canada	Slovenia	Brazil	Ukraine
France	United Kingdom	Hungary	Israel	South Korea
Belgium	Denmark	Hong Kong	South Africa	Indonesia
Spain	Sweden	China		Malaysia
Portugal	Australia			
Netherlands	Norway			
Austria	New Zealand			
Luxembourg	Ireland			
Finland				

There are several interesting points in these two tables. The first is the number of new countries, which entered my radar screen. Second, with the European Monetary Union, the 11 countries forming the charter members (except Italy and Ireland) have risen to Tier One because they will be governed by the European Central Bank, which is supposed to be independent of the individual domestic governments. I have a real problem with Italy and Ireland because of their respective business cycles, and I doubt either country will be able to maintain a monetary union. A third observation is the rise of the Czech Republic, Poland, Hungary, and Slovenia to Tier Three because of their commitment to the European Monetary Union. The fourth observation is the collapse of Japan and the rise of China. This is what the new economy is all about.

Were my real yield charts sound? Yes. In 1988, a few members of the board of directors of GH Asset Management suggested I use my real yield chart to form part of a monthly newsletter. By 1990, we were sending out more than 8,000 copies of our newsletter each month. The real yield newsletter turned out to be one of the best selling tools for introducing myself to prospective clients. I learned at the startup of my business that educating prospective clients was the best way to attract new clients. I held seminars at the Ritz Hotel in London to present our firm to pension funds and pension fund consultants. I explained the importance of going global, the risks, real yield, economic views, and the strategy we were employing. We booked the smallest room, capacity 35, and offered a buffet lunch after the presentation. We started speaking at 11:30 a.m. and broke for lunch at 12:45 a.m.—short and sweet. We held the first seminar in February 1992, after the signing of the Maastricht Treaty (which launched the single currency in Europe). Six people showed up. By the third seminar in October 1993, we had to book a larger room to accommodate more than 60 positive responses. Table 5.6 is an example of the real yield data sheet as of December 1, 1987.

A number of observations can be made from Table 5.6. First, notice the blanks in the Australian economic statistics. The inability to observe all aspects of an economy lessens the likelihood of investing in this government's debt market. Second, France is a Tier Two country and Australia is a Tier Three. France is offering a higher real yield plus France's wholesale prices are falling, which means there is a very good chance that consumer price inflation will fall as well. Also, money supply is growing at an appropriate level in relation to economic growth. I cannot draw these types of investment conclusions from Australia. Australia would have to compensate me with much higher real yields to induce me to invest. Third, Australia has higher nominal yields but a lower real interest rate versus other countries on the data sheet. As I said earlier in this chapter, you do not get something for nothing. A Frenchman investing in Australia, all things being equal, would lose over 2.25 percent per annum in real terms on five-year government bonds. The French investor is much better off remaining in French government bonds rather than diversifying into Australian government debt.

Table 5.6 reflects the new economy. Countries that play by the new international rules will attract greater investment. Those that don't won't. The starting point for my real interest rate analysis is always Tier One countries. Start with the best and see what value the rest of the world can offer. As the line from the movie 'Jerry Maguire' says, "Show me the money." I say, show me real value, credibility, transparency, commitment, and determination to play by the new international rules and, if it looks good and tells a solid story, I will invest.

Here is another way to look at real interest rate tiers. The more a country requires foreign investment to fund its government indebtedness, the lower the real interest rate tier rating. The more these lower tiers require investment, the higher the real interest rate required to attract investment.

Table 5.6: Global Yields (December 1, 1987)

Country Economic Data

Yields	U.S.	UK	Japan	West Germany	Australia	France
3-month	7.50%	9.00%	4.00%	3.75%	11.85%	8.625%
5-year	8.45%	9.00%	4.50%	5.41%	12.50%	9.750%
10-year	8.91%	9.47%	5.15%	6.25%	13.20%	9.850%
30-year	8.97%	9.26%		7.31%		10.220%

Real Rate of Return

	U.S.	UK	Japan	West Germany	Australia	France
3-month	3.00%	4.50%	3.20%	2.85%	3.55%	5.42%
5-year	3.95%	4.50%	3.70%	4.51%	4.20%	6.55%
10-year	4.41%	4.97%	4.76%	5.35%	4.90%	6.65%

Statistics

	U.S.	UK	Japan	West Germany	Australia	France
Discount rate	6.00%	—	2.5%	3.0%	13.00%	8.00%
Prime rate	9.75%	9.0%	Long 5.7% Short 3.75%	4.5%	13.75%	9.25%
CPI	4.50%	4.5%	0.8%	0.9%	8.30%	3.20%
Wholesale price	2.60%	3.9%	0.6%	-1.2%	—	-3.20%
GNP	4.10%	3.7%	2.7%	0.8%	2.00%	1.20%
Money supply	10.80%	5.2%	11.1%	9.5%	—	2.50%

The analysis of global interest rates and real yields on government debt has added another dimension over the past 15 years. The introduction of index-linked government bonds has been extremely helpful in our global analysis.

INFLATION/INDEX-LINKED GOVERNMENT BONDS

The introduction of inflation-linked or index-linked government bonds would make Professor Fisher proud. Index-linked government bonds are negotiable government bonds, which link the coupon and principal payments to a retail or consumer price index. This effectively provides protection to investors who require insulation from future inflation. Index-linked government bonds are quoted and traded on a real-yield basis. Because the effects of inflation are fully allowed for in their valuation, the movements in (real) yield tend to be less volatile than with conventional fixed coupon government bonds. This is because the "residual risk" within a conventional bond's yield moves both up and down according to the market's perception of inflationary risk. Such a risk is not prevalent in index-linked bonds.

One of the difficulties faced as a result of inflation and its future impact is the ability to enter into long-term financial agreements. If we were able to predict the future inflation rate in our business transactions, needless to say, life would be very different and much simpler. In fact, the inflation rate itself is difficult to predict, but the volatility and the magnitude of the annual, quarterly, and monthly changes are even more difficult. There is also another substantial difficulty for investors and business people with the unpredictability of inflation. The additional compensation required by each party in a transaction.

Index-linked government bonds add another dimension for measuring global real interest rates. I was fortunate to learn about these instruments while working at Cigna International Investment Advisors. Although I am no expert on the subject, I regularly used index-linked government bonds and ran portfolios dedicated to these instruments. One of the first papers I read on the subject, published in 1983, came from an old British brokerage firm called Phillips and Drew, now owned by the United Bank of Switzerland. The United Kingdom was the first country in the past 15 years to start issuing index-linked government debt. In the past, Finnish banks offered index-linked deposit facilities as early as 1957. According to the Philips and Drew paper, in 1974, Icelandic pension funds were given the opportunity to invest 20 percent of their disposable cash flow in government bonds with a maturity of 15 years indexed to building costs.[7] The importance of the use of index linking cannot be ignored as a market valuation for inflation expectations. Additionally, the presence of a significant government guaranteed paper based on an index of consumer prices enables parties on both sides of an agreement to measure the cost of inflation into the future.

There is a very big difference between a "conventional" bond and an "index-linked" bond. A conventional bond is a financial instrument which entitles the holder to certain or fixed money payments until its maturity. Index-linked bonds are financial securities whose coupon payments and principal repayment at maturity are tied to a consumer price index.

There is approximately $160 billion in outstanding index-linked government bonds. The United Kingdom and Sweden place 15 percent of their annual government bond issuance in index-linked securities. They are very simple in concept—the indexation of principal and semiannual coupon payments during the life of a bond to a standard measure of inflation, such as the consumer price index. They are the ideal financial instruments in which to protect future long-term liabilities from the exposure of inflation. There is a great deal to read on this subject, and I do not intend to re-hash the details of how they actually work. Instead, I want to look at these instruments in terms of the real interest analysis and how index-linked instruments are a discipline and commitment by fiscal policymakers.

The best way to explain the use of inflation-indexed bonds with conventional bonds is the use or calculation of the break-even inflation rate. Roger Bootle's 1991 book, *Index-Linked Gilts,* best describes the break-even inflation rate, where an investor faces a choice of an index-linked or conventional bond of identical maturity. If the investor buys the index-linked bonds, the nominal return, or money return, will depend on the rate of inflation. The money returns will be higher if inflation is higher with index-linked bonds, and low inflation will cause low returns on the investment. There is an inflation rate, the break-even inflation rate that would generate an identical return on investment for both the conventional and index-linked instrument. Essentially, the break-even inflation rate represents the capital market's forecast or view of the future inflation rate.

If, for example, an investor thought the inflation rate was going higher than the prevailing break-even inflation rate as determined by market supply and demand, investment in index-linked securities would prove better than conventional bonds. Of course, if inflation were expected to be lower than the prevailing break-even inflation rate, then conventional bonds would provide a better return on investment than index-linked securities. In terms of inflation and predicting the true real rate of interest and ultimately its value, global real yields are also determined by supply and demand. A belief and, more importantly, the ability to hedge real interest rates into the future is another market transparency in its best and purest form. Government debt and the real interest rate at which federal governments borrow money from the capital market will reflect the purest cost of real capital in any domestic market. As governments raise capital over 30-year periods, as any consumer, they will forego programs, which might be needed tomorrow for something else today. How often do we read about a government project that was budgeted for one amount and completed five years later for an amount 300 percent higher? But investors must accept the risk that the long-term real interest rate is at a sufficient level.

Another interesting aspect of index-linked government bonds is their statement as an instrument of government fiscal policy. The issuance of index-linked government bonds can also demonstrate a federal government's commitment to low inflationary economic growth. Why? Because if they issue index-linked government debt at the prevailing market price and inflation rises, the semiannual coupon payments and principal payment accrual will rise as inflation rises, causing payments to go higher than budgeted. I suppose it is the taxpayer who loses, but I think you get the idea. In theory, if governments are truly anti-inflationary, they should issue only index-linked debt and save the taxpayer a fortune. Unfortunately, it does not work this way.

The United States is the latest country to issue index-linked government bonds, called TIPS—Treasury Inflation Protection Securities. They have not been as successful in the United States as they are in other government debt markets.

We are getting a very good idea of how to determine the real interest rate and its importance and significance. So what do real interest rates have to do with the new economy? The competition for global capital will become more intense, coupled with freer movement of capital throughout the globe, which, in turn, will create more competition. Real interest rates and real yields are critical. An investor might find it helpful to focus on the real cost of capital before investing in a multicurrency environment.

ENDNOTES

[1] Fisher, I. 1930. *The Theory of Interest.* New York: The Macmillan Company, page 36.

[2] "Gilt-Equity Study." Barclays' Capital, February 2002 and 2003, Exhibit 2.1, page 5.

[3] "Equity-Gilt Study." Barclays' Capital, January 1998, Exhibit 6.1, page 53.

[4] Ibid., Exhibit 6.2, page 53.

[5] Hebling, T., and R. Wescott. "Global Real Interest Rates." Staff studies for the *World Economic Outlook,* September 1995, page 2. Washington, D.C.: International Monetary Fund.

[6] Fisher, op. cit., page 42.

[7] "Index Linked Securities." Phillips & Drew, October 1983.

Chapter 6
INVESTMENT STRATEGIES

INTRODUCTION

This chapter begins by briefly defining terms and concepts that will be used throughout. The bulk of the chapter discusses a few ideas on how to achieve better returns on a bond investment.

The global government bond markets are a very special place—the most active, most analyzed and, in my opinion, the most important to the global capital market system. Government bond markets throughout the world can be as volatile as equity markets, providing an exciting theatre as well. The analysis of bonds and their markets can be intense and at times seem complicated. A bond is an interest-bearing instrument, normally containing a preset maturity date, issued by nations, corporations, and other organizations. They are sold to investors to raise capital. The key distinction between debt and equity is that debt is a contractual obligation of the borrower on which interest must be paid and has a fixed repayment schedule, which can be secured against an asset or be unsecured. No such explicit obligations are made with equities.

The United States Treasury bond market is the largest domestic government bond market in the world, representing approximately 40 percent of all industrial domestic government debt outstanding. Domestic government bond markets present an ironic twist. We need them to invest our most secure funds, in the most liquid market. Unfortunately, to create such a marketplace, federal governments have to behave in a fiscally bad way. In a *Financial Times* article, August 4, 1986, David Lascelles commented on this contradiction:

> *"If President Ronald Reagan's economic policies have produced the largest budget deficits the world has ever seen, they have also created the world's greatest financial market: U.S. Treasury Bonds."* [1]

The U.S. Treasury bond market is enormous, with over $100 billion in turnover each day, and that was 12 years ago! The U.S. Treasury bond market became the first 24-hour-a-day government bond market and the benchmark yield curve for the global economy. In fact, by 1987, more U.S. Treasury bonds were trading daily in the London market than United Kingdom gilt-edged bonds. The proliferation of government debt led to an increase in the use of debt instruments and, more importantly, more professional use of government debt securities.

Numerous varieties and types of bonds throughout the world have been created for investors with diverse preferences for specific cash flow or liability requirements. A gross redemption yield is the convention used when comparing one bond with another. The gross redemption yield is defined as that discount rate which makes the present value of a bond's cash flow equal to its market price.

The gross redemption yield is *not* a good way to calculate the expected return on an investment in a bond, but is useful for comparison purposes at any specific point in time. The gross redemption yield, an iteration calculation, was the first calculation I had to learn, without a calculator, when I first joined Cigna International Investment Advisors. Nick Ritchie, who was responsible for global bonds at Cigna, forced me to understand a gross redemption yield. He made me do the actual calculations by hand for a variety of bonds with varying maturities. When calculating every year of a semiannual 30-year bond, believe me, I learned very quickly how to do it. The definition of the gross redemption yield comes directly from memory. If you grasp the principles of a gross redemption yield and its failings, you will understand an important aspect of bond investments. If you want to check up on someone who is offering you advice on bond investing, ask them to define a gross redemption yield.

There are three potential sources of return on investment when holding a bond with a stated maturity date. The first is the *coupon* or *interest payments* received during the holding period of the bond. The bond may be held until maturity or sold before its maturity date. Second, the *capital gain* or *loss* on the bond. The price change from the time the bond is purchased until it is sold or matures. And third, the *return on investment* that is derived from the re-investment income from coupon payments, which may be invested in a bond itself, another investment asset class, or used for consumption. As an expected return on investment calculation, the gross redemption yield falls down because it assumes that the coupon payments will be re-invested into the bond at the exact gross redemption yield level as at the time of the bond purchase. The value of government debt changes by the second, and therefore the re-investment interest rate will vary each second as well. But as I mentioned earlier, the gross redemption yield calculation is for comparison purposes.

I personally look at each coupon and the principal in and of itself, and use present value analysis to calculate the value of each coupon payment and the principal amount to be received on maturity. This is called a *zero yield curve analysis*. It looks at each cash flow as a separate bond which does not receive interest or is a zero coupon bond. The zero coupon yield curve is discounting each coupon and the principal through present value calculations at an appropriate discount rate which rarely, if ever, equates to the gross redemption yield of the original bond.

Also, as a bond yield rises, the price of a bond will fall. If bond yields fall, prices will rise. Volatility is a concept that was introduced in an earlier chapter; however, to review, volatility is the percent change in price. Three aspects can affect the volatility of bonds. First, as the maturity period increases, so too will volatility in price for a given change in yield relative to a shorter maturity. If we compare a five-year maturity with a 30-year maturity, for every one percentage point change in yield, the 30-year bond's price will be more volatile. That is, the price of the 30-year will change more than the price of the five-year maturity. Second is the coupon rate. As the coupon rate declines, the volatility of the bond rises, all other aspects of the bond being equal. If we compare two five-year maturities with differing coupons, the first with a 5 percent coupon and the second with a 7 percent coupon, the 5 percent coupon bond will be more volatile than the 7 percent coupon bond. Third, the lower the yield of a bond, the more volatile the price. In other words, if bonds are yielding 10 percent today and drop in yield by 1 percent to 9 percent and rise again by 1 percent, the 9 percent yield will have a greater percent change in price than the 10 percent yield falling to 9 percent.

Volatility is an important although simple concept. Measuring, and being able to use the measure to compare one bond with another with all the various constituent parts of a bond, is less simple. A calculation called "duration" is used for this purpose. Duration measures the sensitivity of a bond's price movement in units of time, such as years. There are a variety of calculations for duration, but the one I use is modified duration. Modified duration is the ratio of a value change to a yield change. It is the percent price change, which results from a small change in interest rates, divided by that small interest rate change. The higher the number of years of a bond's modified duration, the greater the price volatility.

INVESTMENT PHILOSOPHY

There are a number of important rules for managing money. David Strecker, my first boss at Cigna International Advisors, taught me the following two rules:

1. Always protect your principal.
2. Don't ever forget rule one.

Another valid rule is:

"Your first cut is always your best cut."

This refers to realizing a loss or reducing an investment position in times of uncertainty or high price volatility. David would tell me:

"Take your medicine when you first realize an investment position is going bad. The longer a bad position is nursed, the worse it gets."

This is so true. Reducing bad investments is a rule everyone should learn and relates to all decisions in life. When decisions, policies, projects, businesses, and investments go totally wrong, when action must be taken, when you first get that feeling that "maybe I'd better do something about this situation," it is probably the time to do something. The longer you put off a decision, which may create a financial loss or loss of face, the longer a bad position is nursed, the worse it gets and the bigger the loss. I have fallen into this trap many times.

Another interesting psychological law of the jungle that I learned from David:

"A person will not know a market unless he is in the market."

Sometimes short-term trading in one market or another helps to get a better feeling for that market's direction. Market makers in government bond markets are generally sanctioned by the central bank for that country to make a two-way price in a government bond, which allows investors to buy or sell their government bonds. One of the important indicators of a government bond market's direction over the short term may depend on the positions that the market makers may or may not have accumulated. To know, feel, and hopefully understand the direction of short-term price movements in government debt often requires an investor to be in the market. Test the market makers. Finding out what prices and amounts of government bonds at a variety of maturity levels that they may want to buy or sell can be very revealing and helpful in gaining an understanding of the market.

The investment philosophy I adopted was always based on long-term investments. I enjoy trading short-term price action, but I never wanted to make a living from trading. I wanted to pick and choose the timing rather than have it defined for me. As I evolved as an investor, my understanding of the science and relationships of economics improved, particularly when managing portfolios of government debt, government bonds being at the most conservative, risk-free end of the investment spectrum. Managing government debt throughout the world gave me unique insight into global financial risks.

As government debt proliferated, the need to attract investment caused Finance Ministers and Central Bankers to be more flexible in their policies to attract the necessary capital to fund their fiscal deficits. Once they became flexible, they had to offer attractions to investors (such as removing withholding taxes on coupon payments) or else face the severe consequences—a buyer's strike. In a buyer's strike, buyers of government bonds stop buying because the bonds do not offer an attractive enough value, because in most cases that government's fiscal and monetary policies stink.

If governments cannot sell their bonds, the only way to fund a fiscal deficit is to print money. Russia provided a perfect example of this situation in November 1998. I described the new international rules in Chapter 2, but if countries do not play by these rules, the cost of borrowing, the real cost of money, will soar. I was a witness to the rising competition for global capital that caused the rise in real yields to attract both domestic and international investors.

I soon realized that currencies are not an asset class. I do not invest in currencies, but I do use foreign exchange agreements to buy another currency to invest in the respective government's bond market. If a specific government debt market reflects poor value in relation to other fixed income markets, there is a good chance that real interest rates will have to rise or the currency price will fall to become relatively more attractive.

No single country is insulated from events throughout the world. The inter-relationships must be studied on an ongoing basis. I do not believe in diversifying in foreign government bond markets for the sake of diversification. Global or multi-currency diversification will work when an investor seeks to add real value to their single-currency return on investment. If, for example, U.S. Treasury bonds are offering the same relative value as Japanese government bonds, why invest in Japanese government bonds? As I move on to the investment process and strategy, seeking to add real value will be the key investment theme throughout.

INVESTMENT PROCESS

My investment process views the global government debt market as a single marketplace. Also, I do not differentiate between asset classes such as cash, domestic government bonds, and international government bonds. I consider these three fixed income categories as a single asset class. In keeping with simplicity, the objective of a fixed income process is to invest as quickly as possible into the higher interest rate or bond yield as interest rates and bond yields are rising. On the other side of the coin, capture the highest yield offered for as long as possible as interest rates and yields fall.

This investment process is much easier said than done. When managing a single-currency government bond portfolio, investors must be aware of the world around them because all government debt markets are interrelated. If the real yield value of the single-currency domestic government bond market is not offering relative value versus other international government bond markets, do not expect strong performance from that domestic government bond market. If, for example, a U.S. Treasury bond portfolio is offering better real value than German, Japanese, and perhaps Mexican government bonds, expect investment funds to be drawn into U.S. Treasury bonds.

Each country has its own story to tell, just as IBM versus Microsoft does. The same is true of France versus Canada, or Mexico versus Argentina. No single country will be the best performing government bond market every year. The three aspects in the investment process are:

1. Country allocation.
2. Capturing the best value each country has to offer through the maturity or duration selection within each country.
3. Currency price risk management.

COUNTRY ALLOCATION

The country allocation is the most important of all investment decisions. Getting this right is essential for the long-term return on investment. It is also essential to out-perform the benchmark index by which portfolio managers are measured. Each country's economy and its growth pattern are different from others. Differences may look slight, but they are there. More often there are crevasses as wide as the Grand Canyon.

In earlier chapters, I talked about differences in each society and problems they will face in the future. Growth, inflation patterns and their effect upon their economy, political leaders and their agenda for future policies, central bank independence or political dependence—these are also unique to every country.

The first step in country allocation is to value and evaluate countries in Tier One (Tables 5.4 and 5.5, page 67). All the factors discussed in Chapter 3 on fiscal policymaking, in Chapter 4 on monetary policymaking, as well as in the previous chapter on real interest rates, are factored into the evaluation process. Once the Tier One countries are complete, then on to Tiers Two, Three, and Four. Credibility of policymakers will become more important and focused on as the time comes for making the country allocation. When moving down the scale of the real yield tier ranking, return-on-investment expectations rise and must be greater than what is available or projected in Tier One countries.

For example, if an investor is U.S. dollar-based and wants to invest and diversify overseas, what countries should he consider? Sticking with country allocation at this time, the economic background in June 1990, as described in my newsletter, *The GIT Asset Management Monthly,* provides the story for the United States:

> *"There is still some uncertainty in the U.S. over just what the economy is doing. The April CPI rose by 0.2 percent, 4.7 percent year-on-year. To the contrary, a 0.6 percent fall in retail sales, a 0.3 percent fall in producer prices, and a 0.4 percent fall in industrial production seem to indicate a positive slowdown. The market really needs an unambiguous series of data to give it any direction. A record $30.5 billion quarterly refunding of federal debt was well received. The Fed has maintained its stance in keeping funds at their targeted 8.25 percent level. The dollar remains stable even though significant problems continue with fiscal policy."*

In other words, uncertainty with real interest rates ranging between 3.5 percent and 3.9 percent.

Another Tier One country, Japan, had a different story;

> *"Four successive discount rate hikes, the stock market crash and a much weaker currency have not as yet had any substantial effect on the Japanese economy. The Bank of Japan is concerned over the high rate of growth of the money supply. April's M2 rise of 13.8 percent would certainly lead us to believe that the Bank of Japan will be in no hurry to ease short-term interest rates. Indeed, the pressure for higher interest rates has not been removed."*

Therefore, the real interest rate ranged from 4.0 percent to 4.75 percent in Japanese government bonds, which, although more attractive than the United States, did not look like an attractive alternative to U.S. Treasury bonds.

In the other main Tier One country, West Germany (that's right, it was then West Germany), the Germans were caught up in their own unique difficulties over reunification. The newsletter fills in the rest of the story:

> *"After a hectic May, signatures have finally been put down on the German Unification Treaty. Details are still being finalized—a 'full take-over' appears to be the best way to describe the reunification process. There was a small modification to the OM [the East German currency] savings conversion rate. The OM 4000 limit for conversion at a 1:1 rate has been altered to a range of OM 2000 to OM 6000, depending on age. The West German markets seem to be taking the estimated DM 115 billion cost of unification in stride. Any concerns over the proposed terms of German Monetary Union have been offset by the reassurance that the Bundesbank will tighten policy if it considers the agreement too inflationary. Although the economy remains strong, broad money supply (M3) growth fell further in April to 4.5 percent."*

The cost for German reunification was rising, causing real interest rates and yields in Germany to soar. The German economy was crowding out global capital with real yields ranging from 6.0 percent to 6.7 percent at the end of June 1990. This was an incredible and historic period of time for the German leadership, and without the balance between the fiscal requirements and monetary discipline, German unification would have been a fiasco. The costs for reunification have been rising and therefore higher real interest rates may be required, which will force the rest of the world to offer very competitive real yields or find themselves stranded for global capital for their fiscal needs.

Now that we have established the stories and credentials for the Tier One countries, we can move on to the Tier Two countries. I will use the United Kingdom and France for Tier Two examples, and Australia for a Tier Three example.

In the United Kingdom my newsletter reported:

"Mrs. Thatcher has added to her problems the dubious honor of having become the most unpopular Prime Minister since 1938. The poll tax riots, accompanied by the further demise in Tory sentiment, have fueled the difficulties lying ahead for the Government and the run-up to the local authority elections on May 3. Unsurprisingly, nervousness is still prevalent in the Sterling markets. March RPI inflation came out slightly worse than expected at 8.1 percent with underlying inflation rising to 6.3 percent. More significant is the city's estimation of April's RPI, unnerving 10.25 percent. There is the impression that inflation may be more of a problem than the Chancellor has yet admitted. Money supply growth (MO) eased slightly to 6.3 percent. The UK current account figure came out a very poor stg 2.18 billion deficit. Long Gilts are continuing to slide down towards a yield of 13 percent which, given no further interest rate rises, should provide support. The currency has remained steady and this must be good news, especially after the gloomy reminder that the UK has some of the worst real rates of return in the world, Argentina and Brazil excepted."

The newsletter comments summarize the story in the United Kingdom, particularly with real yields on U.K. government bonds less than 3 percent.

In France, with real yields in excess of 6 percent, the economic story is very different.

"The Franc remains steady, supported by a strong economy. Inflation fell to 3.2 percent in April, money supply (M2) fell 0.3 percent, 2.5 percent year-on-year, well within the Treasury's 3.5 - 5.5 percent target range. However, any joy from money supply figures was short lived, with April's trade deficit showing considerable deterioration to FFr 4.13 billion. The likelihood of further cuts in short term rates appear to have evaporated."

In Australia the story was somewhat different, with real interest rates of 6.4 percent and real yields ranging between 5 percent and 5.4 percent.

"While there is a feeling that the economy is slowing, there is a stubborn refusal for it to react across the board and certain areas are proving particularly resilient. First quarter GDP grew at 1.8 percent, accompanied by a 1.7 percent, 8.6 percent year-on-year rise in the CPI. There was a small contrac-

tion in the current account deficit to A$1.02 billion. Finance Minister Paul
Keating has firmly reiterated that there will be no short term easing of policy."

I chose this period of time completely at random, and the general economic theme for all six countries is similar, with interest rates rising in response to higher inflation. The German story, unique in every aspect, was causing a huge crowding-out effect for capital throughout the world, and aggravating many economic problems for other countries.

The first country, which offers better real value relative to U.S. Treasury bonds, is Germany. However, due to the historic effects German reunification is having on West Germany, such as the unknown costs and further economic problems and consequences of uniting the two German countries, I think at this stage we should give Germany a miss in our country allocation. Remember, when real interest rates are abnormally high, there must be a good reason. Once the reason is discovered, timing is paramount, because if an investor enters the country too early in the economic cycle, real interest rates and yields may in fact fall, for the wrong reasons, while inflation is rising. The standout country that may offer extremely good value versus the United States is France. France is a Tier Two country. It does not have the economic credibility of Germany, Japan, or the United States, but the French have accomplished an enormous amount in terms of fiscal and monetary discipline. The inflation environment in France is superior to the United States and her European competitors. France looks correctly priced to absorb the intense pressures of the German crowding-out effects.

Australia, a Tier Three country, deserves consideration because Australia is offering value, credibility and commitment to the right policies. These two countries, France and Australia, offer the potential U.S. dollar investor the opportunity to add value relative to the potential return on investment in the United States Treasury bond market.

In simple terms, this is the process I use when making country allocation decisions. With belief in real interest rates along with real yield convergence, I would expect France to converge with Germany, because at this stage (June 1990) France is in better financial shape than Germany. All the countries being considered in the country allocation were going through difficult economic times as economic growth was slowing and inflationary pressures building, but each country had its own unique story and resulting investment environment.

MATURITY OR DURATION SELECTION

Now that the country allocation has been determined, the next step is to capture the best value that country has to offer, investing in the most appropriate end of the yield curve and determining what maturities offer the best real value for money relative to the source currency, in this case U.S. dollars. The maturity or duration selection in each country within the government bond yield curve is vitally important. Depending on the economic and financial fundamental information available, investing in five-year, 10-year, or 30-year maturities can make a big difference in the ultimate performance of the country allocation. If real yields fall by 0.50 percent, 50 basis points, then the best investment will be a 30-year maturity.

CURRENCY PRICE RISK MANAGEMENT

The last aspect of the investment process is managing the currency price risk. I largely learned foreign exchange risk management during the very first days of my career, though I first studied it at the London School of Economics. My tuition was sent to me in U.S. dollars and all my bills were denominated in U.K. sterling. When I first moved to London in 1982, the exchange rate was $2 for every stg 1 (one pound). By February 26, 1985, the exchange rate fell to its lowest level $1.0345 for every stg 1, a nearly 50 percent drop in value. In 1982/83, the U.S. dollar cost of a pint of lager was getting lower every month. I may not have saved much money in actual terms, perhaps $500, but that is big money for a student. Whether exchange rate risks equate to 50 percent on $10,000 or one 100 million dollars, 50 percent is a huge move in a currency's price and will have a 50 percent effect on an overseas investment. Note that I view foreign exchange price movements as a risk and not as an investment opportunity, although it is an opportunity to lose money. I am a global bond investor, not a currency speculator. The currency price is a means to and end, not an asset class. I am happy to accept country and interest rate risks, but not foreign exchange risks. I fundamentally cannot place a value on a currency price, because a currency price is just that, a price to exchange one currency for another. Many commentators will argue that a value can be placed on a currency through purchasing power parity analysis or interest rate differential analysis.

I deal and treat the currency decisions in a very simple way. As a global government bond investor, I seek to add value either to a single currency index or to a global government bond index. I need to get the bond decisions correct and I do not want to get the currency price wrong. I would rather sacrifice return on investment through currencies than risk loss. I will take a view on the trend of currency price movements, and have a currency exposure as well, but the currency decision to allow exposure to risk is rare, or part of a much larger investment strategy. When taking a view on currency price movements, whatever can go wrong will go wrong.

Assessing the best way to hedge adverse movement in currency prices is also straightforward. The money cost to hedge an adverse movement in currency prices is the difference between the interest rate yield curves in one country versus the interest rates in the other country. For example, let's say Country A has a one-year money market interest rate of 6 percent and Country B has a one-year money market yield of 8 percent. If we invest from Country A to Country B—hedge the foreign exchange rate exposure for one year—the cost of hedging the currency risk is 2 percent per annum. However, what if the 3-month interest rate in Country B is 8 percent and we forecast that interest rates in Country B are going to fall to 6 percent, while interest rates in Country A remain the same? The investment strategy regarding the foreign exchange risk is to hedge for three months. If three-month interest rates in Country B fall by 0.5 percent every three months, renewing the foreign exchange rate hedge every three months, the annual costs for hedging against adverse movements in the currency price is 1 percent per annum. As a global fixed income investor, I am supposed to make investment decisions based on interest rate views or forecasts, but I eliminated adverse movements in the currency prices. The scenario outlined above is never this easy, but it is a good example of the proactive approach one can take when handling currency risks.

PUTTING IT ALL TOGETHER

Performance attribution is a term used to describe the origins of returns on investment. During a final question/answer session after my presentation at a major public pension fund in the United States, a panel member from the fund asked why I had invested in another country so early in the interest rate cycle. I hadn't known that I invested so early in an interest rate cycle, but in fact I had consistently invested a calendar quarter too early. I didn't have an adequate answer for him because I never considered looking at this attribute of my investment style in the past.

Another client thought I achieved excellent performance results each year, but that the quarterly volatility in the return on investment was too high. Investment management performance is important, but the way in which performance is achieved is just as important. Performance attribution is another way to measure risk and, more specifically, investment manager risk. The investment philosophy and process that I have adopted show that the total return on investment is attributed to three areas (1) 50 percent derived from the country allocation, (2) 35 percent from the maturity/duration selection, and (3) 15 percent from the foreign exchange decision.

The performance attribution figures also indicate the importance of the country allocation in my investment process. The key to the country allocation is to find countries committed to achieving real interest rate and yield convergence with Tier One countries. Global real interest rate and yield convergence has been amazing, generating wonderful returns on investment along with interesting investment opportunities.

Performance attribution versus a benchmark index is also an important exercise. Benchmark indices are created as a market indicator, like the S&P 500 for the U.S. stock market. There are, however, differences between equity indices and bond market indices. An equity or stock market index represents the average number of stocks based on their total capitalization. Ironically, bond market indices, particularly global bond market indices, are country-weighted averages of the total outstanding government bonds. As companies represented within an equities index create more wealth, the company will command a greater weighted average of the total index. In a global bond index, on the other hand, a country will command a higher proportion within the total index as its total indebtedness increases. Instead of being penalized by leveraging future wealth, a country will capture a greater proportion of the global government bond index. If we follow the investment philosophy and process outlined earlier, my country allocation should heavily favor those commanding a smaller proportion of the global government bond index, and stay away from those increasing their proportion of the total index. Perhaps someone should create an inverse relationship global bond index, so when total outstanding government debt falls in relation to other countries, that country will gain a greater proportion of that index.

There are several global government bond indices, and each domestic government market has its own benchmark index. Similar to equity indices, bond indices are broken down into component indices (such as bonds with maturities of no longer than five years) or sector indices (such as mortgaged-backed bonds, corporate bonds, and municipal or local government bonds). Benchmarks or indices are an important subject because they are used to judge the relative performance of a portfolio manager or the investment firm itself. We used the J. P. Morgan indices at my firm, benchmarking various global bond portfolios. I am no expert on this subject, but it was an important part of my professional survival, and it affected investment management decisions.

Global government bond indices can be denominated in any currency, hedged or unhedged from currency exposures. Similar to equity indices, bond indices are updated as frequently as the underlying instruments' prices change, and therefore the value of the index. A good example of a global government bond index and its composition can be seen in Table 6.1.² The J. P. Morgan Global Bond Index includes its components and each country's global weightings within the index.

Table 6.1: J. P. Morgan Global Government Bond Index

Composition and Statistics

Indices	Number of Issues	Market Value (US$ Mil)	Global Weight (%)
GBI Global	517	5,901,784	100
GBI Broad	561	6,039,448	-
GBI+	621	6.153,428	-
Global Country Indices			
Australia	15	44,597	0.76
Belgium	18	172,101	2.92
Canada	29	147,566	2.50
Denmark	13	102,395	1.73
France	31	530,977	9.00
Germany	64	571,365	9.68
Italy	37	416,420	7.06
Japan	74	809,838	13.72
The Netherlands	27	196,666	3.33
Spain	25	210,553	3.53
Sweden	12	92,936	1.57
United Kingdom	30	422,677	7.16
United States	142	2,183,694	37.00
Broad Country Indices			
Finland	7	44,076	-
Ireland	8	23,487	-
New Zealand	6	8,776	-
Portugal	13	25,693	-
South Africa	10	35,631	-

Indices used as benchmarks are an age-old way to measure investment performance. However, they have to be used correctly to offer the best measure for a money manager. For example, if I had a U.S. dollar-denominated client who wanted to diversify overseas to add value to the prospective or potential returns on investment in U.S. Treasury bonds, the most appropriate benchmark index would be a U.S. Treasury bond index, not a global bond index. A single-currency U.S. Treasury bond index is more appropriate because the investment objective is to outperform the returns available on U.S. Treasury bonds. If I am unable to outperform the U.S. Treasury bond performance, why go global? Another example: A big U.S. pension fund wants to make an overseas government bond diversification to smooth out the total return on investment of their fixed income asset allocation that is invested solely in the United States. In this case, an international government bond index, which excludes U.S. fixed income assets from the index, might be most appropriate.

As an added definition, global indices include the global government bond markets, where an international index excludes the source currency or country's domestic government bond market.

INFORMATION

The following information is important to help make appropriate investment decisions.

YIELD CURVE

The yield curve is chock full of information. The importance of daily information flow is imperative, and the government bond yield curve is the most important. A yield curve refers to the plot, for a given date or time period, of interest rates ordered by the time-to-maturity of the underlying securities (from short to long maturities). The difference between long-term and short-term interest rates provides a simple characterization of the yield curve slope.[3] The yield curve representing the yields of government debt indicates the most creditworthy cost of capital. The yield curve establishes the absolute bottomline real cost of capital.

There are three types of yield curves (1) in an upward-sloping yield curve, long-term yields exceed short-term yields, (2) in a downward-sloping or inverted yield curve, short-term interest rates or yields are higher than long-term yields, (3) in a flat yield curve, short-term yields are the same as long-dated yields. The shape of the yield curve signals economic and inflationary expectations. A positive sloping yield curve anticipates economic growth with higher inflationary expectations tomorrow than today. A negative sloping yield curve indicates an expectation of economic growth slowing, possibly signaling a forthcoming recession, and causing inflationary pressures to fall. A flat yield curve indicates low inflationary economic growth—utopia. Positive yield curves are also known as a *normal* yield curves because they occur most often and represent normal economic and financial anxiety for the future.

There are two theories that explain the underlying relationship determining the slope of the yield curve. The first is derived and summarized in the Fisher equation, which specifies that the nominal interest rate, at any maturity, is the sum of the real rate of interest and the rate of inflation expected over the relevant period. Underlying this equation is the observation that investors with funds to lend have the option of investing those funds in physical assets with its corresponding real rate of return. For a nominally specified loan contract to be attractive, it must offer a competitive real return plus compensation for the expected change—and the associated uncertainty—in the purchasing power of the money with which the loan will be repaid.[4] Sound familiar?

The second way to characterize yield curve movements and direction is summarized in the *expectations hypothesis,* which states that the long-term rate equals the geometric average of the short-term interest rates expected to prevail over the lifetime of the long-term contract. In addition, the long-term interest rate may contain a risk premium (to compensate for uncertainty regarding the future course of interest rates and policy actions, for example) as well as a term premium (to compensate investors for the liquidity lost by locking into a long-term agreement).

The expectations hypothesis is based on arbitrage reasoning as well. An investor can enter into a long-term loan contract or can plan a sequence of consecutive short-term loans, rolling the funds over and earning a market given short-term interest rate each time. If the returns on one of these two strategies were expected to be higher, investors would shift funds to that strategy, and interest rates would adjust.[5] This is a very important concept, because the simplest strategy is often the best one, and sometimes compounding interest in the money market offers a better return on investment than investing in long-term maturities.

The perfect example occurred in 1988 in the United Kingdom. The U.K. economy was over-heating from the over-stimulus provided by Chancellor of the Exchequer Nigel Lawson's reducing interest rates too far in 1987 and allowing an asset price bubble to occur in the housing market. An over-heating economy means that economic growth runs out of control, causing inflationary pressures to build very quickly in nearly every aspect of the economy. Interestingly, the Chancellor was controlling (or "trying" to control) the price of the U.K.'s currency sterling with the deutschemark. This process was known as "shadowing" the deutschemark, because sterling was shadowing the movements of the deutschemark. (I also thought it was called shadowing because the Chancellor's policies were so shadowy.) His efforts to peg the value of sterling with the deutschemark produced a disaster. The policy was supposed to be a secret, but when interest rates go down while inflation rises—well, you get the idea. The U.K. economy's business cycle had peaked while Germany's was in the recovery stages of an economic growth cycle. It was bad policy, poor judgment by the Chancellor, which caused a dramatic and unnecessary economic hardship for the British people and the perfect example of a boom-bust economic cycle. Interest rates in the U.K. were lowered to 7.5 percent on May 17, 1988, because sterling was rising in value versus the deutschemark, and therefore to make sterling less attractive, the Chancellor lowered interest rates. When sterling started to weaken, interest rates were raised to 8 percent on June 10, 1988, and ended the year at 13 percent. By October 6, 1989, interest rates had risen to 15 percent (does anyone wonder why monetary policy should stay out of the control of politicians?). Interest rates remained at 15 percent for an entire year. Only after the politicians pegged sterling within the European Monetary System's Exchange Rate Mechanism were interest rates allowed to fall to 14 percent on October 8, 1990. You would think these people would learn. We'll come back to the fiasco that unwound their membership in the Exchange Rate Mechanism.

Let's return to the example. When interest rates were rising, yields on U.K. government bonds, gilt-edged securities rose as well. The yield curve became negative or inverted. This means that when interest rates rose to 15 percent, yields on five-year gilt-edged securities were 10.75 percent; 10-year maturities were yielding 10.125 percent, and 20-year bonds were yielding 9.5 percent. The yield curve was painting a picture of high interest rates today for lower economic growth and lower inflation in the future. However, at the time—October 1988—Chancellor Lawson waited too long to raise interest rates, and therefore interest rates had to rise much higher and remain at the level of 15 percent for a considerably longer period of time than the market was expecting. The U.K. yield curve was telling a different story which suggested that interest rates would not remain at 15 percent very long.

Needless to say, my investment decision was to remain in short-term money market maturities on behalf of my sterling-based clients. In fact, the decision was to invest in overnight deposits with commercial banks, compounding the interest earned on the principal every day. If interest rates remained at 15 percent for 365 days, the total return on investment would be slightly in excess of 16.1 percent per annum. A one-year money market fixed time deposit of 15 percent would provide a return on investment of 15 percent. Analyzing the return on investment for a five-year gilt-edged bond yielding 10.75 percent in relation to the overnight deposit would require the yield on the five-year bond to fall to 9.25 percent to generate a comparable return. The 10-year gilt-edged bond yielding 10.125 percent would have to fall to 9.25 percent to outperform overnight deposits. And 20-year maturities yielding 9.5 percent would require their yields to fall to 8.85 percent to offer better returns. I did not see U.K. government bond yields falling that far that soon, and therefore thought the best strategy would be the simplest strategy. The other important aspect of this strategy is the evidence at that time suggesting that gilt-edged bond real yields were very low and extremely unattractive in global terms. Therefore, real yields would have to rise to a level attractive to international investors, another reason to keep investments in short-term deposits. To achieve higher real yields on government bonds, either yields must rise or inflation fall. My view was that inflation would remain high along with interest rates, which would ultimately reduce inflationary pressures.

OTHER RELEVANT INFORMATION

When determining the next move in the shape of the yield curve, there are no short cuts. Do you expect me to say, "It's easy?" The use of all available relevant information is essential. What is all available relevant information? It is *everything,* although too much analysis can lead to paralysis. At the end of the day, prices go up or down, it is a 50-50 bet. But all available relevant information comes from fundamental analysis, such as economic statistics, political, economic and financial news, global trends, monetary statistics, and policymaking. It includes newspaper editorials, investment bank or stockbrokerage research, and technical analysis.

Technical analysis is the statistical study of the behavior of historic price movements. The subject of technical analysis has merit and is helpful for the timing of short-term investment decisions, but it is not something I would rely on solely. However, many investors view and follow technical analysis religiously, and consider nothing else. I have classified technical analysis as fundamental because so many investors look at the technical data. It has become fundamental to them, and sometimes becomes self-fulfilling as many traders react to this technical information. Therefore, I had to follow the charts of historical prices, which may signal a particular pattern from historic price movements as to the direction of future price movements. Generally speaking, if a majority of traders are looking at a particular price pattern, and the price action could "breakout" one way or another, I may very well wait to see which way the price will go, depending on my investment confidence. Technical analysis also includes moving averages, which is a trend-following statistic, and the volume of transactions is another technical factor during rallies or sell-offs. Oscillators are helpful in non-trending markets, such as the concept of momentum measures, which look at the rate of price change as opposed to actual price levels themselves. Oscillators are also helpful in determining when a market is overbought or oversold, measured by a calculation called a relative strength index. There is an enormous amount published on technical analysis, and I have personally studied only a minor part of this subject.

I would receive a daily morning report that included all the fundamental and financial events from the United States for the previous trading day, plus all expected economic statistical releases for the forthcoming week for all industrial and emerging markets. The morning report also included technical analyses generated in house, such as relative strength indices and five-day and 20-day moving averages for the industrial government bond and interest rate markets. It also had a spreadsheet updated with the previous day's closing prices and yields, and all the cross-market yield curve spreads and relationships of very major industrial country, along with their money market's forward yield curves and their real rates of return.

We also calculated currency hedging/swap costs and cross-market relationships, forward rate agreement interest rates, and the strip analysis on the related futures contracts, along with a printout of the closing indices of all the global stock markets, including closing levels of commodities prices making up the Commodities Research Board's Price Index and Goldman Sach's Commodity Index, which provided information on commodities price movements from the previous trading day. In addition, the report contained a six-month summary of the price movements with an up-to-date price chart of the *Journal of Commerce's* Industrial Price Index, which paints a picture of the effects of commodities price movements on industry. I also received a summary of all industrial countries' official interest rate levels and the date of their last change. And still more. An annual schedule of government bond auctions around the world, and the European Monetary System's Exchange Rate Mechanism parity exchange rates (in the 1980s and early 1990s, the parity exchange rates would change regularly).

In addition, each morning I received a copy of the names of all Federal Reserve Governors and German Bundesbank Council members, including their voting intentions and meeting dates. The report contained a calendar of political elections for the next two years and, lastly, a volatility guide for a range of maturities and coupon levels. Each day the report included at least 30 pages of relevant information and sometimes it could be longer depending on events. I also read six newspapers every morning and watched CNN, Sky News, CNBC, plus all the necessary information services such as Reuters, Telerate, and Bloomberg.

GOVERNMENT BOND AUCTIONS

I would have to write another book on every bit of information I might analyze at any given time. Without going into every iota of information, there is a situation where timely data can be a great help to investing in bond markets—when governments auction their bonds. One often hears of equity sales taking place on the stock market or, in my case, government bond auctions which are 10 times oversubscribed, two times oversubscribed, or perhaps 1.3 times oversubscribed at auction. When a government issues bonds, let us say $10 billion of 10-year maturities, and it is 1.3 times oversubscribed, the government received a total number of bids representing $13 billion. Another piece of important information at the time of a government debt auction is the spread or tail of the bids. For example, if you hear that a government bond auction is 1.3 times covered with a 3 basis point tail (3 basis points equals 0.03 percent), the 3 basis point tail means $13 billion in bids with the spread of the bids over a 3 basis point yield price. This means that if the 10-year bonds were sold at yield of 6 percent, then the range of bids was as high as 6.03 percent.

A government bond auction is a very important event, as fresh money is raised from the capital markets to fund maturing bonds and to fund fiscal requirements for the annual budget. In the United States, for example, the U.S. Treasury regularized its debt issuance in 1975. The Treasury felt that with the rise of the annual fiscal deficit, there was a need to minimize the cost of issuing Treasury bills, notes, and bonds. And at the same time, maximize the capacity of the market to absorb such large amounts of debt. Also, it was crucial that the issuance of debt securities be made as predictable as possible. The views of the U.S. Treasury spread throughout the world as government debt issuance became more regularized, to the point where investors have an annual calendar of debt issuances for each country.

New government debt issuances represent huge sums of money, and investors must be able to absorb these amounts. If not, the central bank must buy the securities, which cannot be sold, and is, in effect, printing money to fund the annual fiscal deficit. Therefore, government bond auctions are important for a government bond money manager. If a bond auction goes wrong, the capital market reactions can be vicious and cause extreme volatility.

As the day approaches for the scheduled bond auction, the government announces the size or amounts of bonds and the maturity period, such as two-year, three-year, five-year, 10-year, or 30-year. There is typically a time lag between the announcement of a new government bond and its auction. In this time period between announcement and auction dates, the bond is traded on a yield called "wi" ("when, as, and if issued"). The government bond due to be auctioned is bought and sold at a yield during this period and, therefore, the hope is that the bond will be sufficiently and correctly priced to ensure its successful sale on the auction day. Sometimes these auctions go wrong, and I have endured a few. I remember a case in September 1995, during a U.K. gilt-edged bond auction. The U.K. Treasury was auctioning a new 10-year benchmark issue (when the government issues bonds, which represent a maturity reference such as five-years, 10-years, or 30-years, and the bond is a widely traded, it is a very liquid issue within that stated maturity period). This makes the auction most important because it is setting the new benchmark bond for the next 18 months.

In this case, the U.K. Treasury was auctioning the 7.5 percent 2006. The new bond included all the bells and whistles needed to attract investors. It would include paying coupons free of withholding tax. It was also allowed to be *stripped*. A stripped bond is a program started in the United States in 1985. It allows investment banks to separate the ownership of the components of the bond—the coupon payments and principal. The auction was for stg 3 billion, approximately $4.5 billion, and was the largest U.K. government bond auction for that financial year and since 1993/94. The *Bank of England Quarterly* explains, in their view, what happened next:

> *"The auction was just uncovered (with a cover of 0.99 times), and the dispersion of bids received and accepted was exceptionally wide (there was a tail of 7*

basis points). Unusually, the stock did not cheapen relative to other stocks in its sector in advance of the auction, and the prices accepted were unusually far below those recorded in the 'when-issued' trading. The small amount of remaining stock (stg 28.6 million) was held in official portfolios; it was announced that it would not be sold for a period of at least two months, and in any event only in stable market conditions. The result of the auction was seen as disappointing in the market; the gilt future fell 1.5 points between the closing of the bids (at 10 a.m.) and 1:30 p.m., when disappointing durable goods figures were announced [in the United States]. Turnover at LIFFE (London International Financial Futures Exchange) in the long-gilt future was at record levels, with over 125,000 contracts traded.[6]

In common speak, it was a fiasco. The gilt market fell 1.5 points, equal to stg 15,000 for every stg 1 million invested—that is, stg 45 million in losses on stg 3 billion of government stock issued. The information contained in the *Bank of England Quarterly* also suggests that the gilt market would be very weak (prices falling, yields rising) for a considerable period in the future. The total volume in the futures trading pit for that day amounted to stg 12 billion in nominal turnover, representing hedging from the potential losses from the poor auction and the unwinding of optimistic long positions, plus the opening of short positions in anticipation that gilt bonds would fall further.

This is a big move for a government bond market in such a short period of time. Domestic and international investors abandoned U.K. gilt-edged securities because they felt that the Bank of England should be given instructions from the Chancellor of the Exchequer to raise interest rates. Once again, political interference caused havoc in monetary policymaking.

If the U.K. planned to sell more government debt, they had better get their fiscal and monetary house in order; otherwise real yields must rise to levels where the market will accept U.K. risk. Still, bond auctions are good fun, the best and most exciting being the United States quarterly re-funding.

LESSONS LEARNED—THE HARD WAY

Three incidents in the 1980s solidified my views about three types of global financial risk. The first experience dealt with currency risk, the second revolved around credit risk, and the third had to do with over-the-counter derivative products.

Experience is worth more than education, although the tuition is often much higher than any university's. When I did learn something from the markets, I never knew it because I was sweating too much.

CURRENCY RISK

In 1984 I learned how quickly currency losses could mount, and in 1985 I learned how quickly they could reverse themselves. I have described the economic and financial environment in the 1980s, but at some point in 1984 I thought the U.S. dollar was peaking in value. I do not recall the exact date, but do remember that the U.S. dollar/German deutschemark exchange rate was trading around DM 2.80 for every $1. I remember being extremely focused on technical analysis rather than fundamental analysis.

Similar to Latin American countries, the rest of the world was also being affected by the strength of the U.S. dollar, as described in the Introduction. I was trying to fish for a bottom on the U.S. dollar trend and preempt a change in the trend of the dollar. Instead of actually watching for the changes in real yield movements between the United States and Germany, I focused on the currency price. I watched the charts like a hawk.

The first major chart point was DM 2.85 for every $1. Once I started buying deutschemark, I had committed myself to a program where, as the dollar continued to strengthen, I had to double up on the position as the deutschemark weakened. I doubled up the original position when the exchange rate rose to DM 2.94 for every $1, then again at DM 3.04, and finally stopped at DM 3.25. I could not stand any more pain.

The deutschemark continued to its weakest level to the U.S. dollar on February 26, 1985, reading DM 3.45 for every $1. The U.S. dollar had risen 80 percent since the election of Ronald Reagan in November 1980, and rose 19 percent from my initial buying level of DM 2.94.

Playing around with the price of an exchange rate is dangerous. I learned a harsh lesson but, equally, I believed in the position and stayed with it until the end of March 1985, at which time I nearly recouped all my losses (accumulated over the previous nine months) in just over one month. From that point onward, however, I vowed that I would never speculate on pure currency price movements, but would focus on the underlying fundamentals, which drive the movement in currency prices. The real yield differential between the United States and Germany took more than eight months to narrow. Had I waited for real yields to actually start to contract, the return on investment from the currency position would have been considerable. I learned to stick to what I knew best, and currency speculating was not part of that. Any future exposure to currency price movement would be based on the economic and financial fundamentals supporting that price movement or trend and part of an overall global bond strategy.

CREDIT RISK

The next market-related learning exercise came by accident. Once again, the event took place in 1984, the day the United States released its first measure for gross domestic product (GDP) for the second quarter. The GDP data is released in the United States soon after the end of the calendar quarter, and subsequently revised and released at later dates, as data from the economy can be refined. However, this day was the initial release, shortly after the end of the second quarter in 1984. U.S. real interest rates and real yields were very high, and therefore the market expected that U.S. economic growth would slow along with inflationary pressures caused by President Reagan's fiscal policy. At Cigna International Investment Advisors, I was responsible for portfolios that only invested in government debt and its related derivative instruments. My colleague Nigel was responsible for government bond portfolios as well, but he was also responsible for all of the corporate debt instruments called Eurobonds. Nigel was out of the office the day of the GDP release. He did not expect any surprises or fireworks from the GDP figure either. When the figures from the United States were released, he would be on the telephone with me as I sat on the dealing desk. I could not find the actual initial release figure, but when it came out, economic GDP growth in the United States was running in excess of 7 percent per annum. A huge figure with huge market implications for the direction of interest rates and government bond yields throughout the world. The beauty of investing in benchmark government bonds is their liquidity as well as the availability of exchange-traded futures and options contracts, which also adds the ability to hedge the direct financial risks associated with government bond investments. The government bond markets, along with exchange-traded derivative products, are the most liquid markets and instruments in the world.

Corporate debt or Eurobonds are another matter. Eurobond and corporate bond deals are organized, arranged, and underwritten by investment and commercial banks. They also make a two-way price to promote efficient trading in these bonds. Since there is no central bank supporting the market makers, they must protect themselves, particularly during times of uncertainty and high levels of market volatility. There are no exchange-traded derivative instruments available to directly hedge their risks or to improve liquidity during adverse periods. There is also credit risk where yields on corporate bonds can diverge or converge with government debt. In times of uncertainty the yield spread between government debt and corporate debt widens and will compound the losses.

When the GDP figure was released, it showed much stronger than expected economic growth. Bond yields instantly rose because the market expected interest rates to rise further or remain at the high levels for a considerably longer period than had been expected before the release of the GDP figure. I was able to quickly reorganize our government bond portfolio positions, but Nigel also wanted me to see to certain Eurobonds on behalf of his portfolio. The Eurobonds were very difficult to sell, but easy to buy. What happens? When Nigel purchased these Eurobonds, I believe it was $20 million at an average spread between the bid and the offer of approximately 3/8 of 1 percent. In other words, the bonds were purchased when the investment bank/market makers would buy the bonds at, let's say, 95 1/2 and the offer 95 7/8.

After the GDP figure was released, I asked the market maker for a price and size. The size referring to the amount of bonds the market makers are prepared to buy and sell at their quoted price. Nigel wanted to sell half of his position, $10 million. The market maker came back to me with a price of 90 to 90 1/2 in $500,000 on the bid. When I was finally able to sell the entire $10 million position, I had to accept nearly a 4 percent reduction in price relative to market levels to get rid of the bonds.

There is more than one risk when moving up the credit risk spectrum. As an investor, I believe that bonds should be a part of a long-term multi-asset portfolio. However, within the parameters of credit risk, I would invest only in government debt, and also on the opposite side of the spectrum, absolute junk, in special situations. The various additional risks in holding top-grade and medium-grade corporate debt other than credit risk include counter party and liquidity risks. Everything in between junk and government does not make much sense to me.

OTC DERIVATIVES

Another experience I would rather forget occurred in the spring of 1987—a very high tuition fee for this one. Until then, the only derivative instrument that I had ever used was exchange traded. Derivative instruments are futures and options contracts. A futures contract is an agreement to make or take delivery of a standardized amount of a commodity (an ounce of gold, a pork belly, orange juice, an interest rate over a period of time, or a government bond) in the future at a price today. The price for delivery in the future is established in a futures market where contracts for future delivery take place. The generally accepted way to strike a price for a commodity for future delivery is through the open outcry method where for every buyer there must be a seller. The open outcry method differentiates itself from the market makers (who are making a two-way price for buyers and sellers), and is the most efficient market in the world, reflecting, in the most transparent way, a price that reflects all available relevant information at any given time. The futures exchanges provide regulation, liquidity, daily settlement, and arbitration when a transaction is in dispute.

Options contracts are also traded on these exchanges. An options contract is the right, but not the obligation, to buy or sell an amount of a commodity at a specified price before a specified date in the future. Another type of tradable derivative instrument is known as over-the-counter (OTC) products, which is nothing more than a decentralized marketplace where investment banks create derivative products in-house and sell them over the telephone to their clients. The OTC instrument is created for a specific client need and the only seller for the instrument, at that time, is the bank that created it. To my knowledge, there is no regulation or arbitration procedure.

One of my brokers at a large and infamous investment bank (everyone shall remain nameless) was talking with me about the U.S. Treasury bond market. I was minding my own business, yatta, yatta, yatta. I thought U.S. Treasuries would be range bound for a period of time, which is a price action within a tight price range. My broker, a nice guy, suggested a trade, which would use in-house over-the-counter options on U.S. Treasury bonds that would yield me a profit if the price of U.S. Treasuries remained in the tight price trading range. The trade went wrong when the prices on U.S. Treasuries traded right though the trading range. The trade was my fault. I misread the market. I wanted to sell the OTC options position with this bank immediately. My position represented $5 million and my calculations based on market levels indicated a loss of approximately $100,000. Fine, I'll take my medicine and get it right next time. A $5 million OTC options trade with this bank, I was soon to learn, was very small, but it was a big deal to me. When I asked my broker for a price, the answer I received from the market maker meant a $500,000 loss—$400,000 more than expected. I turned white. I felt sick. My broker, embarrassed, could not have been more apologetic and suggested I speak directly to the market maker. He told me the price was firm, no negotiations. Take it or leave it. Remembering rule number one, I took my medicine and have never used an over-the-counter product again. Frankly, I've never needed to. Everything I needed to manage financial risk was traded on exchanges.

THE 1990s

The 1990s were interesting. Folowing is what happened.

EUROPEAN MONETARY SYSTEM'S EXCHANGE RATE MECHANISM (ERM): 1991-1993

The Maastricht Treaty signing in December 1991, dominated investment strategy at the start of the decade. When the United Kingdom became a member of the European

Monetary System's Exchange Rate Mechanism, the strain on pegging one's currency to the strongest member in the Exchange Rate Mechanism became evident. The opportunities to exploit fault lines in the fixed exchange rate regime were plentiful. George Soros is not the only person to exploit the investment environment in European government bond and currency markets. Please remember that currency price movements are a function of the underlying economy of that country. Also, European Monetary Union is about member countries whose economic cycle is moving in the same direction at the same economic speed.

The New Year 1992 started with the U.S. Federal Reserve reducing interest rates, along with the Bank of Japan, as recession hit the U.S. and Japan's bubble economy burst. In Europe, the United Kingdom was entrenched in its worst recession since World War II, France was economically stagnating while Germany was expanding, but worse, inflation was proving stubborn for the Germans as the costs for East and West German unification soared. The collapse of U.K. sterling from the Exchange Rate Mechanism, made famous by the publicity of George Soros' involvement and the subsequent report that his fund made over $1 billion profit, was the highlight of the 1992 ERM collapse.

The crisis in September 1992 did not actually run its course until August 1993. European Monetary Union reminds me of the Quebec Independence vote in Canada. After every referendum for Quebec independence, I recall telling my guys on the trading desk that the independence of Quebec from Canada would never be resolved until Quebec got what it wanted. The same is true for European Monetary Union. Until it blows up, EMU will never be resolved and will remain uncertain.

Regardless, there are a few key dates and events, which helped toward the ultimate collapse in the ERM in 1992 and 1993. But please remember, the ultimate problem was trying to link apples and oranges—pure economic fundamentals. If a weak economy pegs its currency with a strong economy, something has to give. The economic situation can best be described as riding in an automobile with no shock absorbers, bouncing off the roof of the car because there is nothing to cushion or absorb the shock of hitting bumps and potholes in the road. If a country's currency does not act as the economy's shock absorber, its people will be bouncing onto the unemployment lines. When the weak economy fixes its currency with the strong country, and interest rates rise in the strong economy, so too will the interests rates in the weak economy in order for that country to maintain currency parity with the strong economic country. Still, believe it or not, some countries continue to peg their currencies with stronger economies.

This is what the ERM crisis was all about, and ultimately it became an EMU crisis. The ERM collapsed June 2, 1992, when the Danes rejected the Maastricht Treaty by a majority of 50.7 percent. I remember the day well, because I had to cancel one of my famous road trips—I had really started to hate traveling. (After 16 years of it, I could write a travel guide!)

An interesting phenomenon of the markets is that most market players felt there was a good chance that the Danish referendum for the Maastricht Treaty would fail, but when it actually happened, the result was total shock. Chaos ensued, particularly in high-yielding markets such as Italy, Spain, the United Kingdom, and, of course, Denmark. There had been a build up of investments, which were gambling that EMU would move ahead with the high-yielding countries. Therefore, huge investment positions were in place to take advantage of the interest rate and yield convergence with Germany.

When the Danes said "no," all bets were off. I was not surprised by the "no" vote, even though I had convergence trades in place as well, but I'd expected trouble on the way, so I could add to my investment positions.

The fact of the matter was that the Danes hated the Germans. The Danish, particularly the man on the street, were petrified of the Maastricht Treaty. They were afraid Denmark would be swamped with Germans, and in the Maastricht Treaty they negotiated a protocol prohibiting foreigners from purchasing holiday homes in Denmark—Germans loved the Jutland Beaches.[7]

Euro-enthusiasts throughout Europe turned on the Danes, while the London markets proudly patted their Danish brothers on the back. The very next day, Tuesday, June 3, the French announced they would hold a referendum on the Maastricht Treaty on September 20.

In the peripheral European countries such as Finland, Denmark, Sweden, Italy, Spain, and the United Kingdom, bond markets were especially hard hit by the Danish "no" vote. I had positions in the United Kingdom gilt-edged bonds, French thirty-year bonds, and the French European Currency Unit (ECU) denominated bonds, Spanish 10-year maturities, and a small allocation to Dutch 30-year government debt. On behalf of our sterling-based global bond client portfolios, I unhedged the sterling foreign exchange positions to expose sterling to European currencies. I felt strongly about the inevitable collapse of sterling, but now the time was right. All U.K. gilt-edged positions were also sold forward into German deutschemarks to add to the currency exposure. It was not a leveraged position, but it was an exposed one. I had a pretty good portfolio before the Danish vote, but now I had the opportunity to add to the positions in European bonds at yield levels that I never expected to see again. By July I, was really pleased with all of our portfolio positions—a rarity in the life of a money manager. The ERM strategy was in place. Now sit back and wait for chaos to break loose.

The compelling reason for adding to high-yielding European bonds such as Spain was largely the way they handled themselves during the ERM crisis. The Italians panicked, raising interest rates, constantly asking for help from Germany, and arrogantly, announcing they would not devalue the Lire. But the Spanish remained very quiet and kept their fiscal policies in place, accepting the fact that their currency, the peseta, would take the strain, be the shock absorber for their weaker economic situation versus Germany's strong economy growth. The Spanish were realistic and would not inflict hardship on the Spanish people for pegging their currency to the deutschemark. They would allow the peseta to devalue. The Exchange Rate Mechanism straightjacket remained in place throughout the summer.

I realize this book is about the new economy, but the 1992 ERM crisis is important because the new economy went on vacation, and it represents the type of new risks we must protect against.

On July 16, as the summer of 1992 progressed, the German Bundesbank raised its discount rate by 0.75 percent. The Bundesbank interest rate rise could not have come at a more dramatic time. The higher German interest rates went, the more bullish I became for the collapse of the ERM. The European government bond markets were in turmoil. The contradiction for the entire mess were the currency linkages—pegs— whatever you want to label it. The ERM could not last in its present state.

The higher German interest rates went, the deeper the economic recession for those countries that raised interests rates with the Germans while attempting to maintain the currency parities with the deutschemark. The higher real interest rates rose, the bigger the fall in real interest rates later. Real interest rates in the high-yield recession-hit economies were high and getting higher. In Italy, the entire European strategy was based upon the belief that the European Economic Community would bail out Italy or, in other words, the Germans would bail out the Italians. Yeah, right, and pigs fly.

Italy was in a ridiculous economic position. It had raised interest rates in line with Germany's and most of its huge debt mountain was based in short-term maturities. So as its government debt matured, the Italian government had to finance at a much higher yield.

A quick note: At the beginning of the chapter I discussed capturing higher yields when interest rates fall and reinvesting into the higher interest rates as quickly as possible. However, issuers such as governments must try to do the opposite. Whereas investors try to maximize the return on investment, borrowers must try to minimize the cost of borrowing and, in the case of government borrowing, reduce the cost, or burden, for the taxpayer.

In the Italian case, they found themselves in a mess because of their very poor fiscal position. Instead of issuing long-term debt, they had to issue short-term debt and therefore more budget money had to be spent on higher coupon rates. Higher interest rates caused higher unemployment and, once again, more budget monies had to be spent on the unemployed. In addition, to defend the Italian lire's parity with the European Monetary System's Exchange Rate Mechanism, the Italians had to use nearly all their reserves, plus borrow deutschemarks from the German Bundesbank for foreign exchange intervention in an effort to defend the value of the lire.

I remember when we talked about this mess in our offices; we referred to the Italian policies as nothing short of treason, because the Italian policy was absolutely, in no uncertain terms, promoting the destruction of the country. As I said, there has to be a shock absorber—better to let the currency absorb the shock than fix its price and force the economy itself to take the total stress of recession.

There are situations when it is right to take on currency risk. Don't get me wrong, even with a floating currency price, the economy will feel the effect of over-heating or recession, but at least the economic situation will be less dramatic and nothing remotely on the scale that took place in Europe.

The straw to break the camel's back came on August 20 when the Germans announced that money supply (M3) had grown at a stronger rate than the markets expected. As I discussed in Chapter 4, the German Bundesbank targeted money supply (M3) at an annual growth-rate range of 3.5 percent to 5.5 percent. The release of the M3 figure showing an 8.6 percent annual growth was not what the markets wanted, even though the money supply growth rate was down from 8.7 percent in July.

According to the Bundesbank, subsidized loans to East Germany were responsible for M3 growth. But because the Bundesbank placed so much emphasis on money supply targeting, its hands were tied and, from Germany's point of view, rightly so—interest rates in Germany were not going to fall any time soon. The weakest economies suffered the most, particularly their currencies. The financial situation was absurd. Interest rates really could not go much higher, equity market prices were depressed because of the lack of economic growth, and the only place, so to speak, for traders to make money was in currency prices.

In the new economy, the markets were about to teach the silly politicians a lesson. A wall of money built up short positions. The Italian lire, Finnish markka, Swedish krone, Spanish peseta, British pound, Danish krone, Irish punt, and even the French franc came under huge selling pressure versus the German deutschemark.

The 1992/1993 ERM crisis was also an example of having to be in the market to feel the market forces building as capital flows built up against the ERM. The writing was on the wall. The collapse of the Exchange Rate Mechanism, in my mind, was only a matter of time. Two important stories serve as examples. The first, you will hear again and again under different identities, occurred when Italian companies borrowed huge amounts of low-cost currencies, thinking they would get a free lunch because their currency was linked and protected within the ERM. Italian corporations added to their own demise as they panicked to hedge or repay foreign currency loans.

There are no free lunches!

The second piece of bad news for the lire, and Bundesbank support for the lire, came on September 10, 1992 when the lire traded below its official ERM floor—the lowest exchange rate permitted under the rules of the ERM versus the strongest currency. The lire traded below its floor price in New York after Europe officially closed for the day, when the European Monetary System's Exchange Rate Mechanism rules of engagement cease. Therefore, the Bundesbank, as the strongest currency central bank, did not have to intervene in the foreign exchange markets. But to rub salt into the wounds of the ERM, Italian banks and corporations bought lire below its floor exchange rate in New York and presented them to the German Bundesbank the next morning, purchasing deutschemarks at the official ERM floor exchange rate. A very stupid, shortsighted move by the Italians, costing them all support from the Germans, and everyone else for that matter. The Italian lire devalued by 7 percent the next day. The markets perceived the lire devaluation as too little too late for the Italian economy. And the fact that political arrogance would not permit other countries to follow the Italians created an electrically charged marketplace. The European markets were in turmoil again, as all economically weak currencies were heavily sold against the deutschemark. The German Bundesbank finally reduced interest rates—which I did not think a credible move because money supply was high and therefore political pressure must have been enormous on the German central bank to reduce interest rates—however small a reduction. But it was too late. The Finnish markka was floated the week earlier, and the Swedes were going to the wall maintaining their peg against the European Currency Unit, raising their short-term interest rates to 500 percent. It all came to a head on September 16, 1992.

We sat and watched in amazement that everyone was so surprised that the ERM was coming unglued. But I must admit I was shocked by the events of that day. Interest rates were rising in Sweden, and in the U.K. on that day, first from 10 percent to 12 percent and then, at the end of the day, 15 percent (to come into force the next business day).

That day seems like yesterday. Norman Lamont, the U.K. Chancellor of the Exchequer, came outside of the Treasury building in the early evening darkness to suspend sterling's membership in the ERM. The Italians followed the next day. Once sterling broke from its linkage, the economic shock was felt throughout the entire country as it devalued ultimately to nearly stg 2 for every DM 1 over the next few years. The reason for such a huge long-term devaluation is the pegging of sterling in the ERM, which made the economic situation in the U.K. so bad that the currency price had to reflect the additional economic weakness.

The demise of the Scandinavian, Italian, British, Irish, and Spanish currencies did not end the ERM crisis. On the contrary, the elimination of the weakest currencies, or their devaluation, turned the focus on the French "Frank-fort" policies adopted by the Mitterand government and Delor's EEC. The Germans were happy to go ahead with European Monetary Union if it meant control over Europe's economy and protecting German competitiveness. The French accepted it to keep the "old demons" of the German character in check. Besides, Mitterand and Delors would never allow the creation of the monetary union and then hand control of it over to the Germans.[8] So the French franc-German deutschemark parity would be protected at all costs.

I believed that the success of EMU was totally dependent on the French-German axis and invested in French 30-year zero-coupon bonds because the French and Germans would not allow their exchange rate parity to destroy the EMU process. The only way to protect the parity of the exchange rate between the franc and deutschemark was to reduce interest rates in Germany, and raise interest rates in France, a political decision I believed had already occurred. To make a long story short, our investment strategy remained in place throughout 1993 and running into 1994. But the ERM crisis did not come to a general conclusion until August 1, 1993. The European Community Finance Ministers and Central Bank Governors announced a widening of the trading bands within the Exchange Rate Mechanism to +/-15 percent. Real interest rates and yields collapsed, as the shackles that held the currency price movements in place were all removed.

The damage to Europe's economy from the ERM debacle can be seen through the real interest rates and yields. Table 6.2 shows the real interest rates and yields for August 1, 1992. Note the real interest rates and yields for the slow-growth economies of the United States and Japan. Then look at France, the United Kingdom, and Germany.

Table 6.2: Real Interest Rates—August 1, 1992

	United States	Japan	Germany	United Kingdom	France
3-month	0.21%	1.87%	5.51%	6.35%	7.25%
5-year	2.71%	2.49%	4.10%	5.40%	6.28%
10-year	3.80%	5.22%	3.77%	5.22%	6.03%

Table 6.3 has the real interest rates and yields as of November 1, 1992. The real yields in the United Kingdom dropped by 300 basis points, and look at France.

Table 6.3: Real Interest Rates—November 1, 1992

	United States	Japan	Germany	United Kingdom	France
3-month	0.44%	1.86%	5.14%	3.90%	7.16%
5-year	2.79%	2.32%	3.33%	3.51%	5.48%
10-year	3.71%	2.74%	3.52%	5.22%	5.65%

In my opinion, the only reason the ERM was saved at all was the German recession in 1993. Look at Table 6.4 for a before-and-after picture of real yields as of August 1, 1993 and October 1, 1993.

Table 6.4: Real Interest Rates

August 1, 1993

	United States	Japan	Germany	United Kingdom	France
3-month	0.18%	2.22%	2.45%	4.70%	6.97%
5-year	2.23%	2.85%	1.72%	5.59%	4.34%
10-year	2.90%	3.30%	2.26%	6.32%	4.84%

October 1, 1993

	United States	Japan	Germany	United Kingdom	France
3-month	0.29%	0.56%	2.30%	3.98%	4.67%
5-year	1.89%	1.30%	1.49%	4.58%	3.39%
10-year	2.48%	1.90%	1.90%	5.26%	3.89%

The third and fourth quarters of 1993 produced the best performance in European government debt markets, and the collapse of the ERM is a very good example of the power of the markets. However, the European countries such as Italy, the United Kingdom, and Scandinavia paid the highest price because they used Keynesian expansionary fiscal policies to attempt to maintain their currency parities, which had to be repaid through higher taxes.

As extreme as 1992 and 1993 were, so too was 1994, my worst performing year in European government bond markets. The rest of our global positions were fine, except that the Japanese government bond market rally, and the yen's strength, caught me by surprise in 1994, but that was minor compared with what was about to happen with our European bond positions. In the autumn of 1993, the U.S. economy started to rise from its recession. Real interest rates were low but competitive. Money supply started to rise and unemployment was falling. During the first week of November 1993, I had given instructions to sell our U.S. Treasury bond positions, because there was little real value in them relative to the rest of the world. I favored European bonds, because Europe was in such a mess, economically, and the determination for European Monetary Union would ensure that economic growth and inflation would be low for a considerable period of time.

We expected an interest rate rise in the United States in early 1994. Inflation was not a problem with the U.S., but, left unchecked, inflation would infect the economy, requiring higher interest rates than would have been necessary had those pressures been preempted with interest rate rises early in the cycle. I felt that a preemptive strike by the Federal Reserve, raising interest rates sooner rather than later, would be good for long-dated bonds.

The Bank of Japan reported no signs of an imminent economic recovery. As calendar year 1993 came to a close, European economic growth was recovering but still needed a kick-start from lower interest rates, which the German Bundesbank provided. Real yields fell sharply. I believed the Germans would continue to lower interest rates in 1994 although, as 1994 began, I wanted to reduce our European bond positions in preparation for a correction in yield levels. Prices fall and yields rise when U.S. interest rates rise.

I felt all of our portfolios were in order as I headed for another road trip to the United States in late January/early February that would last beyond the Federal Open Market Committee meeting to determine the fate of interest rate policy in the United States. The date was February 4, 1994, and I was in Chicago in the middle of a presentation when my office telephoned with the news that the Federal Reserve had raised interest rates.

During London's afternoon trading session, the markets did not take the news well. Prices fell sharply. Perhaps more sharply than expected.

I was asked to return to London. I returned that evening.

1994

I want to talk about 1994 and describe the events that occurred because it was a very perplexing year. Indeed, it was the first time I had ever generated a negative return on investment for some of our client portfolios.

During February, the Germans reduced their interest rates, along with the French and British. The inflationary outlook in Europe improved, economically grinding better, although Japan remained in the doldrums, as real interest rates and real yields rose. I was looking for a healthy technical correction to what was a marvelous bond market rally in 1993. As the end of the first quarter in 1994, the real yields on 10-year maturities in industrial government bond markets rose by nearly a full 1 percent since the U.S. Federal Reserve raised interest rates in early February. The real yield rise in March was much more dramatic than I had expected, and I felt the real yield level in Europe was too high to sustain the fragile economic recovery just underway.

My view was simple. The higher real yields go, the lower inflation and economic growth. At times there are contradictions regarding economic news and information in relation to government bond markets. During 1994, I felt that economic growth was good for bonds, because the additional tax revenue (which that additional economic growth would provide) would aid the increase in fiscal indebtedness during the recent recession and ERM debacle, thus reducing the annual fiscal deficits. I also felt, and confirmed through research, that the excess capacity of Europe's economies in both supply and demand would not stoke the flames of inflation. On the contrary, I felt very strongly that there was a greater probability that deflationary pressures were more of a risk to Europe than inflation, particularly as real interest rates and yields increased.

In April, the Federal Reserve raised interest rates again as the Germans reduced their official interest rates. In France, the inflation rate fell to record lows of 1.5 percent, adding to my belief that European government bonds were a very attractive investment. I thought that May or June might be the right time to extend European bond positions on behalf of our client portfolios, particularly in relation to the United States and Japan. I have not commented on the emerging debt markets, though I will in forthcoming chapters, but I do want to add here that certain European government bond markets were in fact offering better value than the emerging government debt markets. By the end of May early June, I had extended the maturity profiles for our portfolios to take advantage of the allowable duration/maturity limits approved by our clients.

Projected economic growth in Europe was revised upward in the second quarter to 1.4 percent in 1994 and 2.4 percent per annum in 1995, which I interpreted to be non-inflationary, good for fiscal balance sheets, and therefore good for government bonds. However, real yields continued to rise in Europe. Japan's economy was stagnant, and a confrontation over trade looming between the United States and Japan was causing the Japanese yen to strengthen against the U.S. dollar.

In May, the U.S. Federal Reserve raised interest rates again, but what was happening in the United States was right for America. Rising real yields in Europe was wrong for Europe. For reasons, which even today I cannot understand, the global government debt markets, other than Japanese government bonds, were expecting a huge rise in the rate of inflation. The scope in the rise of bond yields in Europe and the scale of losses staggered me. In the most favored countries, such as Spain, yields on long-dated government bonds rose by 2.8 percent, France by 2 percent, the U.K. by 2.3 percent, The Netherlands by 1.5 percent, and Sweden by 4.4 percent. Table 6.5 compares real yields from January and December 1993 with September 1994.

Table 6.5: Real Yields

January 1993

	United States	Japan	Germany	United Kingdom	France
3-month	0.46%	2.65%	5.30%	3.93%	9.46%
5-year	3.04%	3.11%	3.35%	4.37%	6.11%
10-year	3.74%	3.45%	3.61%	5.40%	6.20%

December 1993

	United States	Japan	Germany	United Kingdom	France
3-month	0.56%	0.91%	2.42%	3.85%	4.23%
5-year	2.26%	1.11%	1.50%	4.61%	3.18%
10-year	2.92%	2.09%	2.15%	5.30%	3.85%

September 1994

	United States	Japan	Germany	United Kingdom	France
3-month	2.07%	2.42%	1.86%	3.08%	3.73%
5-year	4.12%	4.15%	3.71%	6.07%	5.68%
10-year	4.48%	4.84%	3.24%	6.22%	6.17%

An interesting note about Table 6.5 is that the real yield relationships between Tier One and Tier Two countries remains in place. Perhaps where I went wrong is that real yields in the Tier Two countries of the United Kingdom and France required a 50 percent additional real yield premium over a Tier One country. I had thought, wrongly, that the additional real yield premium between Tier One and Tier Two countries would contract or diminish, because of inflation and economic background, during the setback in 1994.

Many commentators and clients thought that 1993 was a fluke year, not only in interest rate and yield convergence, but also in terms of portfolio performance. But as 1994 passed, I became more convinced that 1993 was no fluke. On the contrary, I thought 1994 laid the foundation for a deflationary spiral, particularly with the discipline of European Monetary Union in place, and I did not think we were heading back to the high inflation days that the markets were suggesting. European interest rates and yield relationships stood on average at 890 basis points as of December 31, 1992, according to the Bank of England, as a representative sample of European government bonds. The yield relationship fell to 495 basis points by February 3, 1994, rising to 749 basis points by the end of December 1994.[9]

WHAT REALLY HAPPENED

There are a number of conclusions to draw from this experience. First, 1993 was not a fluke. It represented a new economy because politicians did not change course in 1994 as economic conditions weakened in Europe. Second, inflation concerns and expectations causing real yields to rise were preempting any thoughts of rising inflation pressures. Third, the preemptive interest rate strikes by raising interest rates and tightening monetary policy worked, and therefore became accepted policy. Fourth, even though real yields rose beyond my expectations, the real interest rates and yields of country tiers remained firmly in place. Fifth, when real yields on the "risk-free" asset, government bonds, are two or three times higher than the growth rate of the real economy, something has to give. In this case, inflation fell and unemployment rose. Sixth, many commentators thought the European interest rate and yield convergence was dead in 1994. They were wrong! And finally, leveraging, bloody leveraging, hedge funds, and investment banks—I had no idea it was being allowed on such a scale. To this day I am not quite sure of the exact amounts, but they were huge.

Leveraging investment portfolios and leverage in and of itself was something I knew about. However, to repeat, the scope of leveraging throughout all asset classes was beyond anything I had ever contemplated. I do not believe that leverage, whatever shape or form it takes, is an asset class. When high degrees of leverage take place, fund managers must have stop losses in place. When an investment reaches a certain price level, it requires the reduction of that investment position, or else face, perhaps, bankruptcy. The stop loss amount in price may in fact be a very small percentage movement in price because of the leveraging. As I said earlier, when I have a bad year, I may lose clients and maybe my business will not do so well. However, leveraged funds go bankrupt and take the system with them.

When de-leveraging takes place, fund managers sell at the best price available. They will sell their most liquid investments to reduce their exposure, and will sell profitable trades to offset the sale of their loss-making trades. In July 1994, I was only getting switched on to the amount of leveraging taking place, and who these players were and how they operated. The year was nasty for me, but luckily I stuck by my principles, and 1995 was much better, although I admit that 1994 scarred me for life. I also believe that the 1994 government bond market crash aided the deflationary spiral of 1998.

CONCLUSION

David Strecker used to tell me there are perhaps three days every year when we walk into our dealing rooms with 99 percent confidence that we will make money that day. He also taught me that when you manage a portfolio of risk, not investments, always be aware of your risks and book positions. We will never pick the bottom nor sell at the top, and there are no medals for being a hero in this business. Clients expect good performance, do not accept poor performance, and if you make a big bet and it goes wrong, expect to get fired—but when it goes right, do not expect a pat on the back. The business risk in the money management business is definitely on the down side when it goes wrong. A single year of poor performance can destroy five years of solid performance! Many money managers learn about this concept slowly.

ENDNOTES

[1] Lascelles, D. "The $100 Billion A Day Market." *Financial Times,* August 4, 1986.

[2] Source: J. P. Morgan Government Bond Index Monitor, September 30, 1998.

[3] "Information Contents of the Yield Curve." *World Economic Outlook,* Annex II, May 1994, page 89. Washington, D.C.: International Monetary Fund.

[4] Ibid.

[5] Ibid.

[6] *Bank of England Quarterly Bulletin,* November 1985, Volume 35, Number 4, pages 323-324.

[7] Connolly, B. 1995. *The Rotten Heart of Europe.* London: Faber & Faber Ltd., page 129.

[8] Ibid., page 142.

[9] *Bank of England Quarterly Bulletin,* May 1995, Volume 35, Number 2, page 154.

Chapter 7
GLOBAL FINANCIAL RISKS

Among the harshest realities and aspects of our new global economy are the new global risks. I learned early in my career that "defense wins championships." Risk-taking is all about greed and fear. My approach has always been to look at global risk-taking from the risk side rather than from the return—fear versus greed.

I prefer to defend against the hazards of global risks. The downside hazards are far more numerous than the upside potential. There is more than one risk in the global capital markets. The term "global risk" is generic for all risks to investors. The one important lesson I've learned is to keep investment decisions clean and simple, not to over complicate investment decision-making. The more complicated the investment strategies, generally speaking, the greater the risks—whatever can go wrong will go wrong. At the very least, try to reduce the number of things that can go wrong. Remember, the value of an investment can go only two ways, up or down. There is nothing too complicated about that.

The best and most efficient way to deal with global risk is to eliminate those risks, which are not necessary, focusing on those risks with which one feels most comfortable. More monitoring and analysis is required as investors add additional risks to an investment portfolio.

The global risks I have faced over the past 15 years are much more manageable, understandable, and avoidable today than they were in the early 1980s. *Market risk* is the most well known, talked about, analyzed, and modeled of all the global risks. Market risks relate to the behavior of price movements and the ultimate value of an investment. The next topic in this chapter is about leveraging and derivatives. That is, the use of borrowed money as a means of investing and as an asset class.

Another aspect of global risk is *operational risk,* perhaps the most important and least discussed. Operational risk includes the way a person or organization manages itself internally. Operational risks encompass everything that goes on within an organization and its ability to deal with problems, which might arise from time to time with any transaction, in any part of the world.

Liquidity risk, another important and little-known global risk, refers to the ability to liquidate an investment instrument at any given time, and the cost of its liquidation— another risk which, on the whole, can be avoided.

Lastly, *credit risk*. Credit risk is about the quality of an investment, about default or bankruptcy, the inability to repay interest and/or principal. I tried to avoid credit risk from the very beginning of my business, and later I will explain why.

WHAT IS GLOBAL RISK?

Let's look at some examples of global risk. Remember Nick Leeson? He gambled and lost more than $1 billion in Singapore, causing the downfall of centuries-old Barings Bank. And in late 2001, the story broke about a currency trader at Allfirst Bank, owned by Allied Irish Bank, who lost more than $700 million.

But what is it really all about? I read a report about a major Swiss Bank that lost $689 million in its equity-derivatives department. Within this same Swiss bank, their Singapore office had papered-over a $500 million loss by shifting the losing investments from one balance sheet item to another. Their South Korean operation underwrote complex equity-linked securities, which the bank continues to hold, representing $1 billion of a single line of credit to a single South Korean corporate client. Additionally, this same Swiss bank is holding paper on behalf of its Asian customers, which represents little or no market value. I would say this institution has a global risk management crisis on its hands, because there is no global risk management system.[1]

Another example? A single fund management company in the United States with $4 billion of assets under management had a portfolio under its control with over $100 billion of investment positions, which included swap positions estimated at $1.25 trillion, the equivalent of 5 percent of the global market.[2]

I have not made up these stories nor are they from our historic past. They are not from the 1930s, the Latin American debt crisis of the 1980s, the savings and loan debacle in the United States, the Scandinavian Bank crisis of the early 1990s, nor the bond market crash of 1994. They occurred in 1997 and 1998, and concerned the Union Bank of Switzerland and Long-Term Capital Management of Greenwich, Connecticut.

The most recent financial disaster in 2001 was corporate America's largest bankruptcy—Enron, followed by yet another world record-breaking American corporate history in 2002, the bankruptcy of WorldCom. There are a number of lessons to learn from the Enron disaster. The first is the need to standardize the way in which companies must account for themselves. The second is the ability for Anglo-Saxon economies to rebound from the creative destruction of one of its largest and more inventive corporations. When we talk about the European corporate disasters they seem to fester for many years before their ultimate demise, wasting huge sums of taxpayer monies—I digress.

Did you know that total world exports in goods and services were approximately $6.1 trillion? This represents the amount of foreign exchange turnover required to process those goods and services. So how come there is almost $1.2 trillion in daily foreign exchange turnover? The daily turnover in foreign exchange markets is approximately 50 times the amount of exports of goods and services, which is three times the volume of daily foreign exchange turnover per annum from a decade earlier.[3] Wow! We routinely hear of huge losses at institutions such as Barings Bank, Daiwa, Kidder Peabody, National Westminster Bank, and Allied Irish Bank (Allfirst), to name a few, who have lost money due to operational risks. Major exchange-traded futures and options contracts in nominal value terms traded more than $28.6 trillion in 2000, up from $12 trillion in 1997, 2 1/2 times its traded value levels since 1992, and 17 times greater than the levels of 1987.[4]

There are a whole range of risks within any financial transaction or instruments. I found a good example in a recent journal. Suppose a United States bank lends a Japanese bank a floating-rate loan in yen. The U.S. bank has underwritten foreign exchange risk (market risk), interest rate risk (another market risk), and the risk if the Japanese bank defaults on the loan (credit risk). But the U.S. bank has also underwritten risks in the financial instrument that may be issued on the back of the Japanese loan, which creates liquidity, operational, legal, and settlements risks. If the U.S. bank uses over-the-counter derivative products to hedge any of its risks associated with the Japanese loan, then the derivative contracts themselves contain counterparty, credit, liquidity, operational, and settlements risks.[5] It never ends.

The globalization of the capital markets has created global risks. Global investing will continue to grow. Therefore the need to understand and manage global risks will intensify. A recent IMF report talks about the key elements of an ongoing transformation in our global financial markets. They are, first:

> "... an increase in the technical capabilities for enjoying in precision finance, that is, unbundling, repackaging, pricing, and redistributing financial risks. Second, the integration of national financial markets, investor bases, and borrowers into a global financial market place. Third, the blurring of distinctions between financial institutions and activities and markets they engage in. And fourth, the emergence of the global bank and international financial conglomerate, each providing a mix of financial products and services in a broad range of markets and countries."[6]

I believe derivative volumes would drop dramatically if many investors truly understood the financial risks they were undertaking. But let me organize our discussion and talk about each risk.

MARKET RISKS

Market risks are about the risks to movement in prices of an investment's value. In a global bond portfolio, for example, market risks would include country risk, credit risk, liquidity risk, interest rate risk, yield curve risk, and currency risk. These factors put the value of the investment, the price of the investment, at risk. To a large extent, quantifying the potential losses arising from one's investment portfolio, of one kind or another, is the ability to predict the future. To understand or know with certainty the potential losses of an investment is to know what will happen in the future. Predicting future events with any kind of certainty is just not possible. Probability analysis or informed forecasting, yes. Certainty, no.

MEASURING MARKET RISKS

So how are market risks measured? Over the past few years a model called *value-at-risk (VaR)* was created to help determine the probability of future market risks. The model asks a simple question: "With a degree of confidence, how much money will I lose?" VaR is an amount of money because the model will calculate how much we may lose within a stated period of time. VaR is an estimate based on historic price movements and, therefore, a probability can be attached to future market risks with a degree of confidence. I do not believe that these models, although helpful, are the perfect answer to risk control. Human beings must make the ultimate risk assessments at the end of the day. VaR models provide a means to look at, compare, and measure risk among a broad line of assets. Models are helpful in that they offer a degree of control, and they also focus on the variety of market risks to which client portfolios are being exposed.

I used the J. P. Morgan "RiskMetrics" system at my firm. But even J. P. Morgan adds the following strong health warning or disclaimer with the usage of their VaR system:

> *"We remind our reader that no amount of sophisticated analytic will replace experience and professional judgment in managing risks. 'RiskMetrics' is nothing more than a high quality tool for the professional risk manager involved in the financial markets and is not a guarantee of specific results."*[7]

This is precisely the reason I stress that a person understands the various financial risks, rather than spend a great deal of time on fancy, complicated models. Using models to focus the mind is great. However, they should not be used to make decisions on behalf of a human being. Others will disagree, but I speak from experience. In most circumstances, I am able to look at an investment strategy or instrument, break down the various components of market risk, and determine which are necessary or which are not.

However, risk models are here to stay, and are advocated by regulators. I am in favor of risk models as a way to organize and standardize risk measurement, which ultimately aids the development of transparency in market risk management and accounting. Models try to portray reality, and Mike Brosnan, Deputy Comptroller for Risk Evaluation for the Comptroller of the Currency in the United States, believes that:

> *[models] ". . . are a lot better than the alternative, which is traditional analysis and intuition . . . a model's superior ability to measure economic risks will ultimately become established in regulating capital rules.*[8]

Fair enough, but models cannot replace human judgment. If models, computers, or systems of any kind could predict the future, then everyone would be using them. As a means for managing risk exposures under a standardized formula or format, they are a good idea. We need to standardize our risk measurement practices to enable investors to compare like with like. If risk is measured one way in Asia, another in Europe, and still another in the Americas, for example, investors cannot compare the strength of an American institution with an Asian one—which would be another way of creating transparency for market risk management throughout the global capital markets. Hey, even the "brightest" people in the world cannot predict the future, but hopefully they *can* help build an appropriate standard to measure market risks.

The RiskMetrics system is a set of techniques and data to measure risks in portfolios of fixed-income instruments, equities, foreign exchange, commodities and their derivative instruments issued in over 30 countries.[9] I do not want to get into the technical details about value-at-risk calculations, but its methodology and process are worth describing. In a *Risk* publication entitled, "Understanding and Applying Value-At-Risk," the introduction estimates value-at-risk through a simple four-step process.

1. Determine the time horizon over which to estimate a potential loss. It can be one day, the next business day, or a multiple day estimation of exposure to market risks.

2. Select the degree of certainty required. The confidence interval for the estimate of exposure to market risk. This allows you to know the likely loss to occur over one day, with a 95 percent confidence interval (95 times out of 100).

3. Create a probability distribution of likely returns for the instrument or portfolios of investments under consideration for VaR analysis. I used a simple distribution of historical returns for analysis, and always a portfolio of assets—never for an individual instrument.

4. Read the solution of the VaR analysis. The loss will appear beneath the bell-shaped curve of a normal distribution at the value statistically associated with the confidence level, which is the distance from the center of the bell curve.[10]

I received daily market data from J. P. Morgan to calculate the VaR amount, but the four-step process is how VaR basically works. There are many differences on the basic theme with many software providers, but essentially this is the type of market risk model which we may see incorporated into risk management reporting standards.

Let me emphasize again that the measurements and management of market risks continues to be as much a craft as it is a science. The importance of VaR is for every institution to integrate a model in which to organize and assess global market risks in an effort to create a common and transparent risk measurement tool to help risk managers analyze their global market risks. But VaR is not a shortcut to managing global market risks. Management must be in a position at all times to assess global market risks. In the new economy, models such as VaR will become a standard feature for the regulation of market risks. Public disclosure of financial risks using VaR models could gain acceptance, but there are numerous ways in which to arrive at a VaR amount. The probability analysis must be standardized and understood by all market participants. Value-at-risk cannot just be for the professional elite or technically astute. VaR must become part of an easy-to-understand, credible, reported figure.

From the very first day in the operation of my firm, I adopted one of the more important aspects of value-at-risk analysis—marking-to-market. Marking an investment to its market price at the end of each business day. Simple as it may sound, obvious as it may be; this was something many investors did not do. When managing a portfolio of risks, marking-to-market is essential, including the official markets, such as stock exchanges, government bond markets, official interest rates, exchange-traded futures and options contracts, money markets, and foreign exchange prices—wherever there is an official closing price (normally the mid-price between the bid and offer). But when pricing over-the-counter derivative instruments and non-official investments and markets, there is no official closing price. In most instances, when there is no official closing price, traders who run these instruments must be relied on to provide administrators with a closing price for purposes of evaluation.

Risk managers, management, executives, boards of directors, creditors, and share-holders must have confidence in the data being presented. If not, difficulties will most certainly arise. When all is well, market conditions are normal and relatively stable, complacency in data credibility starts to wane. However, if a crisis or crises erupt, knowing in a simple, concise, credible, and accountable manner for all investment positions is absolutely essential. I was always taught to know my book market positions at all times, more difficult today than 10 years ago, but still an important rule.

Investors buy yield but sell price, meaning that an investor will spend time on the analysis determining the right yield to buy a bond, but when market chaos breaks out, that same investor will seek the best, and perhaps only, price to dump his bonds, equities, currencies, etc., reducing market risks. I have seen investors and institutions with the best 20-year record wiped out in a matter of hours. By marking-to-market, all sorts of global risks are eliminated, or at least easily monitored, which helps avoid extreme situations. This is one of the reasons why I said at the outset of this chapter that not understanding global risks is part of the problem with our global financial system. Once understood, they can slowly be eliminated or reduced one by one. Remember, though, problems in new global risks are going to occur. However, as problems arise, they should be solved as quickly as possible. Administration people need to solve administration problems and provide management with position sheets that reflect reality rather than wishful thinking. Marking-to-market in a true and accurate manner goes a long way to solving and avoiding many global risk problems.

Transparency is a word that I used for government policy, regulation, and accounting standards in earlier chapters. But transparency is also extremely important when managing market risks. And frankly, if individual institutions do not properly execute risk management controls, then, like sovereign borrowers, financial institutions will find it more difficult to raise finance, gain market share, and so on. Internal risk control management must also be clear, concise, and globally transparent. Risk control standards must apply to everyone. In our new global economy, market forces will cause institutions to implement appropriate risk management controls. Those that do and have achieved a level of transparency in their risk control applications and reporting will be rewarded with more and more business. It's natural. Therefore, market forces will perpetuate transparency in risk management controls. In the aftermath of the Enron collapse, commercial firms throughout the world will be requiring better information about their business counterparties. This will include the way accounting standards will be defined along with how the terms and conditions of the newly developed credit derivatives market will be re-thought as J. P. Morgan takes legal action against several insurance companies regarding credit insurance contracts.

Transparency not only includes the data that is used by VaR models and constructing balance sheets and income statements, but must also include a streamlined understanding of all aspects of market risk, such as credit risk, liquidity risk, and counterparty risks. This is an important issue because if our global financial system is going to work, each institution must be responsible for its own profits and losses. I do not believe that public funding for individual institutional losses is acceptable any longer. We need to find the appropriate market risk model with appropriate market supervision, which is made easier if everyone uses the same system for controlling risk. Transparency will be sufficient to allow market forces to keep institutions from straying too far and controlling their own risks relative to everyone else, and thus avoiding public bailouts.

In September 1997, the Basle Committee on Banking Supervision[11] issued core principles for effective banking supervision. In a *Financial Times* editorial of January 2, 1998, it was noted that:

> "... *the introduction by the Basle Committee of new standards for measuring banks' market risk is a significant step forward for banking supervision. The new standards mark the first time that supervisors have allowed banks to use their internal risk management models to calculate how much capital they need as a cushion, rather than applying a centrally determined formula.*"[12]

The Basle Core Principles are 25 basic principles that are intended to serve as a basic reference for supervisory and other authorities in all countries and internationally. In their 1997 document, the Basle Committee's principles deal with seven key areas of banking. In a nutshell:

1. Preconditions for effective banking supervision (principle one).

2. Licensing and *structure* (principles two through five).

3. Prudential regulations and requirements (principles six through 15).

4. Methods of ongoing banking supervision (principles 16 through 20).

5. Information requirements (principle 21).

6. Formal powers of supervisors (principle 22).

7. Cross-border banking (principles 22 through 25).

The principle we are interested in at this point is number 13. It states that:

> "... *banking supervisors must be satisfied that banks have in place a comprehensive risk management process (including appropriate board and senior management oversight) to identify, measure, monitor, and control all other material risks, and, where appropriate, to hold capital against these risks.*"

The new Basle Accords (January 2001) goes to the next step, which will come into force in 2005 after further revision. The new accord will tie the amount of capital banks have to hold in reserve more closely to the actual risks they face. It will require financial institutions to disclose far more risk management information than they do now. In addition, operational risks will account for 20 percent of a bank's risk. There is controversy regarding the Accord's effects on the European asset management community. In particular, the risks related to their operational risks.

The Economist's 'Leader' reported (January 20, 2001):

> "*The new rules tie banks' capital more closely to the actual risks they are taking. That should create a stronger incentive for banks to adopt better risk-management, because they will be rewarded with lower capital requirements. [The original accord fixed banks' capital at 8 percent of their risk-adjusted assets.] The new rules propose three pillars to keep a check on them: the risk based capital rules, better and more stringent supervision, and more market discipline, which includes greater transparency. Bad banks are rarely penalized for*

taking more risks, thanks to government deposit-insurance, privileged access to bailout funds from central banks, and a perception that they are too big to fail. The new rules should make risk-taking more expensive."

All well and good, but if the data and commitment to ensure market valuations is not there, or is very poor, all the fancy models in the world will not protect an institution from unexpected market risks.

DERIVATIVE INSTRUMENTS

Derivative instruments (futures, options, etc.) were created to help enhance returns on investment and reduce or better enable investors to manage their portfolio risks. The growth in these instruments has been phenomenal. We hear and read horror stories about using derivative instruments. Their usage is full of jargon and use complicated, complex mathematical formulae. Derivative instruments are tools to manage financial risks. I would often get into heated arguments with colleagues over the use of derivatives. I viewed them as a tool, a means for managing risk, not as an asset class. Financial futures contracts were used to manage financial risks while options contracts were used to add value to the return on investment. The use of futures contracts is not limited to hedging a cash position. They could be used to manage the duration of the portfolio, to arbitrage the underlying cash security, and for efficient asset allocation.

For example, if overnight deposit interest rates were extremely high, with one-year deposit rates much lower, I could keep my money on deposit while maintaining a long-term bond exposure through the government bond futures contract. This type of trade may add only 0.25 percent to the annual return on investment, but every little bit helps.

Another way to manage risk with futures contracts is their ability to reduce transaction and hedging costs, particularly when investing overseas. By keeping my cash in the source currency and using the overseas futures contract to gain an exposure, I do not have currency exposure, nor do I have to undertake the cost for hedging the currency risk. This is a transaction, which I often used, and it came in handy from time to time, particularly for tactical or short-term strategies. However, I only used options contracts for limited liability strategies, never open-ended or unlimited liability ones. Uncovered options writing, without holding the underlying cash instruments, are theoretically an unlimited liability. In theory, options writing are the same as becoming a "Name" at the Lloyd's Insurance Market, because it is underwriting an unlimited liability. There are investors who use options as a means of underwriting huge amounts of risk, which, if the market goes the wrong way, could result in a massive loss of money. I remember that this happened to a firm in Chicago, which underwrote "put" options on the stock market before the October 1987 stock market crash—they went out of business. When I used added value derivative strategies, they were exactly that—they added value to the overall return on the portfolio. I never bet the house using derivative instruments.

LEVERAGE

Stories about the use of these instruments keep making newspaper headlines. So what's causing all the trouble and fuss? In a word, leverage. Leverage also seems to be at the heart of most financial crises. Leverage is an ability to control a large dollar amount of a commodity or cash instrument with an investment of a comparatively small amount of capital (margin). In the futures market, the margin is merely a good-faith performance bond, while in the cash market the margin is an actual down payment on equity.[13]

There are two types of margin payments (1) initial and (2) variation. *Initial* margin is the amount each participant must deposit to his or her margin account at the time a buy or sell order is placed.[14] A *variation* margin call is a demand for money issued by a commission house to bring the equity in an account back up to the initial margin call.[15]

If variation margin calls are not met, positions are stopped-out, closed-out because the additional monies required to maintain the total nominal amount of financial exposure are not provided. I am concerned that attempts to defend against improper use of derivative instruments for leveraging will focus on restrictions on their use when attention should be on the need for risk-management tools with an overall organizational firm-wide level of exposure.

Leveraging must absolutely be controlled. Not the derivatives market itself, but leverage. The transparency of leverage needs dramatic improvement. I have the right to know if a company has a leveraged position well in excess of its equity value. I must be able to protect my shareholders, firm, and clients. If I am doing business with another firm with, let us say, $1 billion in shareholder equity, but with $1 trillion in financial exposures, I have the right to know about it. Over-the-counter derivative products must be properly valued and accounted for, and off-balance sheet transactions have to be on-balance sheets. If our new economy markets are going to succeed, and they will, the required transparency in the use of derivative instruments of all types and varieties is imperative.

I dealt with and defined leverage and the use of derivative instruments by defining their usage with my clients. First of all, I always used futures contracts in nominal terms. If the size of the contract is $100,000 of a U.S. Treasury bond, then I have a $100,000 U.S. Treasury bond exposure, not an exposure limited to the initial margin amount, $1,000. When hedging or arbitraging between the cash equivalent instrument and the futures contract, it is always duration-weighted, which means that the cash instrument and the futures contract are correctly related to each other. Options contracts were less difficult because their usage was defined in absolute money terms. There were no unlimited liability exposures. Models are not the solution to the problem when using derivative instruments. It is people's greed that creates the leverage and fear when investors deleverage.

Modeling potential market risks is a helpful and important tool for monitoring derivative positions, but human beings must manage their usage and subsequent leveraged positions. You can have all the fancy models for managing derivative exposures, but if that value-at-risk amount is not accurate or reliable, then it is not much good.

OPERATIONAL RISK

Operational risk is:

> ". . . the risk that improper operation of trade processing or management systems will result in financial loss. Operational risk encompasses the risk of loss due to the breakdown in controls within the firm including, but not limited to, unidentified limit excesses, unauthorized trading, fraud in trading or in back-

office functions, including inadequate books and records, and a lack of basic internal accounting controls, inexperienced personnel, unstable and easily accessed computer systems."[16]

Operational risks also include business risk, settlements and reconciliation of transactions, the use and type of global custodians, and, perhaps one of the most overlooked operational risks, performance fees and performance related bonuses.

In September 1998, the Basle Committee on Banking Supervision reported on operational risk. The Committee defined it as the risk involving breakdowns in internal controls and corporate governance. Such a breakdown can lead to financial losses through error, fraud, or failure to perform in a timely manner or cause the interests of the financial institution to be compromised in some other way, such as unethical or risky business activities. The new Basle Capital Accords (January 2001) require that 20 percent of a bank's regulatory capital be set aside for operational risks.

Operational risks are the most interesting to deal with. Market risks, credit risks, and liquidity risks are avoidable. Operational risks are going to happen. The best way to deal with them is to be in a position to troubleshoot them as they occur, not two, six, or 12 months down the road.

I learned early on that buying and selling financial instruments was quite straightforward. It's everything that's happening behind the trade that causes the headaches. Market, credit, and liquidity risks are controllable. Operational headaches are inevitable. I built my firm from back to front, which means that I created the back office operation first with the computer software systems necessary to control operational risks and give my staff the required tools to troubleshoot operational problems as they occurred, or shortly thereafter. I wanted to be able to account, value, settle, administer, check, and balance every transaction on behalf of each client portfolio each business day.

The human factor is clearly a dynamic asking for trouble in any organization, and ego is a major force to help push events into a crisis situation. Dealers may start losing money and hide their dealing tickets, breaching investment mandates, fighting with administration staff, administration staff getting even, and so on. Portfolio managers are under enormous pressure to perform for the client and themselves, and not necessarily in that order.

Portfolio managers and dealers receive a substantial amount of income from annual bonuses, often directly related to their portfolio performance or performance-related fees from the client. If bonuses are geared heavily to individual performance—I am not passing judgment over this methodology—this policy will add greater operational risks to one's firm. Why? Because, in very simple terms, when the annual bonus is measured by portfolio performance, a human being will risk everything to gain that performance-related fee or bonus, and risk nothing once it's achieved, irrespective of market trends. And the portfolio manager generally risks nothing and has everything to gain. A Bank of England article entitled "Remuneration and Risk" adds:

"Many employees in the financial sector receive a significant part of their income in the form of profit-related bonuses. They therefore have a personal stake in the outcome of the activities they carry out on behalf of their employer. If these employees have significant discretion, then a firm's overall risk profile may be influenced by its employees' attitudes to risk."[17]

Corporate chief financial officers must also beware. Salaried employees who are trying to manage their financial risks as they relate to their operational risks, such as the purchase of commodities to build something or the foreign exchange transactions for buying a part in Brazil used to construct the end product, go head-to-head with the professional risk-taker in this type of hedging transaction. Their bonuses are related to the number of transactions and/or trading profits that they produce. Who's going to win this one? Exactly. One key ingredient to being able to manage noncore financial risks is to understand them, which is not every person's core competence in a growing global economic and financial world. In this context, someone recently was talking about the definition of 'globalization' and from what I can see of corporate America is the increase and amounts of business that is being conducted overseas. Instead of having 10 different currency risks, for example, many companies have 40, 50, and 150 currency exposures that relate to 40, 50, or 60 percent of the their bottomline revenue.

From my humble life with GH Asset Management, I understood my strengths and weaknesses very early on in my professional career. In the investment process, currency risk was not the investment motivation for going into global investments. Additionally, operational risks related to the back-office of the firm were outsourced to a professional and well-known custody bank and the internal computer systems were built from scratch, from back-to-front, enabling a fully automated checks and balances system for client accounts.

I believe that the key to our success in avoiding operational risks was due to our internal computer systems, which checked and balanced our work every day. The ability to reconcile every business day for several hundred-client transactions took the human labor intensity out of the administration process. In a nutshell, our systems accounted for every transaction, producing each evening a settlement report for the next business day.

The next aspect of avoiding operational risks was to reduce client fund movements to a minimum. The treasurer at GH organized client fund movements. Any uninvested funds were kept on overnight deposit, and "call" accounts were never used. A "call" account is an interest-bearing account that can be withdrawn on 24-hour notice, but its interest rate is substantially lower than the overnight deposit rate, which compounds interest daily. Call accounts only paid and compounded interest quarterly. Each evening the treasurer reconciled all client fund movements with a zero balance report, which reconciled fund movements with the exact cash on overnight deposit. If the invested or divested amounts of money equaled the difference between the previous day's overnight deposit amount and today's overnight deposit amount, then the operation was in balance. This meant, in a very quick way, that all tickets were inputted. Client funds were in sync. Counter parties and global custodians all agreed. If they differed, something had gone wrong. A ticket written or inputted incorrectly, counterparty instructions were not correct. The point is that at GH we knew there was a problem somewhere. We were then in a position to sort out the problem, find it first, troubleshoot or solve it second. We were in a position to solve it immediately rather than wait for an outside party to bring it to our attention when it was too late to repair and therefore costly to our clients and our firm.

Operational risks are a huge business risk because the firm, rather than the client, normally absorbs them. On the other side of the coin, a first-class administration system allows a firm to expand and provide a cost-efficient service to its clients. The positive aspects of a proper operation will self-perpetuate the positives for a firm, as surely as the negative ones will bring a firm down.

LIQUIDITY RISK

Liquidity risk is one of those hidden risks. They occur when an investor least wants it to happen. An *Economist* column of June 13, 1998 wrote:

> *"No one would buy a house without knowing what the last house in the neighborhood sold for. Buyers in bond markets, however, must do exactly that."*

Liquidity risk has been defined as the risk that the holder of a financial instrument may not be able to sell or transfer that investment quickly and at a reasonable price.[18]

Liquidity risks are not a new problem. On the contrary, they have been a problem and will continue to be a problem. Every global bond trader has experienced liquidity difficulties in one part of the world or another, where the liquidation of any investment position could cost an additional 0.5 percent or 2 percent or no price at all because of the illiquidity of the instrument or market. In the November 1998, issue of *Risk Magazine,* an article entitled "Prepare to Meet Thy Maker," stated:

> *". . . when confidence disappears, liquidity dries up, leading to exaggerated moves in prices."*

Models cannot accurately describe the risks associated with liquidity or illiquidity in any sense of quantitative measure that I know, yet it happens in all the capital markets in every asset class.

For example, when a government bond auction goes wrong, selling government debt in this type of environment can be difficult at any price. One of the problems with liquidity risks is that they are compounded as credit risks are increased. As market risks increase, leveraging increases, so too liquidity risks rise. One of my incentives for investing in only government debt is the ability to sell or hedge portfolio positions adequately. In times of crisis, a central bank will support its domestic government bond market, and portfolio positions can be hedged with exchange-traded futures and options contracts. I reduce the risk of being caught in a liquidity crisis, along with all of the other problems out there.

One of the other benefits of investing in benchmark government debt is being able of keep track of portfolio positions. I always told my team to know their book, to know all of their positions, because when there is a crisis and action is needed, there is very little time to wait for printouts from a computer system. If investment managers do not know their portfolio positions, how can they protect the principal value of their client portfolio? I refer to bond markets, not equity markets, because I have not managed institutional equity portfolios, so my experience is limited to bonds.

But the point is "know your book—always. When investing in small amounts of liquid bonds, the portfolio becomes unmanageable. I can remember on numerous occasions taking over a client portfolio from another money manager and finding huge amounts of investment holdings relative to the portfolio's value. Modern portfolio theory may say diversity, which includes bond investments, but if diversification does not reflect the potential for liquidity risks, then the total return on investment may be put at risk.

Keep the investment strategy simple. Invest in the most creditworthy, liquid, and transparent government bonds. Avoid credit, liquidity, and, to an extent, market risks, because you will be able to better manage the market risks related to the benchmark government debt.

Liquidity risk can be avoided even with derivative instruments. If exchange-traded derivative products can do the job, why use over-the-counter products? *Risk Magazine* (November 1998) reported:

> *"In late August and September, the global over-the-counter fixed income markets suffered a temporary yet terrifying paralysis, and liquidity all but died."*

Next time it may not be so temporary.

CREDIT RISK

I left credit risk for the end of this chapter because, as an investor, credit risks are the easiest to avoid and the most difficult to estimate. Credit risk assessment is only as good as the information used for analysis. If the information is rubbish, the analysis will be no good. This will be true for you and me as well as the ratings agencies who famously apply credit ratings to many types of business counterparties.

Whether sovereign or corporate credit risk, understand that the greater the credit risks, the greater the problems, such as liquidity, counterparty, and market risks an investor undertakes. Investing in less creditworthy investments is fine during periods of stability, or if an investor is planning to buy and hold the bond until it matures, as long as it does not default. For an active bond manager, credit risks create all sorts of problems during periods of volatility, in a rising interest-rate cycle or, most importantly, as an economy slows, so too does the creditworthiness of less creditworthy bond investments.

Credit risk is the financial loss arising from the failure of a counterparty to a financial transaction according to the terms and conditions of a contract.

SOVEREIGN CREDIT RISK

My experience has been focused almost solely on sovereign credits, so I will start with sovereign credit risk. Sovereign debt is the starting point or benchmark to any credit rating for a country and its corporate debt, because governments are able to raise taxes to cover interest payments or to repay the principal amount at maturity. There are two types of sovereign debt credit ratings (1) domestic currency default and (2) foreign currency default. Domestic currency-denominated debt is very different from foreign currency-denominated debt. Domestic debt default can be avoided by raising domestic taxes. However, foreign currency debt goes through two stages toward repayment. The country must first generate the necessary domestic currency to service its debt. Second, authorities must also be able to purchase the necessary foreign currency to meet its foreign currency obligations.

I view domestic and foreign currency debts in a very different light because of the difference between the two bond issues. Foreign currency debts have a whole host of additional risks attached, such as currency shocks or market risks, plus economic risks such as terms of trade and economic growth sufficient to raise the foreign currency required to meet obligations. Domestic currency government debt can be repaid from raising domestic tax rates.

In the aftermath of the Enron collapse, corporate credit risk will be a hotly debated subject, particularly the way companies report and account for themselves. When a company offers its financial reports to a counterparty, those reports and accounts must reflect its true financial position. The ratings agencies, such as Standard & Poor's or Moody's Investor Services, along with all the fancy risk management tools, are only as good as the information they are provided. A corporate default such as Enron is really no different to an extent than the fundamental causes and events during the collapse of the Asian countries in 1997. Moral hazard means doctoring the books and the standards that nations attain must also filter down to the private sector. The transparency and standardization of statistical data measured and announced by the U.S. Treasury department must also work its way down to the corporate sector to ensure that all available relevant information about that company are accounted for and reported in a standard way to accord professional analysis.

In a *Wall Street Journal* article by Ken Brown (February 21, 2002), "Creative Accounting: How to Buff a Company" provides a good summary of the post-Enron environment.

> *"Accounting never has been an exact science. Auditors must distill a company's many broad and often complex transactions into a few key numbers, making dozens if not hundreds of judgment calls along the way, in an effort to reflect accurately its underlying financial condition.*
>
> *Now in the wake of Enron Corp.'s collapse and subsequent revelations of accounting irregularities at other big corporations, it has become increasingly clear that number crunchers often present a company's finances in the most flattering way."*

No doubt better accounting and reporting standard will be an end product of the Enron collapse and, as with public policy making, market forces will require greater transparency and timely reporting in a fair and consistent manner.

CONCLUSION

My point regarding the subject of global risk is the way the various components of risk can be avoided while enjoying a very good return on investment. But as an investor throughout the global financial system, I am concerned by many of the unaccountable risks being underwritten and not marked-to-market.

ENDNOTES

[1] "Just a Few Loose Screws." *The Economist,* May 30, 1998, page 75.
[2] "Meriwether's Meltdown." *Risk Magazine,* October 1998, page 34.
[3] "Globalization of Finance." *International Capital Markets,* September 1998, Annex V, page 188.
[4] Ibid., page 192.

[5] Ibid., pages 191 and 192.

[6] Ibid., page 180.

[7] J. P. Morgan, "Risk Metrics Technical Document," 4th Edition, December 18, 1996.

[8] Brosnan, M. "United We Stand." Enterprise-Wide Risk Management Special Report, November 1998, page 12. London: *Risk* publications.

[9] J. P. Morgan, op. cit.

[10] "Understanding and Applying Value-At-Risk," 1997, pages 19 and 20. London: *Risk* publications.

[11] The Basle Committee on Banking Supervision is a Committee on Banking Supervisory Authorities, which was established by the central bank governors of the group of 10 in 1975. It consists of senior representatives of banking authorities and central banks from Belgium, Canada, France, Germany, Italy, Japan, Luxembourg, The Netherlands, Sweden, Switzerland, United Kingdom, and United States. It usually meets at the Bank for International Settlements in Basle, Switzerland, where its permanent secretariat is located.

[12] "This Year's Basle Model." *Financial Times,* January 2, 1998.

[13] Rothstein, N. H. 1984. *The Handbook of Financial Futures.* New York: McGraw Hill, page 597.

[14] Ibid.

[15] Ibid., page 606.

[16] "Globalization of Finance and Financial Risks." *International Capital Markets,* Annex V, September 1998, pages 194 and 195. Washington, D.C.: International Monetary Fund.

[17] Davies, D. "Remuneration and Risk." *Financial Strategy Review,* The Bank of England, Issue Two, Spring 1997, page 18.

[18] "Globalization of Finance." International Capital Markets, Annex V, September 1998, page 194. Washington, D.C.: International Monetary Fund.

Chapter 8
CURRENCY AND LIQUIDITY CRISES

INTRODUCTION

In this chapter I will talk from my experience about currency theory, models for predicting currency price movement and crisis, commodity-based currencies, the fixed versus flexible or floating exchange rates, and present the arguments for each position.

A liquidity crisis is similar to not having enough money in a checking or current account, even though there are plenty of assets on the balance sheet. A short-term requirement to finance the current cash shortage can turn into a liquidity crisis, and when the balance sheet assets are not enough to finance the short-term cash requirements, the situation can turn into a debt crisis. Liquidity crises in themselves are not normally short run events, because often times a liquidity or currency crisis becomes a debt crisis, which will be a real long-term problem. There are a host of terms and definitions used during these crises, so I first want to clear up all the terminology.

TERMINOLOGY

A *currency crisis* is a speculative attack on the exchange rate or currency value resulting in a sharp fall, devaluation, and depreciation in the currency's price. The currency devaluation can be left to the market, or may force government authorities to defend its currency value by using central bank reserves to intervene in the foreign exchange market, and/or to raise interest rates in an attempt to attract investors with a higher real interest rate on their savings. Another event that may occur is a banking crisis.

A *banking crisis* is a situation when depositors withdraw savings from banks as quickly as humanly possible. Bank runs cause banks to fail to meet their liabilities and to suspend internal convertibility of their liabilities (banks cannot liquidate their loan portfolio to meet the demand of depositors for withdrawal of their savings), and/or compels government authorities to intervene by offering assistance.

A *systematic financial crisis* is simply the inability of the entire financial system to function properly. This can have large adverse effects on the real economy.

Lastly, a *foreign debt crisis* is a situation where a country cannot service its foreign debt, whether sovereign or private debt.[1]

I will discuss the latter three definitions separately, because debt crises of any kind require me to think very differently from liquidity or currency crises.

A currency crisis or a run on a currency, which simply devalues the nominal exchange rate, has enormous repercussions to an entire economy. In the Introduction, I gave an example of what happens to a country's tax revenue from a major commodity exporting country such as the United Kingdom with North Sea Oil, when the currency, sterling, would rise or fall. Businesses also feel the pinch as terms of trade with overseas markets radically change. If a company is exporting a good or service to another country, which has seen its currency devalue 10 percent within a week, its terms of trade with the counterparty in that country has been adversely affected by the same amount. The cost of servicing overseas debts rises by the devalued amount. Everyone involved with specific overseas markets or generally throughout the world must find an extra 10, 15, or even 50 percent more profit margin, or find cost savings to afford the additional cost in doing business overseas. Currency crises happen so quickly that, often times, decisions to hedge the currency exposures take too long to make, or are too late in implementation. The ability to find the appropriate cost savings takes time as well.

Therefore the obsession over movements in currency prices may very well be justified. Table 8.1 shows the number of currency crises that occurred from 1976 to 2002. Table 8.2 shows the number of currency crises that occurred with each country from 1975 to 2002.

Table 8.1: Currency Crises: 1976-2002[2]

Year	No. of Crises	Year	No. of Crises
1976	11	1989	2
1977	9	1990	3
1978	6	1991	5
1979	2	1992	7
1980	4	1993	2
1981	3	1994	3
1982	10	1995	3
1983	9	1996	0
1984	7	1997	6
1985	7	1998	3
1986	8	1999	0
1987	3	2000	1
1988	4	2001	1
		2002	3

The tables stipulate that only one currency crisis could occur in each country each year. Frankly, the numbers surprised me, and I remember many of the crises. There is no question that every year the global financial system is learning more and more about currency price movements. The global financial and economic system has come a long way since the days of the classic gold standard, when only a few economic powers could proj-

Table 8.2: Currency Crises per Country[3] (from 1975 to 2002)

Country	No. of Crises	Country	No. of Crises
Argentina	8	Mexico	5
Australia	5	Morocco	5
Belgium	1	New Zealand	4
Brazil	7	Norway	3
Chile	4	Peru	9
Columbia	3	Philippines	4
Denmark	1	Portugal	5
Ecuador	7	Singapore	3
Finland	4	South Africa	1
Greece	1	Spain	5
Indonesia	4	Sweden	5
Ireland	2	Thailand	2
Italy	3	Turkey	6
Korea	1	United Kingdom	2
Malaysia	2	Venezuela	6

ect and flex their financial muscle on the less fortunate. In the new economy, economic and financial power will become more displaced globally as it becomes more concentrated institutionally. A country's individual identity has become regional identity and now we will build a global identity. We need one another more today, a dependence that will increase in the future.

The power of market forces will create the new economy. With our understanding of the science of economics improving each year, so also is our understanding of currency crises. I am not suggesting that we can predict the future, but we do have the resources and understanding of many of the leading indicators and underlying factors that cause currency crises.

A LITTLE HISTORY

A great debate is occurring over whether a country should adopt a fixed or floating exchange rates regime. Whether government authorities control capital flows, fix or anchor their currency's value against a commodity or another currency, is an argument as old as the classical gold standard itself. The classical gold standard, dating from about 1870 to 1914, represented the longest period of high capital mobility between the major capital exporting countries—the United Kingdom, France, and Germany—and the newly emerging markets in North America, Latin America, the Middle East, Africa, Eastern and Central Europe, and Scandinavia.[4] But what ultimately happened was that more and more funds were invested in emerging markets because rates of return were so high. The convertibility of the currency into gold at a fixed and known price made this easy.

Why would anyone invest in the capital exporting country while being guaranteed the value of his investment by the price of gold? The capital exporting country had to raise interest rates to attract the capital back, therefore protecting the convertibility of currency.

Please remember the discussion on currency boards from Chapter 4. The colonies of the capital exporting countries linked their currency to the capital exporting currency, which in turn was linked to the value of gold. The music was stopped by World War I, protectionism, deflation, and social unrest because the cost of pegging the currency's value to the value of gold. In other words, a fixed exchange rate allowed absolutely no flexibility in domestic fiscal and monetary policies. Of course, after the gold standard came greater competition, regular competitive currency devaluation, depression, and World War II.

The world re-entered fixed exchange rates once again when the Bretton Woods meetings took place—a new gold standard. A central banker once told me that government authorities and their policies were always based on the last economic or financial crisis. If the last crisis were inflation, the next policy would be anti-inflation, or, vice versa, if the last crisis was deflation. The policy after World War II would be government intervention, control, and greater collective or social policies. Hence, Bretton Woods was founded on the fears of the great depression and not based on the reasons for the difficulties and ultimate collapse of the gold standard prior to World War I.

INDICATORS OF CURRENCY CRISES

What causes currency crises or liquidity crises? I don't know! But I recognize the symptoms, warning signs or leading indicators of an impending bout of currency weakness or liquidity difficulties. My view on currency risk-taking is, avoid it.

A currency or a foreign exchange value relative to other currencies is not an asset class but rather a means to an end. It is a means of exchanging goods and services from one country with another by purchasing a domestic currency with our country's currency. But the value of the currency will rise and fall; sometimes its price will keep falling or rising. One of the fundamental difficulties I faced as an investor during currency crises is, once started, they are difficult to stop until the liquidity requirements for those investors involved is raised to sufficient levels to attract buyers to come back into the market. A currency does not represent value but is a relationship between one country and another. If I gamble on the value of a currency price movement, I am not investing in something but gambling on a change in a relationship between one thing and another thing.

The leading indicators and causes for currency crises are the relationships between two countries. It is like comparing one company versus another, one country versus another. One country will offer better economic value and represent stronger financial health than another. I rely on certain statistics more than others, but do not rule out any single economic or financial statistic from my research radar screen. An investor must keep abreast and track a wide range of information and data about each country.

These leading indicators can be broken down into various categories, such as:

- Macroeconomic relationships.
- Financial positions.
- Political stability.

In addition, any other category that can affect the perception of investor expectations for that country and lead to currency weakness should be considered.

Macroeconomic instability may take the form of excessive fiscal expansion of fiscal policies (e.g., causing the budget deficit to rise). An inappropriate monetary policy will cause other statistical signals to alert the investor to other warning signs for the potential currency weakness. The key statistics to keep an eye on relate, first of all, to public finances relative to other countries and real interest rates. Examples of public sector statistics include (1) the annual budget deficit as a percentage of gross domestic product and (2) total outstanding debt as a percentage of gross domestic product. In emerging market countries, short-term capital flight may be related to the total amount of foreign debt as a percentage of GDP (look at the interest payment requirements and payment dates). Also, the relation between the money supply M2 to a central bank's foreign currency reserves shows the extent of foreign currency reserves on hand to convert or defend a run or excessive demand on the domestic currency. The analysis that goes into emerging market debt is much more intensive than for industrial countries. Because of size, liquidity, transparency, and infancy of the financial system, small mistakes can lead to big price movements in the value of their currency. A *Euromoney* article (August 1998), "Unknown Killer on the Loose," shows that short-term foreign debt is a clear indication for future difficulties from newly developed and emerging markets.

Often I have tried to obtain as much information available on outstanding short-term debt, local money supply figures, and hard currency reserves. Unfortunately, the relevant information would be unavailable, or out of date, and three months later the financial situation would have deteriorated dramatically, causing panic and ultimately a currency crisis.

The *economic* health of the financial sector of an emerging economy can be useful as a leading indicator of the health of the financial system. A currency can react to the financial inability of local governments or financial sector companies when they get into financial trouble and have difficulty meeting their obligations. If a central bank is intervening to help the financial system, credit will grow, expanding the money supply. If interest rates are held steady or reduced and if these additional local currency credits are used to buy hard currency to repay hard currency debts, the balance sheet of any emerging country can quickly find itself in trouble. In an effort to attract new hard currency investors, interest rates must rise. This is contrary to the needs of the financial system and the health of the overall economy, and an example of how quickly a liquidity crisis can develop into a debt crisis.

One of the key strategic factors at the outset of a liquidity and currency crisis is the country's *political* "will" to defend its currency's value. Government authorities can intervene in the open market by using hard currency reserves to purchase domestic currency. Intervening in the foreign exchange markets and purchasing one's own currency will provide support, but as soon as the intervention is complete, the currency price tends to fall again. And, in theory, if the hard currency reserves do not equal the quantity of local outstanding currency, once the central bank uses up its hard currency reserves, hyperinflation will occur. The central bank must then print money to fund foreign liabilities and, as inflation rises, so too does the inflation-adjusted fiscal spending. Government authorities can raise interest rates to attract foreign investors, but the high interest rates will slow domestic growth, which causes unemployment to rise, along with the necessary fiscal unemployment support. The other problem with the interest rate weapon is that once used, it has to be carried through to the end to be successful, no matter what happens to the domestic economy. The same is true for hard currency reserves, but intervention serves only the speculator and not the domestic economy. If government authorities show no commit-ment, the currency will weaken and drop very fast in value.

When a currency crisis occurs, the problems build slowly but surely, unless the gov-ernment takes action. Or authorities may decide to take no action and let the market find the right level for the price of their currency. Investors will seek to protect themselves from the crash in the currency's value, while government officials will tell these investors what they want to hear—it brings out the worst in everybody concerned.

Another fundamental factor is the state of the *current* account. If the domestic econ-omy is importing more than it's exporting, a trade deficit is created, which means more domestic currency is being sold to purchase another currency to finance and pay for the difference between imports and exports. When invisible earnings are incorporated into the trade account, which are derived from the service industry, the total balance of goods and services (which, put another way, are the actual currency transactions that pass through the central banks' current account) will create either a current account surplus or deficit for that country. But if the current account is in deficit, it needs to be financed from some-where. Using hard currency reserves, borrowing hard currency reserves, attracting foreign direct investment, or merely allowing the currency to devalue, which has, in theory, a knock-on effect—slowing imports, increasing exports, balancing the trade deficit in finan-cial terms but not necessarily in economic terms. If, on top of a current account deficit, an annual fiscal deficit is added, the sums of money required to finance the so-called "twin deficits" could be difficult. If perpetuated year after year, it becomes an enormous sum of money in relation to a country's gross domestic product. The ability of an economy to pro-duce enough output, economic growth, to induce foreign direct investment becomes more difficult over time.

Every year, if the problems persist, the forces within the economic and financial sys-tem build, particularly if the currency's value is held in parity with its trading partners. The problem becomes acute as the current business and economic cycle moves in a different direction or at a different speed from that of her trading partners.

One of the last leading indicators or warning lights is the *appreciation* of the *domes-tic* currency in real terms. In terms of its real value adjusted for inflation rather than at its face value or nominal value. I cannot remember a situation where a currency's real exchange rate occurs in absolute isolation. Meaning that there were no extreme fundamen-tal problems associated with a massive real exchange rate misalignment. There are always factors behind the scenes, built up over years of fiscal and monetary neglect, that cause a sustained real exchange rate appreciation. They inevitably end in tears with a big bang.

Currency crashes and liquidity crises do not pop up out of thin air. A sustained policy of maintaining an exchange rate's nominal value will actually cause the real value of the currency to rise, if inflation is higher than that of her trading partners. A number of models have been developed in an effort to predict currency crises, and currency theory has also attempted to explain the long-term movement and trends in currency prices and values.

CURRENCY MODELS AND THEORY

From my experience and understanding, recent currency models attempt to predict emerg-ing-market currency crises, while general currency theory tries to explain currency price movements over longer periods of time for all countries. Since currency theory is nothing really new, I will start with the theoretical models, which try to predict currency crises. These currency models were developed in response to the emerging market currency crises starting in the 1970s. However, the currency crises of the 1970s and 1980s were not the same as those that occurred in the 1990s in the emerging market countries. The theoretical explanations in the late 1970s and early 1980s relied on the view that a currency crisis was unavoidable and predictable when excessive fiscal deficits were used to stimulate economic growth. The fiscal deficits would be financed by a central bank that printed the necessary money.

If the exchange rate was fixed, a balance of payments deficit would create more and more pressure on the exchange rate's parity. The deterioration between the economic fundamentals in relation to a contradiction of a fixed exchange rate made the currency crisis predictable. These models were known as the first generation models.

FIRST AND SECOND GENERATION MODELS

The first generation models and research were developed in response to the Mexican Crisis (from 1973-1982) and Argentina (from 1978-1981).

After the currency crises in Europe in the early 1990s, and the Mexican peso crisis subsequently known as the "Tequila Crisis" because of its spread throughout Latin America in 1994 and 1995, the second-generation models came up with alternative explanations for currency crises. They held that even in the absence of deterioration in economic fundamentals, a currency crisis could occur. The second-generation models studied the acceptance of self-fulfilling crises, which occur when the sheer pessimism of a significant group of investors provokes a capital outflow that leads to the eventual collapse of the exchange rate system, thus validating the negative expectations.[5]

I do not rely heavily on models for predicting the future, but they are helpful for examining specific relationships of one kind or another. In other words, they explore the pure speculative aspects of major and sudden currency price movements. All of these models use a variety of leading indicators that have been discussed earlier.

Leading Indicators

A Sachs, Velasco, and Turnell paper in 1996 identified three relevant leading indicators forewarning a currency crisis. They note that high real currency appreciation, an increase in bank lending, and a high ratio of money supply M2 relative to hard currency reserves are key indicators.

Also, in 1996, Frankel and Rose argued that currency crises in emerging markets occur when foreign direct investment (FDI) dries up, hard currency reserves are low, domestic credit is high, interest rates in the industrial countries are high, and the real exchange rate is over valued. Their paper is also interesting because the authors do not find that either current account deficits or budget deficits add significantly to a currency crisis.

I believe the "twin deficits" are an important leading indicator for potential liquidity problems in the future, particularly if they mount year after year. No country can afford a sustained accumulation of a fiscal and current account deficit without consequences, particularly if the country in question has a fixed exchange rate regime. Some models say differently, but they will not sway my thinking.

Lastly, and more recently, Kaminsky, Lizondo, and Reinhart used a signals approach to predicting currency crises. Basically their paper monitored a number of economic and financial indicators that showed unusual behavior prior to a currency crisis. A good signal is one that is followed by a currency crisis within 24 months. Fifteen economic and financial indicators were used, showing that certain indicators send stronger signals than others. The loudest is the appreciation of the real exchange rate, money supply M2 as a percentage of hard currency reserves. The growth rate of money supply is second, while the real interest rate comes in the middle of the range—the real interest rate differential places last.[6] The actual list of 15 is as follows:

1. The real exchange rate.
2. M2/hard currency growth rate.
3. Export growth rate.
4. International reserves growth rate.
5. Excess M1 balances.
6. Domestic credit/GDP growth rate.
7. Real interest rate.
8. M2 multiplier growth rate.
9. Import growth rate.
10. Industrial production growth rate.
11. Terms of trade growth rate.
12. Lending rate/deposit rate.
13. Bank deposit growth rate.
14. Stock price index growth rate.
15. Real interest rate differential.

As a leading indicator, the appreciation of the real exchange rate offers the loudest signal. A J. P. Morgan paper, "Event Risk Indicator Handbook" (January 29, 1998), states:

> "... a key condition for a currency crash is a loss of international competitiveness. A trade deficit or the path of the real (inflation-adjusted) trade-weighted exchange rate can measure this. The timing of the loss of competitiveness turns into a currency crash and is determined by two factors: the credibility of the government's commitment to defend the exchange rate—which is related to growth in domestic economic activity and the size of foreign exchange reserves—and the force of financial contagion. An overvalued currency can remain overvalued for a long time if output growth is strong, reserves are high and there is no 'contagion.' ... There are two elements to contagion. There is the contagion that spreads along the economic avenue of falling competitiveness caused devaluations in a country's trading partners. The path of the real trade weighted index can capture this. Another element to contagion is a currency crash everywhere which reduces investors' appetite for currency risk everywhere."

An example of the effect of the real exchange rate can be seen in the following simple scenario. Country A and Country B start off life in a perfect world (for our example) with interest rates the same with an exchange rate of A1 to B1. Both countries are equally balanced in terms of trade and trading accounts. Country B starts to show signs of inflation of 2 percent per annum more than country A, and therefore Country B raises interest rates by 1 percent. In real terms, after inflation, the exchange rate of Country A adjusted for the inflation difference between A and B should strengthen to 0.99 for every 1.0 of country B's. It takes less, after adjusting for the inflation rate difference, of currency A to buy goods and services in Country B. But because a higher interest rate is more attractive to investors, Country A invests in Country B and, in fact, the exchange rate between the two currencies rises to A1.15 for every B1.0 instead of the inflation-adjusted exchange rate of A0.99, the difference between the inflation-adjusted, real exchange rate of A0.99. However, the actual or nominal exchange rate of A1.15 or A0.16 cents difference is a 16 percent real exchange rate appreciation. This is the most reliable leading indicator for potential currency crises. Actually, it would cause a liquidity crisis first, and then a currency crisis.

When I study the real exchange rate, I always look behind the figure to see what is going on, but never do I consider the real exchange rate in absolute isolation. The "signals" study does state and accept, however, that real exchange rate misalignments are occurring all the time, but the study suggests, and I agree, that:

> *". . . an increase in the real exchange rate misalignment is expected to increase the risk of a currency crisis."*[7]

It is a rise in the annual percentage of the real exchange rate that sends the signal rather than the real exchange rate in and of itself.

But I continue to argue for the need to be aware of all available relevant information, which includes first and foremost, the real value offered by that country—real interest rates. I discovered an interesting chart in a Merrill Lynch publication that paints a pretty good picture (see Table 8.3).

Table 8.3: Causes in Currency Crises[8]

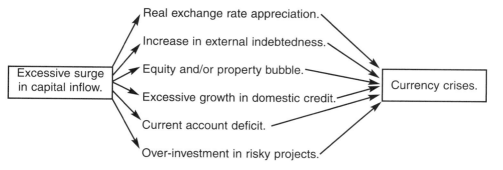

Currency crises, liquidity crises, do not magically happen out of thin blue air. There is always a strong fundamental reason when capital flows out of one country and into another. That is why my starting point in any multi-currency investment environment is the real value of money. If a country I am looking at does not represent value to others, then I believe that, ultimately, funds will flow out of that country, seeking better value elsewhere, and therefore currency weakness will occur and perhaps cause a liquidity crisis. I will never pick bottoms, sell tops, nor predict the future, but I can certainly manage my risks better and be better informed about my own process to managing global capital markets risk.

CURRENCY THEORY

I want to turn to currency theory next because currency theory tries to explain the movement in currency prices in a more general manner. It is interesting and helpful to understand currency price movements and trends. The arguments presented by currency theory only cause me to stay away from currency risks even more.

The most substantive and interesting currency theory is *purchasing-power-parity* theory (PPP). PPP theory is not new. David Ricardo studied and analyzed it around 1917.[9] In a flexible-rate exchange rate system, according to PPP theory, a currency such as the U.S. dollar will purchase the same goods and services in the United States as abroad. If you have ever gone on vacation abroad and found yourself doing the currency equivalent calculations to determine whether the item you are about to purchase abroad is more or less expensive than at home, that is PPP theory in action. PPP suggests that if goods were cheaper in another country, trade arbitrage would create greater demand for the good, thus causing greater demand for that country's currency, and thereby raising its value until the PPP of the two currencies were equal in purchasing-power terms. If inflation rises in one country versus another, then, according to PPP, the nominal or face value should reflect the changes in real purchasing power.

Let's go back to my perfect world of Countries A and B, both of which have an annual inflation rate of 5 percent, but then the annual inflation rate of B goes to 10 percent. The theory goes that the currency of A should rise in value, while that of B will fall in value. In purchasing power parity terms, if the exchange rates between the two countries are 1 to 1, then adjusting for inflation and domestic purchasing power, with inflation running at twice the annual rate, the appropriate purchasing power exchange rate should be currency A0.50 for every B1.00.

The Economist magazine provided my favorite PPP model or standard where their basket of items is a McDonald's Big Mac, which is produced in 110 countries. Table 8.4 is the Big Mac Index as of January 16, 2003.

The Economist's Big Mac Index is based on the theory of "purchasing-power parity." Under PPP, exchange rates should adjust to equalize the price of a common basket of goods and services across countries. *The Economist's* basket is the Big Mac. Relative to its Big Mac PPP, the Euro is now 8 percent overvalued against the U.S. dollar, the U.K. sterling is 21 percent overvalued. In contrast, the Australian dollar is 34 percent undervalued. The cheapest Big Mac hamburger is in Argentina, at $1.18, against the average price in the United States of $2.65, which implies that the Argentine peso is 55 percent undervalued to the U.S. dollar. The most expensive Big Mac is in Iceland, costing $5.51.

Table 8.4: The Big Mac Index (as of January 6, 2003)[10]

Country	Big Mac Prices (U.S. Dollars)*	Country	Big Mac Prices (U.S. Dollars)*
Argentina	1.18	Mexico	2.10
Australia	1.76	New Zealand	2.12
Belarus	1.28	Peru	2.27
Brazil	1.38	Philippines	1.22
Britain	3.19	Poland	1.66
Canada	2.08	Russia	1.26
Chile	1.81	Saudi Arabia	2.40
China	1.20	Singapore	1.90
Columbia	2.13	Slovakia	1.61
Croatia	2.11	Slovenia	2.07
Czech Republic	1.83	South Africa	1.59
Egypt	1.58	South Korea	2.73
Estonia	1.93	Sweden	3.46
Euro area	2.87	Switzerland	4.56
Hong Kong	1.44	Taiwan	2.04
Hungary	2.21	Thailand	1.29
Iceland	5.51	Turkey	2.18
Indonesia	1.82	UAE	2.45
Japan	2.23	Ukraine	1.26
Malaysia	1.33	United States	2.65
Malta	3.03	Venezuela	1.83

*Local currency exchange rates as at January 15, 2003.

But then there are the arguments that the Big Mac Index should be adjusted for individual tax rates or subsidy costs. I do not subscribe to this argument. A price is a price. I talked about country attractiveness in terms of tax breaks or lower taxes and basically offering companies and their executives a competitive and profitable environment in which to work. If a government wants to tax, subsidize the price of a McDonald's Big Mac, then so be it. The PPP theory has to be taken at face value.

PPP theory has fared pretty poorly since my time living overseas. In fact, the U.S. and U.K. exchange rate has only come close to what I believe to be a resemblance to a PPP on February 26, 1985, when the U.S. dollar reached approximately $1.0345.

Living outside the United States is much more expensive in terms of purchasing power and income tax rates. Why doesn't the U.S. dollar fall into place with its PPP throughout the world? Exactly, it doesn't. Still, PPP theory is interesting. I enjoy keeping up with the research on the subject, but otherwise my interest is purely academic—never practically applied.

FIXED VERSUS FLOATING

This is the mother of all debates, shaping and re-shaping our global economic and financial system. The question is, should national currencies be fixed or anchored to a commodity, another currency or basket of currencies, or should they be free floating? My views are clear, but let me first present both sides of the argument. To control or not control, that is the question. Should the government or market forces determine the price?

An exchange rate is "fixed" when the domestic currency is pegged to one or more foreign currencies or when, during the gold standard, it was pegged or anchored to the value of an ounce of gold. An exchange rate is "flexible or floating" when market forces determine the value of the domestic currency.

A great deal of terminology is used to describe a variety of exchange rate regimes—it's time to clear it all up and categorize the differences.

There are three main groups of exchange rate regimes (1) a pegged exchange rate, (2) limited flexibility, and (3) a flexible exchange rate.

In a *pegged exchange rate,* the currency price is fixed to a single currency or a currency composite. *Limited flexibility* means the exchange rate is allowed to move within bands around a single currency or within a cooperative arrangement. A *flexible* system allows the exchange rate to float freely. There are a variety of names attached to the three currency regimes around the world, defined by the IMF in its publication "Exchange Rate Arrangements and Currency Convertibility Developments and Issues" (1999). They are as follows:

- *Exchange arrangements with no separate legal tender.* The currency of another country circulates as the sole legal tender, or the member belongs to a monetary or currency union in which the members share the same legal tender. Adopting such regimes is a form of ultimate sacrifice for surrendering monetary control—no scope is left for national monetary authorities to conduct independent monetary policy.

- *Currency Board arrangements.* A monetary regime based on an implicit legislative commitment to exchange domestic currency for a specified foreign currency at a fixed exchange rate, combined with the restrictions on the issuing authority to ensure the fulfillment of its legal obligation. This implies that domestic currency be issued against foreign exchange and that new issues are fully backed by foreign assets, eliminating traditional central bank functions, such as monetary control and the lender of last resort, and leaving little scope for discretionary monetary policy; some flexibility may still be afforded, depending on how strict the rules of the boards are established.

- *Other conventional fixed-peg arrangements.* The country pegs its currency (formally or de facto) as a fixed rate to a major currency or basket of currencies, where the weighted composite is formed from the currencies of major trading or financial partners, and currency weights reflect the geographical distribution of trade, services, or capital flows. In a conventional fixed pegged arrangement, the exchange rate fluctuates within a narrow margin of at most +/-1 percent around a central rate. The monetary authority stands ready to maintain the fixed parity through intervention, limiting the degree of monetary policy discretion; the degree of flexibility of monetary policy, however, is greater relative to currency board arrangements or currency unions, in that traditional central bank functions are, although limited, still possible, and the monetary authority can adjust the level of the exchange rate, although infrequently.

- *Pegged exchange rates within bands.* The value of the currency is maintained with margins of fluctuation around a formal or de facto fixed peg that are wider than +/-1 percent around a central rate. It also includes the arrangement of the countries in the exchange rate mechanism (ERM) of the European Monetary System (EMS). There is some degree of monetary policy discretion, with the degree of discretion depending on the bandwidth.

- *Crawling pegs.* The currency peg is adjusted periodically in small amounts at a fixed, pre-announced rate in response to changes in selective quantitative indicators (past inflation differentials vis-à-vis major trading partners, differentials between the inflation target and expected inflation in major trading partners, for example). The rate of the crawl, the devaluation of the exchange rate, can be set to generate inflation adjusted changes in the currency's value (backward looking), or at a pre-announced fixed rate below the projected inflation differentials (forward looking). Maintaining a credible crawling peg imposes constraints on monetary policy in a similar manner as a fixed peg system.

- *Exchange rates within crawling bands.* The currency is maintained within certain fluctuation margins around a central rate that is adjusted periodically at a fixed pre-announced rate or in response to changes in selective quantitative indicators. The degree of flexibility of the exchange rate is a function of the width of the band, with bands chosen to be either symmetric around a crawling central parity or to widen gradually with an asymmetric choice of the crawl upper and lower bands. The commitment to maintain the exchange rate within the band continues to impose constraints on monetary policy, with the degree of policy independence being a function of the bandwidth.

- *Managed floating with no pre-announced path for the exchange rate.* The Monetary authority influences the movements of the exchange rate through active intervention in the foreign exchange market without specifying, or pre-committing, to a pre-announced path for the exchange rate. Indicators for managing the rate are broadly judgmental, including, for example, the balance of payments position, international reserves, and developments in other markets.

- *Independent floating.* The exchange rate is market determined, with any foreign exchange intervention aimed at moderating the rate of change and preventing undue fluctuations in the exchange rate, rather than establishing a level for it.

In these regimes, monetary policy is in principle independent of exchange rate policy.

In thinking about the difference between a floating and fixed exchange rate, picture an off-road four-wheel drive vehicle. If the suspension system of the vehicle is fixed in place, and if you drive over rough terrain, then folks inside will be bumping against the roof of the vehicle. They will be absorbing the shock of the rough terrain. Sure, drive over a smooth surface and the passengers will not feel a thing, but any bump along the road will be felt much more than had the vehicle been fitted with a four-wheel independent suspension system, which absorbs most of the shocks and bumps.

The four-wheel independent suspension system is the floating rate currency system. The suspension system absorbs the shocks of the terrain—although people inside the vehicle are bounding around, it's nothing like the rough ride when the suspension system is fixed.

Domestic economies rise and fall, and economic cycles provide the longer distance terrain, while the business cycle provides the shorter-term bumps in the road year after year. No economy is exactly the same as another—therefore its economic strength or weaknesses will influence other economies as well. But as domestic economies rise, certain economic and financial events will occur and, similarly, as economic growth falls other economic events will be triggered. The bottom line: economies bounce around. And depending on what government authorities choose as their shock absorber (fixed or floating exchange rates), the passengers riding along will feel the bumps in the road very differently if the exchange rate is fixed or if it is floating. Theoretically, there are reasonably good arguments for each exchange rate system. For example:

> *"In general, a fixed exchange rate (or a greater degree of fixity) is preferable if the disturbances impinging on the economy are predominantly monetary—such as a change in the demand for money—and thus affect the general level of prices. A flexible rate (or a greater degree of flexibility) is preferable if disturbances are predominantly real—such as a change in tastes or technology, which affects the relative prices of domestic goods—or originate abroad."[11]*

An exchange rate regime must work hand-in-hand with a monetary policy framework coupled with appropriate fiscal policy. We discussed the different monetary policy strategies in Chapter 4. They are exchange rate anchor (an absolute fixed exchange rate regime, delegating monetary policy to another major country), monetary aggregate anchor (targeting money supply), or an inflation-targeting framework.

The argument between the two exchange rate regimes moves on to credibility versus flexibility. In monetary policymaking, particularly with the use of currency boards, a fixed exchange rate regime, with the help of the appropriate economic and financial structure, can help improve a country's credibility. After saying that, whatever the exchange rate regime, a country's long-term economic success will be dependent and judged on the social as well as the political commitment to its success. A fixed exchange rate, from my point of view, is all about earning credibility and getting one's economic and financial restructuring sorted out.

A fixed exchange rate regime must be supported by a firm fiscal policy commitment for a balanced budget and a monetary policy focused on maintaining the fixed exchange rate peg. Government authorities are not allowed to borrow money nor can they reduce interest rates to increase employment, at a time when the currency's value is falling. There is no flexibility in a fixed exchange rate—none. If government authorities do not have the support of their people and/or if investor confidence does not support the fixed exchange rate parity, the process will not work. It will only make things worse. On the other hand, if the people and investors support a fixed exchange rate regime, inflation expectations will fall, and fall very rapidly. Once a low inflationary environment is achieved with stable economic growth, coupled with fiscal and monetary discipline on the part of government authorities and society, then a more flexible arrangement may be required and may be more useful to that country.

However, once again, whatever the exchange rate regime, discipline on the part of government authorities on society, and vice versa, is necessary if a fixed regime becomes a floating rate regime. More flexibility does not mean less policy discipline. On the contrary, greater exchange rate flexibility requires more discipline. Fiscal and monetary policies must be absolutely clear and decisive in their objectives to ensure social and investor credibility. As credibility wanes, policy choices decline. Flexibility, however, also allows government authorities to react to economic and financial difficulties, or to fine-tune their policies.

In a fixed exchange rate regime, fine-tuning policy is not possible. And if maintaining a pegged currency caused interest rates to rise too high, credibility may wane because the longer the interest rates remain high, defending the currency's fixed value, the greater the economic and financial damage they may cause on the domestic economy. Therefore, the high real interest rates required to hold the currency's value are not sustainable, nor is the currency's peg. The high real interest rates may in fact undermine the fixed exchange rate peg itself.

SHAPING EXCHANGE RATE REGIMES

There are many ingredients to shaping either a fixed or flexible exchange rate regime. One of the most important aspects of a fixed exchange rate regime is the state of the domestic financial system or banking system. The financial system must also support the fixed exchange rate with hard currency reserves and strong banking institution balance sheets. Hard currency reserves will more often than not be used to defend the value of the currency rather than the value of the economy. If hard currency reserves fall, then interest rates must rise to attract hard currency investors to rebuild reserves, which could end up hurting the domestic economy. This, simply said, is why the banking system must be financially stable and well capitalized to endure the difficulty of higher real interest rates in an effort to maintain the fixed exchange rate regime.

The political costs for developing a fixed exchange rate regime are much higher than for a flexible one. So, for politicians thinking about a fixed exchange rate regime, if they do not have a strong banking system, the currency parity will not hold, the credibility they want to achieve will fail, and they will actually worsen credibility.

The swing from fixed or pegged exchange rate regimes to flexible ones since the breakdown of the Bretton Woods agreement in the 1970s has recently intensified. As an *Economist* article (November 18, 2000) pointed out:

> *"No exchange-rate system is ideal. Whether governments fix, float or 'manage' their currencies, problems arise. Today's preference for the extremes—pure float or absolute fix—is overdone."*

It can be a very confusing subject. However, one aspect is crystal clear. The exchange rate alone is not a policy, but a mechanism supported by fiscal and monetary policy—an absolute commitment.

As I stated in Chapter 4, policymakers are reacting and creating new policy based on the last economic and financial crisis arising from the Bretton Woods fixed exchange rate regime. I agree with Bernard Connolly when he argues in an *Euromoney* magazine article

(September 1998) that policymakers and the architects of the Bretton Woods fixed exchange-rate system:

> *". . . failed to recognize that the factors that contributed, via the classical gold standard, to World War I were similar to those that led to the breakdown of the inter-war gold standard: international capital flows in a regime of credibly fixed exchange rates made deflation—and thus debt problems and economic, social and political strains—the inevitable consequences of any dip in the domestic rate of return on capital relative to the world rate of interest. 'Competitive Devaluation' in fact provided relief from the strains that led to the depression of the 1930s by engineering, in a non-cooperative way (always the best) a world monetary expansion; unfortunately it came too late."*[12]

In the early 1970s, the Bretton Woods system broke down, allowing a flexible exchange rate regime to evolve. For example, according to the International Monetary Fund, 87 percent of the developing countries had some form of pegged exchange rate in 1975, but by 1995 this proportion had fallen to below 50 percent. A more telling statistic is that in 1975 currencies with pegged exchange rates accounted for 70 percent of the developing world's total trade, and by 1996 that figure had dropped to 20 percent.[13]

The fixed exchange-rate system devised at Bretton Woods failed. Patterns in economic and business cycles are never the same between one country and another. A global fixed exchange rate regime was created, but once the comparative advantages of post World War II Europe and its government policies disappeared versus those that were implemented in the United States and Japan, the system tried to adjust but could not. Like any great earthquake, once the crack starts to open in a fixed exchange rate regime, market forces soon engulf it, as in the case when the gold standard fell apart in the 1970s.

The other major difficulty in the politics of a pegged exchange rate is the political capital spent on the fixed exchange rate and policies geared towards maintaining that fixed currency value. In a keynote address for the annual World Bank Conference on Development Economics in Washington, D.C., in April 1998, James Tobin offered the following reasons for the failure of the Bretton Woods fixed exchange rate system:

> *". . . that the rate of exchange of the key currency with the other currencies could not be devalued without the concurrence of the governments. The United States wanted [the currencies of] Japan and Germany, in particular, to appreciate (by lowering the price of gold in their currencies), and they [Japan and Germany] thought that adjustment was the responsibility of the United States."*

> *". . . which complicated the currency rate conflict, was the peculiar role in the system. Dollars held by foreign governments were convertible into gold at a fixed price. Private dollars were not supposed to be convertible, but they became so de facto as the United States and the United Kingdom, until 1968, fed the private gold market to keep the free-market gold price from getting out of line. U.S. balance of payments deficits increased dollar debt in official hands and depleted the U.S. gold reserves available to redeem dollars. In an ultimate impasse in 1971-1973, the United States abandoned its commitment to pay gold for dollars. Unlike Herbert Hoover, Richard Nixon was not willing to sacrifice American prosperity for the gold standard or for fixed currency exchange rates."*[14]

The move toward a more flexible framework and system took time after the collapse of Bretton Woods.

Basically, countries with higher inflation rates would try to control devaluation with hard currencies through "crawling pegs" to ensure that trade competitiveness did not erode. A floating peg, crawling peg, or managed floats can be defined together. The International Monetary Fund, in a document entitled "Exchange Regime Choice: Emerging Markets and Beyond" (2000), said:

> *"Pegged exchange rate regimes imply an explicit or understood commitment undertaken by policy authorities to limit the extent of fluctuation of the exchange rates to a degree that provides a meaningful nominal anchor for private expectations about the behavior of the exchange rate and the requisite supporting behavior of monetary policy. Quite a broad range of regimes share this general characteristic, with a varying degree of permissible exchange rate flexibility, ranging from very hard, single-currency pegs, to basket pegs and bands, to managed floats."*

The idea is that trade competitiveness needs to remain on equal terms with hard currency countries. Even though the country in question has underlying fundamental economic and financial problems that need to be addressed, which create inflationary pressures, adjusting their exchange rate in relation to the inflation rate differential or real interest rate differential ensures that trade competitiveness is not disturbed. A "crawling peg" is acceptable over the short term to alleviate stress to the economic and financial system while structural reform is taking place. The markets will test any moving or crawling peg.

Smaller countries that do not have the depth of financial resources to defend their country's value find themselves in a precarious position. When I invest in smaller countries, I look at the economic and financial fundamentals, not necessarily at the currency regime that the government authorities have in place. A country must have the economic and financial fundamentals to support their currency's value. The fiscal and monetary policies must work together to support the currency value or the real value of the country's assets.

Once a course is chosen, then absolute support is necessary—there are no options. If it is a fixed exchange rate regime, then there is the opportunity to put the house in order. Get the fiscal budget under control and the supply of money as well. Financial institutions must be well capitalized with hard currency reserves on the rise. Once accomplished, with inflation under control and globally competitive, they should move away from a fixed currency system because a fixed exchange rate regime is only a means to an end, unless the end is to achieve currency union with the associated hard currency peg. It is, however, a serious way to reduce inflation, restructure the economy, and become competitive, and prepares the way to floating the currency once again. As the day to flexibility draws near, public policy must be more diligent and society must be educated to the realities of a floating currency.

In Israel, a great deal of effort is being expended on the state of its exchange rate regime, and the discussions on the fundamental differences between the two exchange rate regimes are fascinating. A *Ha'aretz* newspaper article on November 19, 1998, sums up Israel's dilemma, but also shows the lack of understanding in achieving some form of exchange rate stability.

"There are two ways of conducting monetary policy: either the key item that is managed is the exchange rate and interest rates protect it . . . or manage interest and then the exchange rate will go along. The choice is between large mobility in the exchange rate, which will cause price instability, or large fluctuation in interest rates . . ."

This is just the type of thinking that will get a country into trouble. Exchange rate policy is not about monetary policy, and monetary policy is not all about exchange rates, whether fixed or floating. The policy that is appropriate for any exchange rate system is fiscal and monetary policy working in harmony to reduce inflation and maintain steady economic growth. Neither monetary policy nor an exchange rate policy is the source of all economic success. Even a country such as Israel, with 75 percent of its GDP dependent on international trade, will not achieve its stated objectives without a balanced policy making their exchange rate management mechanism (whatever it is). If a country wants to control short-term capital movements, this policy is a very different subject with very different consequences and objectives. An exchange rate regime is not a policy. It is a tool for both fiscal and monetary policymakers. Fixing the value of a currency is not a solution nor will it automatically solve fiscal and monetary issues. Capital should be allowed to find the best long-term return on investment throughout the world.

I will always be suspicious of fixed exchange rates because I continue to wonder about the long-term effectiveness, objectives, and intentions. This suspicion is not the same with a currency board in its correct form, but fixed or pegged exchange rates. The true real interest rate analysis, credit risk, and searching for the best value for money is only possible when exchange rates fluctuate, allowing real interest rates to reflect the real value that country has to offer. A fixed exchange rate is another form of government subsidy—taxpayers' money being used to finance economic and financial inefficiencies, in a similar way as most nationalized industry operates. Market forces always prevail, or so my friend Peter Maconie tells me.

A fixed exchange rate regime can be central government intervention in the free market system at its worst. The political capital is much higher than any policy towards a nationalized industry, which means even greater dangers. The markets are best equipped to reassess values of one country or another—not government authorities dressing things up to look like something they are not. Real interest rates adjust, exchange rates adjust, and therefore, capital flows adjust, though perhaps not in that order because of perception or expectations. If the exchange rate is allowed to find its own market level, absorbing part of the shock of any economic and financial stress, and with the appropriate fiscal and monetary adjustments, the country can get back on track. The cost will be nothing like the cost or shock when government fixes prices or subsidizes global capital speculators. When major currency crises occur, when a fixed exchange rate system collapses, the fiscal and monetary costs are far greater than necessary had the currency been allowed to float freely.

THE EURO

After all is said and done on this subject, particularly the argument against the use of fixed exchange rates, why, you are probably wondering, are the Europeans creating a single currency? I will discuss this question in the next chapter, further clarifying not only my belief that a monetary union in Europe will have difficulty but also my continued dubious expectation and strategy towards it. The Europeans have fixed their currencies with the introduction of the Euro on January 1, 1999. These eleven countries, with different histories, with very different economic and financial cycles, have a group of politicians who hang their hats on the view that bigger is beautiful when it comes to improving life on the European Continent. Only time will tell. I am very patient and very suspicious. Creating a fixed exchange rate or monetary union is all about credibility. Without the right policy, credibility will fly right out the window. This is the reason Europeans also need political union in conjunction with monetary union to give the idea of a single currency a real run.

IMPORTS VERSUS EXPORTS

Countries, which depend on one commodity or another for their main export or import, will have a major impact on currency values. Table 8.5 offers an example of those countries that depend on commodities as a large proportion of their trade balance.

Table 8.5: Share of Commodities (percentage of imports and exports per country)[15]

Country	In Exports	In Imports
Norway	65	17
New Zealand	63	17
Australia	60	13
Denmark	51	21
Netherlands	33	26
Canada	28	13
Hungary	28	23
Spain	21	26
France	18	21
United States	16	17
Belgium	15	22
United Kingdom	14	16
Finland	13	23
Sweden	12	18
Germany	7	20
Japan	2	41

When commodity prices fluctuate, there is a national dimension to these changes. As tax revenues fall, hard currency reserves may dramatically fall, with economic growth slowing and profit margins falling. Particularly if the chief export of a country is a single commodity such as oil, copper, etc., the negative consequences can be severe.

I mentioned in the Chapter 1a situation regarding the price of North Sea oil and its interrelationship with the United Kingdom's currency value, and therefore the government's tax revenue. A commodity-linked currency is the positive correlation of the currency's price movements with the price of a specific commodity or a basket of commodities. When the price of a commodity falls, the currency price will undoubtedly fall as well. If the value of the currency does not fall, the trade balance between exports and imports will deteriorate, causing the current account to contract, reducing the surplus or increasing the deficit. Additionally, tax revenue from the sale of raw material will diminish, which harms the fiscal budget finances as well, which, if in deficit, must also be financed from somewhere. The tricky part of this situation is the direction of monetary policy—should it protect the value of the currency or should it allow the value of the currency to fall? On one hand, domestic economic growth must slow to cool the amount of imports coming into the country. On the other hand, economic growth cannot be slowed too heavily so its finances are not strained, because then interest rates, real interest rates, will have to rise to attract capital to its country to fund its government finances. But if the currency is allowed to find its own level, at a lower value, this will take part of the strain off the current account and also allow the government's revenue to be less harmed than otherwise with a strong currency. The lower commodity-related prices fall, so too must the value of the exchange rate, which acts as a shock absorber for the economy and lessens the economic and financial hardship for society.

I have found that most government authorities make fundamental mistakes during the budgetary process when projecting the annual revenue stream derived from the commodity price. For example, in the case of Norway, the export of oil and petroleum products represents 13 percent of the country's GDP, and 43 percent of all exports. When the price of North Sea oil falls substantially, 13 percent of the country's GDP and 43 percent of all exports are going to be affected. And, therefore, hard currency earnings will fall accordingly. But you may say that the falling price of oil is good for the rest of the economy. True, but Norway is so dependent on oil revenues that what is good for one country or industry is not so good for Norway. Budget revenue, which is dependent on oil tax revenue, must be found elsewhere, or budget spending must be reduced, or taxes must rise to recoup the oil tax revenue losses. Additionally, if the exchange rate is fixed, a potential current account and fiscal budget deficit must be financed. Interest rates, real rates, would have to rise to attract the required capital. If an economy dominated by a commodity has a floating exchange rate, the currency's value will find an appropriate level when a shock to the price of the commodities occurs outside the control of the country in question. For government authorities, the process of currency adjustment will cause less difficulty than those associated with a fixed exchange rate. If a current account deficit does rise, financing it under a floating rate regime will be less difficult than under a fixed exchange rate regime.

Flexibility is the key to floating exchange rates, but it requires much greater responsibility because flexibility can turn into zero credibility very quickly. Commodity-linked countries should use floating rate exchange rate systems. In 1998, the average price of a barrel of oil reached a 22-year low at $14.5 per barrel. That is good for the Japanese importers of oil, who will benefit from the drop in oil prices, but what about Russia? Russia's energy exports account for half of export receipts and about 40 percent of the central government's budget revenues. The Russian budget crisis was dominated by the deterioration in oil revenues due to the collapse in the price of oil, among other things, which caused the subsequent collapse of the Russian ruble.

During the days in 1984 outlined in Chapter 1, I carefully watched the price of oil relative to the value of the currency, the sterling/dollar exchange rate, to keep track of the government's revenues derived from oil production in the North Sea. The sterling/dollar exchange rate actually fell far beyond the necessary relative devaluation level, and therefore U.K. tax revenue derived from oil production actually grew. There is no doubt in my mind that the U.K. economy benefited greatly by sterling's devaluation in 1984. And this came at a time in Prime Minister Thatcher's tenure when economic difficulties were holding back her restructuring policies. The subsequent fiscal surplus, future tax reductions and economic prosperity came at a time when I was investing my personal monies into the U.K. to start my various businesses.

Another interesting commodity-linked currency is the Australian dollar. Australia is the world's largest exporter of coal, iron-ore, wool, and beef, with nearly 60 percent of the total foreign exchange hard currency income from commodity exports, and over 50 percent of those exports destined to Asia. According to a leading investment report in December 1998, coal, Australia's largest export with 145 metric tons exported in 1996-1997, represented 20 percent of the total mineral exports earnings, approximately A$7.3 billion. Over 85 percent of Australia's combined coking and thermal coal exports are destined for the Asian markets, Japan being the largest end-market. If demand in Asia for these commodities falls, Australia has A$7.3 billion of hard currency revenues at risk, which, if hedged (allowing the value of the currency to fall), will protect their hard currency revenues. This is precisely happened what in Australia in 1997 and 1998.

THE CURRENT ACCOUNT

A nation's current account is very important, and a great deal of discussion is spent on determining the importance of current account deficits. The current account describes the state of a country's balance of payments and trade with the rest of the world. When trade figures are released, they are a nation's balance of payments, defined by merchandise trade (visible) and services (invisible). The total accounting for imports and exports of goods and services is called the 'balance on current account.'[16] The current account of a country are similar to a personal checking account or current account as it is called in the United Kingdom. It represents the actual sums of money coming into and out of the country. If the current account is positive, more money is coming into the country than going out. When it is in deficit, more money is leaving the country. When goods and services are purchased or sold overseas to trading partners, each party must buy the other's currency, selling its own to purchase goods and services in foreign markets. Like a personal checking account, if more money goes in than is paid out, then there will be a current account surplus. If more money is paid out than paid in to the checking account, then the current account deficit or overdraft must be financed.

We lowly individuals can use our cash savings to fund the deficit, sell assets, or borrow the money to take care of the current account overdraft. Nations or sovereign states can use their hard currency reserves to finance a current account deficit, sell assets to finance it, borrow from the domestic savings pool, or borrow hard currencies from foreigners to finance the deficit or domestic tax rates rise. A particular current account deficit may be a short-term event, in which case hard currency reserves could be used to finance it, particularly under a floating-rate exchange rate regime where the currency can be expected to find an appropriate level to offset the current account deficit.

There are models, which try to determine this exchange rate, called the Fundamental Equilibrium Exchange Rate (FEER), which is the exchange rate that produces a sustainable current account balance. However, if a current account deficit builds and is allowed to fester into a long-term event and financial burden, then the costs for servicing it could rise, causing a liquidity crisis and ultimately a debt crisis as the country cannot afford to finance the current account deficit any longer.

As I mentioned at the outset of this chapter, there are a host of economic and financial indicators that I use and monitor that better enable me to anticipate future difficulties—not all the time, but more often than not. I think that the current account is an important warning sign. Professor Stiglitz describes its importance in very simple terms. The long run consequences of persistent trade deficits will cause:

> *". . . increased foreign indebtedness, leading eventually to increased interest and dividend payments abroad, and if foreign borrowing is not used to finance additional investments that yield returns sufficient to pay the increased interest and dividend payments, lower living standards."*[17]

As an indicator, current account data is very useful, and there are three important ways to look at the data. I explained earlier how current accounts are defined in terms of trade. But I also look at it as the difference between a country's ability to save or invest monies. If a country spends or consumes more than it saves, then that spending will have to be financed. When consuming from abroad, the domestic currency is sold to purchase foreign currencies to fund the gap. Offsetting this capital outflow of the domestic currency is usually by way of foreign direct investment. Another way to look at it is the addition to or deduction from a country's claims on the rest of the world.[18] In this instance, I find that watching where the current account surplus is going and how it is invested is more interesting at times than when the liability of the current account deficits are due.

In terms of industrial countries, I am more concerned about whether and where that country is being held hostage in financial and economic terms, such as the Japanese ownership of U.S. Treasury bonds, or the dependency on oil from the Persian Gulf. Also, those with the greatest trade deficit with the United States (Japan and China) have substantial claims on the U.S. by way of their ownership in U.S. Treasury bonds and in other equity investments in the United States. These countries have maintained a positive trade balance and have built up a considerable net foreign asset position versus their trading partners. These statistics, discussed in Chapters 2 and 3, are important because they paint a long-term picture of an industrial nation's potential behavior with developing and emerging market countries.

A current account surplus or deficit is not a statistic that stands on a soapbox screaming and shouting at you at Speakers Corner at Hyde Park in central London on a Sunday morning. But, when a current account deficit starts to develop, depending on a number of factors—such as whether the exchange rate regime is fixed or floating—investors should take heed. Is the current account deficit being financed by short-term hard currency borrowings or through long-term foreign direct investment? What is the hard currency reserve position and how will it be used during the period of a current account deficit? If external debt levels and burdens rise each year without offsetting domestic economic growth, the cost of servicing the debt could be worrisome. There are a variety of relationships, such as the real exchange rate level, which also must be observed and monitored.

In 1996, Frankel and Rose found that current account imbalances were not statistically significant in predicting currency crashes. Also in 1996, Sachs, Turnell, and Valascio found that current account imbalances were not helpful in determining which currencies were vulnerable to contagion effects (when a currency crisis spreads to other countries). Statistically, this may be true. But the current account is important, and does start painting a picture of early and potentially difficult economic times ahead. It also shows a particular direction for a portion of the capital flowing into or out of a country.

Chapter 2 defined the weight of capital flowing throughout the world. If a current account deficit represents 5 percent of a country's gross domestic product, for example, that is a proportionally big sum of money to go out and to find once a year, let alone year after year. The more a country needs foreign capital to finance its economic and financial difficulties, the less likely anyone will invest unless the real return is very attractive. If another country has a 5 percent current account surplus but does not invest its entire surplus into the country that has the deficit, then something has to give. In other words, the real rate of return must rise in the deficit country to attract the surplus country to invest its surplus.

As an investor, I have noticed that reducing a current account deficit will create a difficult period for a country, but a policy to reduce the current account deficit will bring good news in the future. Reducing a current account deficit requires an increase in private savings. Additionally, if the federal government is also running a fiscal budget deficit, which also must be reduced, then investment will slow as the savings pool is used to pay off the fiscal and current account deficits, and therefore private consumption along with overall economic activity. The hardship a country suffers will be substantially less if government authorities take early care to correct a current account deficit, rather than waiting for a liquidity crisis and the weight of global capital to start flowing out of the country. Waiting will cause much greater hardship and more difficult policy decisions.

There are other details within the current account pie, particularly when an emerging country is in deficit. A current account deficit can be financed in five different ways in emerging countries, in addition to allowing their currency to devalue relative to their trading partners. The first and most secure is official lending from international bodies such as the International Monetary Fund. The second most secure method for financing a current account deficit is foreign direct investment (FDI), which is foreign investment in building new factories or providing private finance in various infrastructure projects, which can receive additional financing support from the World Bank. The next level of financial support comes from portfolio inflows in which foreigners invest in domestic companies, although the country starts to become hostage to foreign portfolio managers as they build up their equity stake in that country. The fourth level represents the short-term inflows or "hot money," which is attracted to a country's bond market investment because interest rates and real yields rise to a level attractive to foreign investors. When government authorities have to go this route, raising real interest rates and yields as their reliance on meeting short-term financing needs intensifies—the trouble has long been underway. All-out foreign exchange intervention and dramatically raising real interest rates is the last layer of finance available—an act of desperation, more often than not.

When government intervention gets to this stage a liquidity crisis and, often times, a currency crisis is already in full swing. Once at this stage, I advise analyzing the possibility of a debt crisis—a sovereign default on interest and principal repayments in hard currency obligations. For example, one of the shocking and surprising aspects of the Mexican crisis in 1994 and Malaysia in 1997 was the speed at which hard currency reserves were used to finance current account outflows in those years. Once the hard currency reserves dried up, investors left behind would not be able to get their monies out of the country in question. The central bank basically provides the hard currency liquidity to get out of a liquidity and currency crisis. Once it runs out of money, there is no more hard currency counterparty to sell hard currencies for the local domestic currency.

But also in industrial countries, current account deficits must be carefully scrutinized. In the United States, for example, the current account deficit is worrisome. One billion dollars is required every day to finance the U.S. current account deficit. According to a *Financial Times* article, "The Deficit Trap" (August 5, 1999), the U.S. current account deficit accumulation of 20 deficits in a row means that the U.S.

> *". . . is likely to be a net debtor to the tune of $2 trillion early in the next decade, despite having been a $350 billion creditor in 1980."*

This is a debt burden that must be repaid. The higher it goes, the more disruptive it will become to future generations of Americans. By 2005, the U.S. foreign debt will be equivalent to 30 percent of its gross domestic product. The current account deficit can be financed by economic growth at the moment, but once the economy slows the current account deficit must reduce. At some stage, as the United States becomes deeper in debt to foreign investors, Americans may have to address their foreign liabilities in a similar fashion that the budget deficit was tackled.

I will review the Japanese debt crisis in a later chapter. But until foreign investors require their monies at home, and I suspect Japan may shortly be arriving at that stage, the United States can go on running a current account deficit. But, as with any indebted position, the music will stop eventually. The state of the current account is very important and, when in deficit, may not seem like a problem. However, how the current account deficit is financed will be part of the difficulties in the future. I want to run through two good examples (1) a liquidity crisis and (2) a currency debate regarding a "pegged" currency regime, which should be a flexible system. I am referring to Mexico in 1994 and Israel in 1998.

MEXICO 1994

I was able to avoid the Mexican currency crisis in 1994, along with the lead-up to the widening of the foreign exchange intervention bands on December 20, 1994. The economic and particularly the financial situation deteriorated rapidly. Within days, the Mexican peso collapsed, and along with it the economy, adding another failed policy to the fixed exchange rate system. Investing in emerging market debt did not enter my radar screen in 1994. I had my hands full with industrial government debt, whose value was in free-fall.

There were a number of factors that caused the Mexican crisis. If the United States had not stepped in to help, it would have turned into a full debt crisis. One of the lessons I learned from this crisis was the real failure of a fixed exchange rate regime.

After the Latin American debt crisis in the 1980s, Mexico embarked on an economic reform, which consolidated fiscal policymaking, reducing the role of the public sector. With an inflation rate of 160 percent in 1987, government policy was focused on reducing inflation. To achieve this objective, Mexican authorities fixed the Mexican peso to the

U.S. dollar at 2.2 pesos for every one-dollar. The Mexican government was servicing $62 billion of foreign debt that would fall to $22 billion by 1992. The Mexican authorities fixed the exchange rate of the peso to the U.S. dollar in 1988, and from 1989 until 1991, the peso's crawling peg, as it was known, was devalued at pre-announced rates because of the difference in inflation rates between Mexico and the United States. But for all intents and purposes, the peso was fixed. Inflation fell and fell fast, to 52 percent in 1988, 20 percent in 1989, with a hiccup in 1990 rising to 30 percent before falling to 7 percent by 1994. The Mexican one-month Treasury bill yield, called the Cetes, also fell substantially from 122 percent to under 12 percent by 1993, while Mexico's economy grew steadily over the same period, with an annual budget surplus as well.

Stabilizing the peso was the key to achieving a successful low inflationary environment. Private capital inflows picked up as hard currency reserves rose from $6 billion to $25 billion in 1993. The trouble started as a spark—the Mexican people consumed too much from abroad, and private savings fell. Private savings, according to official statistics, fell from 19 percent in 1988 to 9 percent in 1993. The Mexican current account started to widen because the Mexican people were not saving enough money to finance their economic growth.

The Mexican current account rose as the savings rate fell. In 1988 the current account rose from 2.3 percent of GDP to 4.8 percent in 1991, 6.8 percent in 1992, fell to 6.5 percent in 1993, and rose to 8 percent in 1994. The actual current account sums of money grew at an enormous rate—from $7 billion in 1990 to $14.5 billion outflow of funds in 1991, $24.5 billion in 1992, $23.4 billion in 1993, and nearly $30 billion left the Mexican economy in 1994. The exchange rate regime remained fixed throughout this period of time, with Mexican monetary assets offering no real value. This is one of the indicators that started to concern me. The real effective exchange rate rose by over 60 percent from the end of 1987 until 1992, according to the IMF, causing the terms of trade between Mexico and the United States to deteriorate.

Entering 1994, Mexico seemed to be economically and financially cruising along without too much difficulty, particularly after the passage of the North American Free Trade Agreement (NAFTA). What could go wrong? The first thing was a rise in interest rates in the United States in February 1994. I described this event in an earlier chapter, and the behavior of the industrial bond markets, which caught me by surprise, and certainly added to the difficulties for the Mexican authorities. Using hindsight, the barn door opened on Mexico on March 23, 1994, when presidential candidate Colosio was assassinated. Although history also mentions the rise of the Chiapas rebellion in January 1994, I clearly remember not being overly concerned about Chiapas. But when Colosio was assassinated, international hard currency reserves started to flow out of Mexico, causing the Bank of Mexico's reserves to fall by $11 billion.

The Mexican financial situation quickly got out of hand, and I was encouraged by clients and brokers to buy Mexican paper; but real interest rates and yields were zero. When real yields reversed their dramatic fall in early 1994, one of my favored Tier Three countries, which I believed would rise to Tier One on due course, Spain, was offering a 7 percent real yield, while Mexico was minimal. In early 1994, the Mexican Treasury bill yields, Cetes (Certificados de Tesoreria), were 2 percent rising to 7 percent after the Colosio assassination. Mexico did not even show up on my potential investment radar screen because in 1994 its real interest rate was very poor. Going back to the basics of real interest rates, a Tier Three country, Spain, was offering a 7 percent real interest rate while a Tier Four country, Mexico, was much less. My advice for clients at that time, regarding Mexico and most emerging debt markets, was stay away. There was definitely trouble ahead for Mexico. But something did not make sense. I am an avid supporter of the NAFTA agreement, and the economic and financial convergence it ultimately would bring the North American region. But in 1994, something was wrong, and I could not put my finger on it.

I do not want to beat this event to death, but let me summarize the Mexican situation heading into late 1994. The first problem for Mexico was the maintenance of its fixed exchange rate system. The IMF states:

". . . typically, an exchange rate based stabilization under capital mobility leads to a fall in the real interest rate and an expansion in aggregate demand that cause protracted current account deficits and a real exchange rate appreciation."[19]

The IMF conclusion:

". . . at some point a real exchange rate depreciation is needed to restore the initial level of competitiveness and a current account equilibrium."[20]

The IMF report also stated:

"It can be argued, however, that large current account deficits and real exchange rate appreciation are not, at least to some extent, the equilibrium response to the process of stabilization and structural reforms."[21]

If this is correct, why not float the exchange rate? If the equilibrium response is a rise in the current account deficit and real exchange rate appreciation, why not let the markets find the right level for the peso? If everything is in equilibrium, so to speak, and I hate the term "equilibrium," the Mexican peso would not have collapsed as it did.

Another important factor driving a nail into the coffin was a huge outflow of peso-denominated debt holders into dollar-linked Mexican debt. One of the most peculiar psychoses, if I can use the term, of a fixed exchange rate regime, is the belief in the "free lunch." When interest rates rose substantially in April 1994, many debtors switched from the high costing peso-denominated debt securities into the much lower costing U.S. dollar debt, because of the fixed exchange rate regime—it was a free lunch. The Bank of Mexico was offering peso borrowers the ability to sell their pesos at a guaranteed fixed price for switching to dollar debt, and the borrowers did not hedge their currency risk because of the fixed exchange rate. And the chance of the Bank of Mexico's floating its exchange rate was minimal, so they thought. After the Mexican Presidential elections in August 1994, President-elect Zedillo was adamant about maintaining the fixed exchange rate, even after his swearing into office ceremony on December 1, 1994. If the President says everything is OK, and the fixed exchange rate is going to stay in place, no doubt everything will be just fine, right? So, peso debtors continued to borrow U.S. dollars.

Like all good things, it had to end. In addition, the global capital market's crisis would eventually catch up with Mexico. The single most shocking aspect of this entire event, which I mentioned earlier, was the enormous amounts of hard currency reserves that had been used to prop up the value of the Mexican peso. The use of hard currency reserves allowed so much money to flow out of the country and the conversion of peso-denominated debt into U.S. dollars.

The Bank of Mexico had not published its reserve figures for many months and when they were released, they showed no reserves left—it was a blood bath! I recently read that Mexican authorities spent $1 billion per week from October to December, 1994, to intervene in the foreign exchange markets, in an effort to maintain their fixed exchange rate regime—an annualized $52 billion dollars! Hard currency reserves fell to $6 billion before they gave up and allowed the peso to float freely on December 22, 1994. By the end of January 1995, the peso had fallen, devalued by 40 percent against the U.S. dollar.

What could have been done differently? In very simple terms, interest rates and real interest rates should have been rising in early 1994. The government should have either reduced fiscal spending more aggressively, or they should have raised taxes, or both, to slow consumption, and raised the private savings rate, thus reducing the current account deficit to take pressure off the peso. If the Mexican authorities wanted to hang on to their fixed exchange rate, then a move toward reducing overseas liabilities should have been occurring in 1994, rather than the opposite. In addition, building hard currency reserves rather than depleting them through peso intervention should have strengthened the financial system. There is also the argument that the Mexicans should have been moving toward a floating rate regime. Indeed, all these actions should have been carried out. Allowing the currency to float would have provided a necessary shock absorber as fiscal policy was tightened and real interest rates rose, rather than fixing the currency to the U.S. dollar. Knowing when to move to a floating rate regime from a fixed rate system is a tricky timing question, but not a philosophical one. The alternative is a currency board or currency union with a hard currency country.

In Chapter 3, flexibility in policymaking was shown to be necessary during difficult periods, rather than allowing the status quo. Mexico hung its hat on a fixed exchange rate system and its anti-inflation objective, anchoring the peso against the U.S. dollar. This policy had no flexibility. The current account, manageable under normal circumstances, aggravated the liquidity crisis rather than helping or protecting the Mexican economy.

I am sure many would argue against my suggestion that Mexico should have raised its interest rates in early 1994, rather than allowing them to fall. However, my argument is simple. Higher real interest rates may not have saved the peso from devaluation, but they would have enhanced the anti-inflationary credibility, slowing economic growth, and reducing the current account deficit. Perhaps the peso would have devalued, but at a slower rate, and much less than the 40 percent in January 1995. Once the currency speculators start to unravel and unwind their positions, selling pesos, they buy dollars to repay outstanding dollar loans and interest as well as outright speculative position.

When the U.S. dollar devalued against the Japanese yen, it also fell by 40 percent over a two-year period in the 1990s without a liquidity crisis, nor was it a newspaper headline event. It did receive a great deal of discussion and press coverage, but did not create a global financial crisis. Indeed, everything is relative. Therefore, I believe emerging economies can better handle economic and financial difficulties and avoid situations such as Mexico's.

In March 1995, I was invited to participate in a roundtable discussion on "Bargain Hunting in Emerging Markets," hosted by *International Bond Investor.*[22] I was asked the implications of the Mexican liquidity crisis on emerging markets, and replied:

> *"Because of the freedom of capital movement that we did not enjoy in the 1980s under fixed foreign exchange regimes, because of fashion, we could very well see liquidity crises become more fundamental. And the knock-on effect could be some very dramatic problems for these countries. I was in Mexico in January [1995], and everyone thought this problem was going away overnight. I saw nothing particularly different in Mexico to what we see in Europe when there is a convergence of economies."*[23]

I was referring to "convergence," that Mexico was facing the same problems that Europe had during 1992 and 1993 when exchange rates were fixed. The Europeans did not have shock absorbers available for policymakers to enable them to handle the way their economy was changing in relation to the countries to which their currencies were fixed. There was no flexibility in Europe in 1992 or in Mexico in 1994.

ISRAEL 1998

Over the past six or seven years I have discovered the investment opportunities in the Middle East North Africa (MENA) region of the world. MENA represents Turkey, Jordan, Morocco, Lebanon, Egypt, and Israel. The entire North Africa—Southern Europe—Middle East region is one of the last great geographic regions of the world, where very little trade among themselves exists (e.g., such as in the EEC or Nafta regions). This situation will certainly change, but that is another story. The debate in Israel over its exchange rate regime, the mechanism employed to control inflation, finally boiled to the surface in terms of policy debate during 1998. The debate is a classic example of the difficulty of knowing when to use a fixed exchange rate system, and also knowing when to move on to a more flexible or perhaps a floating rate system.

The debate and difficulties faced are not too different from many countries, because the root of the problem for Israel's fixed exchange rate was that its inflation rate was significantly higher than her major trading partners. Israel is a small, yet open economy with imports and exports representing approximately one-half and one-third of the gross domestic product respectively, amounting to $75 billion in 1994.[24] Israel experienced hyperinflation of 400 percent per annum in 1984. In July 1985, the government introduced the Economic Stabilization Programme (ESP), intending to eliminate the budget deficit, which peaked at 14 percent, and moved to a fixed exchange rate as an anti-inflation anchor. The role of monetary policy was to defend the fixed exchange policy. Israel chose to use a basket of currencies, which reflected the currency's trading partners. The basket was revised regularly. At year-end 1998, it was 62 percent U.S. dollar, 19.7 percent deutschemark, 8.2 percent Sterling, 5.3 percent yen, and 4.8 percent French Francs.[25]

On January 3, 1989, the Bank of Israel moved away from a constant exchange rate, allowing for adjustments from time to time, to a more flexible system. The new Israeli system was similar to the European Monetary System's Exchange Rate Mechanism, which in effect allowed the Israeli Shekel to fluctuate around a midpoint value, exchange rate price. To this day, Israel continues to have an underlying structural inflation disadvantage versus its major trading partners. The labor unions have considerable political clout, which has created a rigid wage system-an index-linked wage system—which keeps the inflationary pressures imbedded within the economic system. The tax burden in Israel is very high. From my calculations, government expenditure represents over 40 percent of the country's GDP. Although one of the unique features of Israel is its ability to absorb new immigrants, particularly in the early 1990s when 550,000 immigrants from the former Soviet Union (350,000 in 1990-1991 alone) made their home in Israel. This added approximately 10 percent to the general population of the country. Needless to say, employment was a major issue and policy objective, which caused the public deficit to rise substantially to nearly 7 percent of GDP in 1991. To protect employment and prices, the state controls the prices of nearly 15 percent of consumption goods represented in the Israeli consumer price index through government subsidy. Also, government influence over apartment prices continues as the government controls the supply of land for building apartments, and does not allow the market to find its own levels. So, whatever mechanism is used to create disinflation forces will only go so far in the fight against inflation. See Table 8.6 for Israel's inflation record, and note that the progress in reducing the annual inflation rate has only been able to fall so far before getting stuck because of structural problems.

Table 8.6: Israel Rate of Inflation (in percent)[26]

Year	Inflation Rate	Year	Inflation Rate
1980	132.9	1993	11.2
1981	101.5	1994	14.5
1982	131.5	1995	8.1
1983	190.7	1996	10.6
1984	444.9	1997	6.8
1985	185.2	1998	6.4
1986	19.7	1999	5.4
1987	16.1	2000	4.5
1988	16.4	2001	1.4
1989	20.7	2002	5.8
1990	17.6	2003	4.1 e
1991	18.0	2004	3.5 e
1992	9.4		

As I mentioned in Chapter 3, every country has its own unique story and set of problems to resolve, along with priorities to settle. From the January 1989 decision until December 17, 1991, the Israeli currency devalued every few months, but on March 1, 1990, the currency bands were widened from 3 percent plus/minus from a midpoint exchange rate to plus/minus 5 percent. On December 17, 1990, a crawling peg exchange rate system was introduced. A crawling peg is the setting of a predetermined devaluation rate for a year, rather than making the real interest rate adjustments every other month or so. A crawling peg is a pre-announced devaluation slope, which was initially set at 9 percent. A crawling peg reduces uncertainty, but achieving a low and competitive inflationary environment was the ultimate goal. The other important argument for Israel's crawling peg was setting the slope of the exchange rate band in accordance with the gap between the inflation target in Israel and expected inflation abroad, indirectly expressing commitment to maintaining the real exchange rate.[27]

I mention this because one of the indicators used for warning against potential currency crises is the value of the real exchange rate. The Israeli authorities thought this through. Each year the Bank of Israel, the Israeli government, and a cabinet vote agreed on the annual inflation targets and therefore a devaluation rate for the slope of the country's crawling peg. Table 8.7 lists the announced annual inflation target.

Table 8.7: Israeli Inflation Target[28]

Year	Inflation Target Rate (%)
1992	14.5
1993	10.0
1994	8.0
1995	8.0-11.0
1996	8.0-10.0
1997	7.0-10.0
1998	7.0-10.0
1999	7.0-10.0
2000	4.0-7.0
2001	3.0-4.0
2002	2.5-3.5
2003	2.0-3.0

Once the inflation target is set, the crawling peg adjustment rate can be determined. The value of the devaluation rate would be the upper limit for the slope of the crawling peg. The slope for the Israeli currency's upper limit devaluation was set at 9 percent in 1991, an 8 percent slope in 1992, and 6 percent annually thereafter. The trading range allowed under the crawling peg around the mid-price was plus/minus 5 percent until May 31, 1995, when it was raised to plus/minus 7 percent and then to 15 percent on June 18, 1997. The debate in 1998 going into 1999 was what to do with the exchange rate mechanism, what should the inflation target be in 1999 along with the crawling peg's upper devaluation limit? However, once a currency reaches its upper limit and lower limit, policy must support those limits. Otherwise, what is the point of having limits? Monetary policy must be restrictive at the upper limit, and accommodative at the lower exchange rate limit.

But at the end of the day, all the fancy calculations and policy initiatives will not detract from the fact that the new international rules in the new economy will cause the rest of the world to move on to bigger and better things. Israel will be competing with the likes of the Czech Republic, Hungary, Poland, and Slovenia, who are the next members to join the EEC and European Monetary Union. If structural change does not occur soon, Israel's cost for raising capital may soon rise in real terms relative to her competitors in Eastern and Central Europe, Asia, and Latin America, let alone the industrial world.

Israel's debate heated up in 1998 and it is an interesting one. This currency debate, not too dissimilar from many developing and emerging countries, is whether the solution will be politically introduced or allowed to be market driven. But as in many countries, the debate over the cost of government, the burden on society, taxes, and the means of moderating the inflationary impact cannot continue in perpetuity. The harsh reality for the private sector is picking up the tab, and the financial and economic burdens from the public sector become more difficult and real with every passing year.

On January 1, 1998, the Bank of Israel introduced a series of currency liberation measures, allowing Israelis to invest overseas and also to hold non-shekel bank accounts. The inflationary environment in Israel was extremely favorable as the annual rate fell to between 4 and 5 percent in the first half of 1998—until, of course, the Israeli Shekel depreciated in value in the second half of 1998 to end the year 20.4 percent lower against the currency basket and 17.6 percent versus the U.S. dollar. On August 6, 1998, before the shekel devaluation in October, the Bank of Israel and the Ministry of Finance announced a proposed inflation target of 4 percent in 1999 versus 7-10 percent in 1998. But all went wrong in October 1998. The problems causing the difficulties for Israeli decision-makers are no different from those experienced by any other country using a form of fixed exchange rate regime.

The issue in Israel is about who should bear the cost for financial and economic volatility. In full-page articles in the local press in October 1998, opinions were many, but they all pointed to a classic misunderstanding of the global capital markets. One commentator, Professor Avi Ben-Bassat, said about the currency crisis:

> *"There is no doubt that the trigger for the crisis here is the international crisis, foreigners want to leave emerging markets and Israel is defined an emerging market."*

Professor Ben-Bassat is perhaps correct in his observation but very wrong about Israel's currency regime. The Israeli currency was not offering a high real value, real rate of return, or return on investment.

Israeli decision-makers fall into the same trap as other countries. The reason money is leaving the country, or foreign direct investment is not coming in, is that there are better places to invest, better returns on investment. There is also the free lunch mentality regarding a fixed or crawling peg exchange rate system. An Israeli analyst in another article on October 7, 1998, describes the free lunch mentality prevalent that has come back to haunt borrowers and investors:

> *"For the past three years, Bank of Israel Governor Jacob Frenkel has warned that many of the companies taking out foreign-currency loans . . . those who took out cheap foreign-currency loans did not always take into account the possibility of a large depreciation that would inflate the size of their loans in shekel terms and cause them large losses."*[29]

To make matters worse, although I agreed with the Governor of the Bank of Israel, the central bank did not intervene in the open foreign exchange markets to prop up the value of the Israeli currency (Boy, did Governor Frenkel make a lot of people angry!) The Governor took the correct action, but the scary aspect of this episode is the belief in Israel that:

". . . the most effective method is to intervene in currency trading. Over the past four years, the Bank of Israel has accumulated $15 billion, and reserves have reached $22 billion. What do you need this mountain of reserves for, if not to use it to stem a flight of foreign currency."[30]

Wow! The government authorities should not be bailing out the market free-loaders who think they can keep having their free lunch as borrowers and investors. But that is what foreign exchange intervention does. It allows investors like me to reposition and take advantage of a situation during periods of official foreign exchange intervention.

The government should be aggressively making itself more attractive for foreign direct investors. Government authorities should be pushing the private sector to position itself better and to be more responsible for its own actions—not to expect a government handout every time the financial environment gets a little too tough. As in so many countries and situations throughout the world, a decision must be made in Israel—give up its fixed exchange rate system, or create a currency board or monetary union. But with capital reforms regarding the freedom of movement in Israel, and fiscal restructuring, the time is right to move on to a floating rate system. The private sector in Israel, as in many other countries, must become more responsible and credible. A free lunch has to be paid out of somebody's pocket.

In early 1999, the political view was to allow inflation to achieve the "usual 8-10 percent" and raise the 5-7 percent inflation goal for 1999. The debate of exchange rate regime is still stuck with the view that:

". . . another slight surge in the shekel, and the real devaluation will be gone, along with the profitability of exports."[31]

As economic growth slowed in Israel with the global high-tech crisis causing GDP to fall by -0.9 percent in 2001 and -1.0 percent in 2002, inflationary pressures subsided allowing the government to set lower inflation targets, with inflation falling to its lowest level of 1.9 percent in 2001. Unfortunately, inflation rose dramatically in 2002 to 6.5 percent. The view at the Bank of Israel for the sharp rise in inflation from 2001 to 2002 was "attributed to the exceptional reduction in the interest rate at the end of 2001 which led to accelerated depreciation [of the Israeli Shekel] and a rise in uncertainty in the foreign-currency market." In their Inflation Report (December 2002), the Bank of Israel sites that an additional cause to rising inflation was due to the rising budget deficit, after achieving balance in 2000, rising to 4.0 percent in 2002.

A PRELIMINARY SUMMARY

A quick summary is in order. There are clearly two very different types of currency crises, although interrelated. The first is the long-term movement in the relationship between industrial currency values, such as the United States and Japan, from a 1971 level of yen 360 for every one U.S. dollar, to Y250 per U.S. dollar by 1983, to a low of Y83.6 per U.S. dollar in 1995. I have witnessed several currency pacts, which may have worked over a short period of time, but not over the long term. The Plaza Accord in 1985 allowed the U.S. dollar to fall in value. The Louvre Accord in 1987 tried to stabilize the U.S. dollar's fall. The third formal pact was in 1995, the multinational intervention that tried to reverse the trend in the rising Japanese yen. These long-term movements can be extremely damaging economically and financially. Whether a long-term trend or whether a sudden short-term sharp devaluation of an emerging market country's currency, the indicators of currency vulnerability remain the same. My view in both cases is to be aware of a range of indicators. Table 8.8 shows the various indicators and symptoms, along with an explanation of potential currency and liquidity difficulties.

The ways to solve currency crises range from central bank intervention, capital controls (restricting the movement of capital in and out of the country), or the use of Chilean-style taxes on short-term flows into the country. I believe the only way to be aware of potential currency crises is to keep an eye on the leading indicators as listed in Table 8.8. Often times, currency crises occur when the fixed exchange rate system is left in place too long. The transition from a fixed exchange rate system to either a full-fledged currency board or a fully flexible exchange rate regime is required. Trouble starts when countries adopt something in between. Do not forget that converting an exchange rate regime from one to another is not the answer for economic ills in itself. Structural and financial economic reforms are required first and foremost.

CENTRAL BANK INTERVENTION

Whenever a central bank or a group of central banks intervene in the foreign exchange markets to help prop up the value of a currency, the news makes headlines. For example, on September 24, 2000, the *Financial Times* headlined:

> *"Euro's relentless decline prompts world's central banks to step in."*

These central banks included the European Central Bank, the U.S. Federal Reserve, the Canadian Central Bank, the Bank of Japan, and the Bank of England. All made an attempt to prop up the value of the European currency—the Euro. Central Bank intervention in the currency markets has a long history with questionable results. These include:

- *September 1985.* The Plaza Accord, when G7 countries intervened to push down the U.S. dollar.

- *February 1987.* The Louvre Accord, when G7 countries intervened to push up the value of the U.S. dollar.

- *September 1992.* The Bank of England tries to prevent sterling from falling out of the European Monetary System's Exchange Rate Mechanism.

- *July 1995.* U.S. Federal Reserve and the Bank of Japan intervened to push the U.S. dollar higher against the Japanese yen.

- *June 1998.* The Bank of Japan and U.S. Federal Reserve intervened to prevent the yen from falling against the U.S. dollar.

- *From 1999.* The Bank of Japan intervened unilaterally to prevent the yen from rising (which was aided by a G7 policy statement).

Central banks intervene particularly during periods of currency price volatility. They will intervene in the spot market that is the cash foreign exchange market, purchasing either their own currency or a relevant hard currency, such as the U.S. dollar. Central

Table 8.8: Indicators of Currency Crisis Vulnerability[32]

Symptoms	Indicators	Brief Explanation
Real exchange rate over-valuation.	Behavior of real exchange rate relative to trend, exports, trade balance.	In the period leading up to a crisis, the real exchange rate is substantially higher.
Terms of trade shock.	Price of exports, price of imports, commodity prices.	In the period leading up to a crisis, there is significant deterioration in export performance.
Current account imbalance.	Real exchange rate, savings, investment.	Foreign exchange reserves decline as crisis approaches.
Weak economic activity/rising unemployment	Real GDP, output gap, unemployment rate, real interest rate.	
Overly expansionary fiscal policy.	Government spending, budget deficit, volume of credit extended to public sector.	Currency crises are often preceded by boom-bust equity cycles.
Overly expansionary monetary policy.	Domestic credit expansion, reserves, money-supply, growth, money multiplier.	Inflation is rising or significantly higher in pre-crisis periods. Broad money growth in nominal and real terms tends to rise sharply in the two-years leading up to a currency crisis.
High ratio of M2 to reserves.	M2, international reserves.	The ratio of M2-to-reserves tends to rise in the 24-month period leading up to a crisis.
Banking crisis.	Equity and property prices, non-performing loans, lending/deposit rate spread, bank share prices.	
Debt crises.	Total debt, domestic debt, foreign-currency debt, short-term/total debt.	
Contagion.	Foreign growth, foreign interest rates, crises elsewhere.	

banks can also intervene in the forward foreign exchange market, which is similar to a futures contract—an agreement to buy a currency for another currency at a future date in time. For example, during 1997, the Bank of Thailand sold forward U.S. dollars for their own currency, the baht. The bank had built up a $25 billion position. The Bank of Thailand had total reserves minus gold, as of the end of 1996, of $37.7 billion—the forward foreign exchange position of $25 billion represented the sale of an enormous amount and proportion of the central bank's hard currency reserves. This strategy was a vain attempt to prop up the value of the Thai baht.

The Mexicans fell into the same trap a few years earlier in 1994, and the British in 1992, in an attempt to maintain sterling's membership in the European Monetary System Exchange Rate Mechanism. Central banks perform their foreign exchange intervention both overtly and covertly, in a transparent manner or a non-transparent, secretive manner, both of which make me suspicious of their motives. I always wonder why they want me to know that they were intervening, or why they wanted their currency intervention transactions to be secretive. If central banks were made completely transparent in their foreign exchange intervention policy, then my suspicions would perhaps be eased.

Transparency in central bank monetary policy does not necessarily translate into transparency in central bank foreign exchange intervention policy or activities. But in fairness, there are two countries involved in foreign exchange intervention, perhaps even more. Therefore, intervening in the currency markets must be sensitive to this situation and respect the privacy of the other intervening party or parties. On the other hand, hard currency reserves belong to the people, the government being responsible for their usage. The government and the people have the right to know what is going on with their hard currency reserves, which should not be identified as "state secrets."

My suspicions are simply based on the thought, "What do they know that I don't?" On a serious note, an IMF paper on policy analysis and assessment by Charles Enoch, "Transparency in Central Bank Operations in the Foreign Exchange Market." March 1998, suggests that covert intervention occurs when authorities do not want to signal their involvement. Examples are:

- Authorities are comfortable with their overall policy stance and feel they are facing a temporary shortfall or glut in demand for currency, and are seeking to avoid having those temporary conditions built into market expectations.

- The central bank is not sure of its own commitment or ability to defend a particular rate, and therefore does not wish to jeopardize its credibility by being seen to support a rate that is subsequently not held.

- The central bank is concerned that its appearance in the markets may in fact prompt increased market pressures against it.

- A country is operating within a foreign exchange rate band regime (such as the exchange rate mechanism of the European Monetary System) to avoid the speculative pressures that might emerge if the rate were permitted to move to the edge of the band.

- A central bank tries, like a typical market participant, to get the "best rate" it can, not wanting to risk its actions being perceived as "distress buying," which might encourage market counterparties to offer worse terms.

And the reason for overt actions:

- It wishes to signal to the market that it has a policy preference about where the rate should be and has sufficient credibility that this signal will encourage expectations that this rate will be achieved.
- It aims to avoid overreaction to market fluctuations brought on by large discrete trades.
- It believes it will be unable to conceal the intervention and thus considers that giving the market accurate information on intervention would be preferable to the markets' generating inaccurate information on its own.
- There are uncertainties about the overall policy stance. Information about its foreign exchange market activities may improve the credibility of the stance.

I hope you can see why I am often so suspicious about the central bank's intentions at any given time. They clearly know something I do not, and I will spend a great deal of time trying to figure out their intentions, whether overt or covert. But to hide foreign exchange activities, particularly when something is going wrong (i.e., Mexico, 1994, Thailand, 1997) is not right. When a central bank has the ability to be covert or overt, then I have to wonder why overt versus covert, or vice versa? I do not believe that once a problem occurs, central bank foreign exchange intervention will stop the flow of capital. On the contrary, it helps the flow of capital to leave a country. In currency markets, the weight of capital in the new economy will prevail!

CAPITAL CONTROLS

Controlling human behavior, individual choice, is at the heart of government policy to control the flow of capital into and out of one's country.

There are two types of controls (1) exchange controls and (2) capital controls. Currency convertibility simply allows both residents and non-residents of a country to exchange their domestic currency for a foreign currency. Exchange controls impose controls on the ability to exchange a domestic currency for a foreign currency. Exchange controls are the more general, and restrict the exchange of domestic and foreign capital in both the current and capital account. Controls restrict only the capital account of a country's balance of payments, rather than exchange controls, which affect the spending on imports and the use of the foreign currency earned on exports. Exchange controls govern an individual's behavior, or restrict individual liberties, while capital controls govern more short-term movements in the way domestic and foreign currencies are bought and sold.

Another way of looking at the differences between the two was illustrated earlier. Total world exports in goods and services are approximately $6.1 trillion per annum. However, the daily foreign exchange turnover is $1.2 trillion. If I assume 250 business days per year, the annual foreign exchange turnover is about $300 trillion. So, out of the annual foreign exchange turnover, only $6.1 trillion is for trading purposes, while $293.9

trillion is used for purely financial purposes. Capital controls try to control the movements of the $293.9 trillion, which represents the investment capital flowing throughout the global capital markets, some of which will be genuine long-term investment, and the other will be the short-term speculative transactions.

As I mentioned, in theory, the idea is that capital, the global savings pool, will always seek out the most profitable and productive investments in the global economy. I will argue, in due course, that with freedom also come added responsibilities by all parties concerned. But even the best of intentions can go terribly wrong, as with the case of currency convertibility and open capital accounts. Short-term capital movements into relatively small economies can be very destabilizing. Prior to discussing specific pros and cons for capital controls and recent events, a little more explanation is necessary.

There are two directions of capital flows (1) going into or (2) going out of a country—keeping resident money in the country or keeping foreign money out. Each directional control provides the authorities with an additional policy instrument or tool to control certain flows of capital. If controls prevent domestic money from leaving the country, then the exchange rate will be kept artificially higher because domestic currency is not being sold for foreign currencies. If interest rates are very high in a small economy, foreign capital may be attracted by the high domestic interest rates in that country, and therefore "hot money" will flow into the country. Controls on foreign inflows to a country will dissuade or prevent foreign speculators from buying the domestic currency, thereby driving the price of the exchange rate up and flooding the domestic money markets with domestic currency purchased with foreign money. And, of course, once interest rates start to fall, the flow of funds will reverse itself.

In my view, foreign funds will cause more problems and a "boom-bust" cycle than the risk of resident outflows. It is foreign inflows, which I will return to shortly, that hurt the most—particularly the smaller developing economies of the world. Capital controls are used to reduce the volatility of much needed foreign investment monies, channeling them into longer term, more positive and predictive purposes. The countries using them employ a variety of techniques, including minimum time periods for investment, non-interest-bearing time deposits, taxes, and penalties for early withdrawal.[33]

From my point of view, there are two bubbles that can burst, both of which seek the proverbial free lunch. The first bubble is created when domestic interest rates are very high and the currency is fixed or tightly pegged, which causes domestic companies to think they can borrow foreign currencies at a much lower interest rate. On the other side of the coin, the high domestic interest rates, which detract domestic companies from borrowing from their own domestic currency market, is attractive to foreign currency investors. As the funds flow in from both sides of the equation, life is relatively good, at the moment, for that domestic economy, but often the music will stop as interest rates start to fall in that country. When the music stops, often there are no options left except central bank intervention. Whatever the economic and financial scenario, and there are many, domestic companies scramble to cover their foreign currency loans while foreign currency investors sell their domestic currency at the best price and flee the country. This is an aspect of the global capital movements that needs to be addressed and refined.

This is why at the outset of this section I suggested that greater responsibility must be achieved if we want to enjoy the freedoms of movement of capital.

I suppose the global economy is no different from a domestic economy, in that the stronger, larger, wealthier citizens must protect the weakest and smallest. The lesser-developed, emerging countries require certain protections from the onslaught of short-term global capital inflows, which will ultimately result in their reversing themselves as capital outflows. Capital controls on foreign inflows are a useful policy to help authorities avoid "boom-bust" economic cycles. An International Monetary Fund working paper of September 1998, asked:

"Can short-term capital controls promote capital inflows?"

My answer is yes. Because true long-term investment capital will continue to flow and actually be protected from short-term ''hot'' money inflows coupled with "panic" out-flows, resulting in the extreme boom-bust business cycles. The Chinese model welcomes foreign investment in factories and business, but imposes strict controls on currency trading. The trick, as World Bank Chief Economist Joseph Stiglitz pointed out, is that capital controls should be considered, provided they can be designed to discourage short-term investments (such as bank loans or short-term currency trades) without disrupting foreign investment in factories and infrastructure.

As I explained earlier, I am a long-term investor, although I do use short-term strategies to add value around the long term. Capital controls, therefore, can add a layer of comfort for me, but they do not replace the need and the fact that prudent and appropriate macroeconomic policies cannot be replaced with capital controls. Capital controls protect the macroeconomic policies in place or, during a period of restructuring, the economic and financial system, but they are not a substitute for those policies. One of the most successful emerging countries that have imposed a form of capital controls in conjunction with an economic and financial restructuring is Chile.

CHILEAN-STYLE TAXES

Chile is a fascinating economic and financial story—a successful story. Although many economic commentators may disagree today about its success, no one denies the Chilean model and its accomplishments since the 1970s. When General Pinochet overthrew President Salvadore Allende, Chile was economically devastated by Allende's policies of socialism and nationalization. The country was left with a 500 percent annual inflation rate, nearly no hard currency reserves, and extreme foreign investor hostility arising from the nationalization of American-owned copper mines. With the help of University of Chicago Professor Milton Friedman, General Pinochet led an economic revolution when in the 1980s the Chilean authorities embarked on a set of economic reforms designed to stabilize the economy and financial system to rebuild shattered investor confidence. The task was enormous, and in 1982 and 1983 recapitalizing the banking system in Chile cost 41 percent of its gross domestic product. Political leaders and economic policymakers labeled inflation as public enemy number one at the very outset in their 1980s policy. Additionally, the central bank set a reference exchange rate (Dolar Alvedo) for the peso, which was changed in January 1997, from 45 percent U.S. dollar, 25 percent yen, and 15 percent deutschemark to 80 percent U.S. dollar, 5 percent yen, and 15 percent deutschemark. I remember very well how the Chileans maintained their tight fiscal and monetary policies throughout the late 1980s and 1990s.

This is also a country where copper accounts for approximately 40 percent of exports and 10 percent of government revenues. With the annual inflation rate standing at 500 percent in the early 1980s, it fell to 27 percent in 1990 and to a 37-year low of 6 percent in 1997. Approximately 80 percent of Chile's gross domestic product is derived from the private sector. Chile's belief in the free market system was unheard of in the late 1980s. During a massive inflow of foreign capital in mid-1991, the Chilean authorities needed to stem the massive short-term inflows while not offending long-term investors. They implemented a reserve requirement called "encaje," which required that 30 percent of all non-direct foreign direct investment funds be deposited into a non-interest-bearing deposit with the central bank of Chile—an implied tax on short-term capital inflows. The reserve requirement or implied tax was best described to me as a back-end load commission, similar to those charged by mutual funds to encourage investors to keep their monies in the fund for longer periods of time. The same concept holds true for Chile, encouraging investment for longer term. It really worked! Another important capital control prevents the use of foreign credits to finance direct foreign investment projects, which, prior to October 7, 1997, was set at 70 percent and then reduced to 50 percent of the total investment. This capital control reduces the risk of using cheaper foreign currency loans as leverage in domestic investment projects.

Chilean policies helped achieve three important economic and financial outcomes. First, high domestic real interest rates were used as a fundamental anti-inflationary tool without causing the "boom" effects of enormous short-term capital inflows. Second, the capital controls on inflows allowed the authorities to protect Chilean financial institutions from the capital withdrawals that ultimately occur after huge capital inflows. Third, the exchange rate did not appreciate in real terms from the tidal wave of "hot" foreign capital that allowed Chile to remain competitive with her trading partners. Although many Chilean economic commentators do not take a similar view, it was a stunning success.

In 1998, with the Asian economic crisis in full swing and commodity prices deflating, Chile's copper trade and earnings collapsed. With every drop of 10 cents in the price of copper, the gross domestic product of Chile loses 1 percent or $800 million. Copper prices fell from $1.19 per pound in mid-June 1997, to $0.72 per pound in July 1998.

With China and Japan accounting for 25 percent of world copper demand, Chile did indeed have a problem. But its problems are a symptom of a global economic crisis, not a result of their economic and financial policies. As a result of the Asia crisis, the trade deficit rose to 17 percent with the current account rising above 7.5 percent of gross domestic product. In 1998, 20 percent of Chile's hard currency reserves were used, protecting the value of the peso as copper prices fell.

A number of research studies and economists suggest that the capital controls on inflows did not have the positive effect on capital inflows, along with the economic and financial impact on the economy, as first thought. I disagree. First of all, the capital controls employed were implemented only after a massive economic and financial restructuring of the Chilean economy. The progress up to 1991 was tremendous, and the economic and financial results proved that the gain was worth the pain. Second, foreign hard currency borrowing did not occur as it did in Asia or other emerging countries (had it occurred, there is no telling how destructive short-term hard currency borrowing might have been). Third, capital controls on inflows being initiated as capital controls on outflows were lifted and eliminated. Fourth, capital controls were used as a tool, not as a core policy, which aided the successful economic and financial restructuring process. Lastly and perhaps overlooked, is the rise of the private sector in Chile. Some 80 percent of the gross domestic product acts as the shock absorber for the Chilean business cycle, rather than central government intervention, which tries to reduce the strain caused by a downturn in economic activity.

Chile was in a much better position to deal with the global economic crisis than her Brazilian neighbors. Perhaps, too, the time has come to lift the capital controls on capital inflows, but they certainly will go down in my view as having a positive impact on Chile, not a negative or negligible impact.

But the important lesson learned from Chile is the progress achieved on the macro economy, for which the capital controls provided a very useful fine-tuning mechanism. Before drawing a conclusion, remember that the Chilean model worked for Chile. It may not work for everybody, but Chile's experiment makes for a very good Harvard Business School case study.

SOLUTIONS

The Deutsche Morgan Grenfell weekly, *Market Issues* from July 21, 1997, summarized the problems facing government authorities in emerging markets regarding the risks of severe currency devaluations. Their research suggests:

> "In cases of a fixed parity, where the exchange rate is allowed to move within a
> small trading range only, the risk of a sudden devaluation is particularly high.
> This is independent of the fact that it is pegged to one currency or a basket of
> currencies, or whether it is a fixed rate, a pre-announced target range, a
> 'crawling peg' or a 'managed float' revealing a peg to a major reserve curren-
> cy. . . . Sustaining such an anchor implies that monetary policy is not independ-
> ent and has to be subjected to exchange rate stability. Whenever doubt arises
> that this link may be loosened, due to domestic problems, devaluation expecta-
> tions in the market can easily lead to a self-fulfilling prophecy. Central bank
> intervention in support of the currency, interest rate hikes to induce short-term
> inflows and discourage short-term borrowing, or even capital controls can
> delay devaluation but ultimately not stem the tide in the face of general percep-
> tion that a policy correction is necessary. . . . Flexible exchange rate regimes,
> by contrast, reduce the danger of such events taking place. However, a freely
> floating exchange rate may not be acceptable to most governments. Due to the
> impact of capital flows, the volatility can be excessive, in terms of its costs for
> policy-makers as well as for trade and investment."

A good summary, which continues:

> "Exchange rate stability is thus a question of the quality and consistency of
> economic management. If a central bank lacks independence and a track
> record of sound currency management, it will have a hard time in stabilizing
> expectations. It will have to resort to administrative controls (i.e., restrict the
> free flow of capital, at least for a period of time). However, this means forego-
> ing the benefits of accessing the international savings pool to promote inward

investment. One way to liberalize capital flows at an early stage of develop-
ment is to use the exchange rate as the stability anchor, as a substitute for an
independent monetary policy. Pegged systems and 'currency boards' can be
rational choices. . . . But relying on a currency-peg as a nominal stability
anchor has serious drawbacks. Its sustainability will always be subject to spec-
ulation, unless it is a small open economy that can gain little from an inde-
pendent monetary policy. That is why domestic interest rates tends to be always
a notch above the rates in the currency it is pegged to. This in turn creates
incentives for domestic companies to borrow in foreign currencies and for
banks to finance their domestic lending on the international markets. This is
profitable as long as the risk of devaluation is low, due to the currency peg.
With rising risks of devaluation, however, maturities will shorten rapidly, as
both lenders and borrowers seek to minimize their exchange rate risk, ultimate-
ly leading to massive outflows as lenders become reluctant to rollover. Hence,
watch countries with relatively rigid exchange rate regimes, weakening politi-
cal support for the central bank and large exposures to external liabilities!"

That is good advice.

I do not subscribe to the argument that the Chilean model did play a minor part in avoiding the contagion effect of the 1994/1995 Mexican liquidity crises—the tequila crisis. Remember that the principal objectives of the Chilean model are extremely relevant for the freedom of movement of capital throughout the emerging markets. It is therefore useful to sum up the Mexican crisis to see what Chile was able to avoid.

At the time Chile put into place its capital controls, Mexico was receiving an enormous pool of capital inflow, nearly 20 percent of all developing country capital inflows. When the United States started raising interest rates in 1994, economic and financial uncertainty started to build regarding Mexico's future. Two-thirds of these capital inflows represented portfolio investments. The Mexican authorities had to raise interest rates to continue to attract portfolio inflows, but when economic growth stalled, yields had to rise further to continue attracting foreign and domestic investment capital. External financing needs rose as their current account deficit rose to 8 percent of Mexico's gross domestic product. Needing to be more creative, the Mexican authorities issued a new form of short-term debt called "Tesobono," denominated in the local currency, pesos, with a high peso yield, but containing an exchange rate guarantee and therefore very attractive to foreign investors. Thus you can see how the snowball builds and, needless to say, the difficulties that Chile was able to avoid.

Chile employed capital controls as a risk management tool. The Tesobonos issued in Mexico maturing within one year in 1995 rose to $67 billion at a time when Mexico's foreign exchange reserves declined from $30 billion in February 1994 to $6 billion by December 1994. That's what Chile avoided. Perhaps Chile did not benefit from the initial windfall from the huge mountain of capital inflow, but it certainly avoided all the trouble when the capital started leaving emerging markets economies. In an article in the *Bank of England Quarterly* (August 1997), Jon Shields, Alternate Executive Director for the United Kingdom at the International Monetary Fund, summarized the feelings of international investors about Mexico:

"The problems that Mexico faced in 1994 were viewed by the international community not as the consequences of a failed economic framework, but as arising from errors made over a relatively short period."

When the IMF and the United States bailed out Mexico, they, in fact, provided a payment for holders of Tesobonos. The holders of Tesobonos were fully protected, instead of being put at risk, and compensated for their risks by receiving high peso yields. I did not invest in Tesobonos and would not do so for reasons I explained earlier, even though certain clients wanted me to, because of the risk associated with that country and the real interest rate offered at that time in Mexican debt securities. Chile avoided a doubling of its unemployment rate, avoided output falling by 6 percent in 1995, which cost the Mexican banking system 6.5 percent of the country's gross domestic product, with inflation rising to over 50 percent at one stage. If Chile had experienced the full effects of the Tequila crisis in 1995, it would have been in terrible shape, particularly after their fiscal restructuring in the late 1980s.

So what are the solutions to currency crises? The essential ingredient is the ability to assess all available relevant information released at regular and predictable intervals of time, preferably weekly and monthly. Investors must be able to determine their own "early warning indicators" and be responsible for the end results—transparency and responsibility. Without transparency, investors will always shout "foul" and expect and receive government assistance. The quality of the data and standards of the data are also vital. The IMF has established the Special Data Dissemination Standard (SDDS), which identifies a set of minimum requirements for macroeconomic data. Transparency is therefore the predictable timely release of economic and financial data, which is globally consistent in terms of standard of calculation and quality of data. An IMF working paper, "Working for a More Transparent World," declared that:

". . . transparency encourages a more widespread discussion and analysis of policies by the public. And it facilitates the underlying and efficient functioning of financial markets. . . . Financial markets must be able to respond more continuously and smoothly to economic developments if dramatic corrections are to be avoided."[34]

Lawrence Summers, Deputy Secretary of the U.S. Treasury, describes transparency as:

". . . a fair bet that the single most important innovation shaping [the] market was the idea of generally accepted accounting principles."[35]

If government authorities provide all available relevant information, then investors have no excuse to avoid the responsibility for their actions. I always found central bank actions to intervene as ludicrous, particularly when economic and financial shocks occur that result from a lack of timely information for market participants. So, central bank intervention is neither a solution nor a cure for major fluctuations or crises.

What about capital controls? If used properly, such as with the Chilean model, the success or failure of Chilean-style capital controls is not a function of its future after 1999. It is the protection provided during a successful reconstruction of the economy from 1991 to 1999. They were tools enabling the Chilean authorities to rebuild and reinvent themselves. The outlook for Chile to cope with further falls in copper prices, a sluggish global economy, and global deflation, does perhaps indicate the need for a re-think of their capital control policies on capital inflows.

An open letter from Paul Krugman to Prime Minister Mahatir of Malaysia on the eve of Malaysia's instituting exchange and capital controls on September 1, 1998, describes currency controls as:

"*. . . a risky step, with no guarantees of success. It is . . . a stopgap measure.*"

Professor Krugman suggests four guiding principles for implementing currency controls. First, the implementation of capital controls should not disrupt ordinary business. Second, controls create economic distortions, which will get worse over time. Third, they will not work if they are used to defend an overvalued currency. Finally, they must aid reform, not an alternative to economic restructuring. I believe that the last point was the key for Chile's success.

What about a fixed exchange rate regime, or a global monetary union leading towards a single global currency? The problem with a fixed exchange rate regime is that it has to be fixed to something. If fixed to the U.S. dollar, then the United States would hold every country in the world hostage—that won't be allowed to happen. If fixed to something else, the currency policy must supersede everything else—I don't think this will happen either.

What happens when costs such as labor and commodity prices start to displace from one region of the world to another? Without total and complete political union, fiscal transfers, with the necessary means to help one region of the world as opposed to another, then a world currency is unworkable. European Monetary Union will be an interesting test—very interesting.

So that leaves us with floating exchange rates enabling each country to determine its own destiny. Public and private authorities and investors have the absolute freedom to invest and choose as they see fit. I believe that with the appropriate and necessary transparency, investors will become better informed and therefore better able to decide how to manage their own affairs, which include risk management. Investors must also become more responsible for their actions. They must face the ultimate risk of default. Automatic intervention by the IMF or other government or international bodies cannot always be the end game for every currency crisis. Sure, there is a need for an institution to provide liquidity in times of need and crisis when it comes to balance of payments, but not for the balance of speculators.

Countries and investors must play by the new international rules, which will provide the outline for an appropriate check and balance system for portfolio capital flows. But the latest idea for currency targeting and global monetary union is not workable, and not in anyone's interests, except for those who rely on trade to fuel economic growth. If this is the case, then these countries must strike the right balance between fiscal and monetary policy to ensure that their currency offers value to investors and importers, and competitive value for the exporters. This process is a dynamic moving target requiring flexible and visionary thinking to keep up constantly with the changing new economy.

ENDNOTES

[1] "Currency and Banking Crises: Characteristics and Indicators of Vulnerability." *World Economic Outlook,* Annex IV, May 1998, page 111. Washington, D.C.: International Monetary Fund.

[2] Esquivel, G., and F. Larain. "Exposing Currency Crises." IMF Working Paper, June 1998, page 15. Washington, D.C.: International Monetary Fund.

[3] Ibid., page 16.

[4] "Capital Flows to Emerging Markets—A Historical Perspective." *International Capital Markets,* Annex VI, page 234. Washington, D.C.: International Monetary Fund.

[5] Esquival and Larain, op. cit., page 4.

[6] Berg, A., and C. Pattillo. "Are Currency Crises Predictable? A Test." IMF Working Paper, November 1998, page 10. Washington, D.C.: International Monetary Fund.

[7] "Currency Crises in Emerging Markets." Merrill Lynch, July 21. 1998, page 19.

[8] Ibid., page 19.

[9] Samuelson P. A., and W. D. Nordhaus. 1985. *Economics.* New York: McGraw-Hill, Inc., page 875.

[10] "Big Mac Currencies." *The Economist,* January 6, 2003.

[11] Caramazza, F., and A. Jahangir. "Fixed or Flexible," April 1998, page 6. Washington, D.C.: International Monetary Fund.

[12] Connolly, B. "The Spectre of Intervention." *Euromoney,* September 1998, page 88.

[13] Caramazza and Jahangir, op. cit., page 2.

[14] Tobin, J. "Financial Globalization: Can National Currencies Survive?" Keynote Address, Annual World Bank Conference on Development Economics, April 1998, page 3.

[15] Source: J. P. Morgan.

[16] Samuelson and Nordhaus, op. cit., p. 898.

[17] Stiglitz, J. E. 1997. *Economics.* New York: W.W. Norton & Co., page 629.

[18] "Figures to Fret About." *The Economist,* July 11, 1998, page 84.

[19] "Factors Behind the Crisis in Mexico." *World Economic Outlook,* May 1995, Annex I, page 96. Washington, D.C.: International Monetary Fund.

[20] Ibid.

[21] Ibid.

[22] "Searching for Value in the Bargain Basement." *International Bond Investor,* March 1995, page 2. Euromoney Publications.

[23] Ibid., page 5.

[24] Ben-Bassat, A. "The Inflation Target in Israel: Policy and Development." Bank of England, 1995, page 16.

[25] Source: Bank of Israel.

[26] Ibid.

[27] Ben-Bassat, op. cit.

[28] Source: Merrill Lynch.

[29] Rolnik, G. "Pressure on Frenkel: Foreigners Scent Blood." *Ha'aretz,* October 13, 1998.

[30] Bassock, M. "One Expert's Opinion: Central Bank Should Intervene in the Market." *Ha'aretz,* October 13, 1998.

[31] Tal, A. "The Governors Interest Rate Threat." *Ha'aretz,* January 11, 1999.

[32] Source: Merrill Lynch.

[33] "Cooling Hot Money." *International Investor,* September, 1998, page 120.

[34] Anjaria, J. S. "Working for a More Transparent World." IMF Working Paper, January 11, 1999, page 1.

[35] Summers, L. "Go With the Flow." *Financial Times,* March 11, 1998.

Chapter 9
WHAT IS EMU?

European Monetary Union (EMU) is the monetary system of the European Union, which introduced a new single-common currency for Europe, the "Euro," on January 1, 1999, and is likely to affect nearly everyone's life. Even though the Euro existed on this date, the actual notes and coins were introduced on January 2002, at which time EMU members abolished their own domestic money. A new European Central Bank (ECB) governs monetary policy.

The European Union as of January 1, 2000, consists of 15 countries:

1. Germany.
2. France.
3. United Kingdom.
4. Italy.
5. Spain.
6. Netherlands.
7. Belgium.
8. Austria.
9. Finland.
10. Sweden.
11. Denmark.
12. Greece.
13. Portugal.
14. Ireland.
15. Luxembourg.

Only 11 joined the single currency at its inception. The U.K., Denmark, Sweden, and Greece opted out of EMU, technically remained out, or did not qualify for membership.

Let there be no doubt. EMU has created a New Europe. Having said that, it must be added that it is not the solution to Europe's present difficulties—EMU is not a quick fix. It is, however, the first step and catalyst for *political integration*. Without that, monetary union may not succeed, as we shall see.

It can be said without exaggeration that European Monetary Union could become the most significant economic event in the world, at least since Bretton Woods after World War II. It is the biggest, boldest economic experiment regarding a currency union in history.

Still, problems abound. The true story of EMU is very different from that published in newspapers or aired on television, as a careful study of the history of monetary union and the events leading up to the signing of the Treaty of Maastricht in December 1991 will reveal.

MAASTRICHT TREATY

The Maastricht Treaty, named for a small town in Holland where it was negotiated and signed, produced an agenda leading to a single currency in Europe. It detailed a desire for currency stability and currency union that dated from the 19th century when the Latin Monetary Union brought France, Belgium, Switzerland, Bulgaria, and Greece together.[1] It didn't work then, and Professor Rudi Dornbush, writing in the September/October 1996 edition of *Foreign Affairs,* doesn't think it will work now:

> *"The battle for the common currency may be remembered as one of the more useless in Europe's history. The Euro is hailed as a solution to high unemployment, low growth, and the high costs of welfare states. But the deep budget cuts required before integration are already causing pain and may trigger severe recessions. If the European Monetary Union goes forward, a common currency will eliminate the adjustments now made by nominal exchange rates, and the central bank will control money with an iron fist. Labor markets will have to do the adjusting, a mechanism bound to fail, given those markets' inflexibility in Europe."*

Whose idea was it to create a single currency and monetary union in Europe? The finger can be pointed at Germany and France. The notion of a single European Economic Community could be found in Nazi and Vichy doctrine during World War II. Prominent Nazi professor Dr. Bernhard Benning and the Reich Economics Ministry agreed that the Reich mark would be the leading currency in the German Economic Area, and, along with the U.S. dollar, would be one of the two reserve currencies in the resulting global economy.[2] The Fuhrer himself pointed out that there is no geographic definition of Europe, and the only possible aim of economic cooperation must be the establishment of the European Economic Community.[3] Nazi economic doctrine also intended to confront the evils of the Anglo-Saxon markets-oriented economy and its self-indulgent culture.

The Hitler government intended a fixed exchange rate leading to the creation of a European Central Bank. Nazis envisioned fixed global spheres of influence, including a Reich mark Zone, under German Central Bank control, comprised of Austria, Bohemia, Moravia, Netherlands, plus Belgium and Luxembourg (which had had a monetary union in place since 1926). The Reich mark Zone would stretch over Denmark, Norway, Sweden, Slovakia, Romania, Hungary, and Bulgaria.

In the Nazi vision, Italy's sphere of influence would be Spain, Greece, and Turkey.

Britain and the U.S. would control the Americas.

Japan would rule in much of Asia.

In accordance with the Ribbentrop-Molotov Pact, the Soviet Union would be master of Finland and the Baltic's.

Left out of the mix was France.[4] Hideous as the Nazis were, given today's realities, they may have been onto something where France was concerned.

From 1944 to 1973, the economic debate focused on Bretton Woods, but ultimately the battle among German Corporatism, French Socialism, and British Anglo-Saxon Capitalism pushed Europe toward the next phase of monetary union. That push came from the Germans and French. The British looked on in horror.

France's traditional socialist policies had failed the French, while German Corporatism helped Germany's economy grow in strength, year after year. German Corporatism is the system of large battalions—the industrial-financial complex, banking cartels, big business associations with large trade unions.[5] French Socialism, on the other hand, based itself on Keynesian intervention by the central government to control the business cycle, aimed at ultimately providing jobs for all.

An interesting difference between the German and Anglo-Saxon Capitalist systems involved their labor policies during periods of slow economic growth. The Germans reduced the hourly working week and the Anglo-Saxon model allowed market forces to increase unemployment.

The French believed they had no choice between national economic self-sufficiency and subservience to the German way of doing things. Siding with Germany on European Monetary Union, France echoed the 1940 view that it was:

". . . doomed to defeat, and would be forced to change for the better only by being under the tutelage of the victorious Nazis."[6]

The European Union is more divided than it appears. In particular, France still believes that monetary policy is a matter for politicians and central bankers. It continues to argue that the central bank should target economic growth along with inflation, and is determined to design and develop the new Europe, with its political agenda topping the list and economic issues coming second.

EMU ISSUES

Members of EMU face several unresolved issues, including:

- Fiscal policy coordination.
- High unemployment.
- Tax harmonization.
- The evolution of the European Central Bank (ECB).
- EU expansion.
- The opt-out currencies.

How to deal with new members of EMU in the coming years.

The battle between differing capitalist systems poses a significant problem for EMU. One need only remember 1997 when Renault tried to close a plant in northern Belgium—the company had lost nearly a billion dollars the year before, and had a huge over-capacity in the global production of automobiles—this only six months before the Asian economic crisis. Belgium Prime Minister Jean-Luc Dehaene demanded that the European Commission draft legislation "to stop outrageous corporate misbehavior."[7] European Commission President Jacques Santer "denounced Renault for breaching the spirit and letter of European laws which require prior consultation with workers."[8] Also, the EU's Social-Affairs Commissioner wanted to propose new legislation to improve worker protection, and the Competition Commissioner denounced Renault for its response to competitive pressures![9]

THE RHINE AND ANGLO-SAXON CAPITALIST MODELS

The difference between the Rhine and Anglo-Saxon capitalist models comes down to the state's role in the economy and the extent of social safety nets. The Rhine model proposes more government intervention. The Anglo-Saxon design prefers market forces. The European Union intends a corporate super state governed from Brussels.

Recent research by Deutsche Morgan Grenfell revealed that shareholders in Germany received two percentage points less in return on equity than those in the U.K. and 4 percent less than in the United States. Werner Seifert, Chief Executive of the German Stock Exchange, noted that although Germany invested more per capita than the U.S., the capital was 35 percent less productive. Clearly, capital markets must develop along the Anglo-Saxon model, fueling an industrial revival and encouraging more shareholder value.[10]

To further illustrate the difference between German Corporatism and Anglo-Saxon Capitalism, look where money must come from to fuel economic activity. According to the *Financial Times* (January 25, 2000), Germany's bank assets were virtually the same as the United States, but the German people had one dollar invested in stock to every $13 in the United States. Traditionally, banks are less likely to loan money on anything but sure things.

Corporatism does not encourage entrepreneurs, yet these have been the reasons behind the success of the Anglo-Saxon system. The flexibility and transparency of Anglo-Saxon capital markets has demonstrated their ability to create jobs, while the inflexibility of labor markets in Europe, plus the cost of doing business there, cannot be resolved through more European Commission regulations promulgated from Belgium.

Europe's problems will begin disappearing when capital becomes more flexible, and corporatism gives way to market forces.

The Rhine Model (the German version of corporate capitalism) has protected industry for a much longer time than Anglo-Saxon capitalism. The results have been higher costs in the protected industries. Also, capital markets develop more slowly under the Rhine Model. The banks in Europe monopolize the distribution of capital, which limits its access. Take a look at Table 9.[11] and note the differences between the two capitalist systems:

It should be realized that the collapse of the Asian economic miracle (the Asian system is similar to the Rhine model) points to the need for the ECB to be more open and transparent. Maybe that will happen. The *Financial Times* on July 28, 1998, noted:

"The ECB feels culturally different from other institutions. Its official language is English, which is unusual in an otherwise French-dominated network of

Table 9.1: Distribution of Capital

Country	Population (mil)	GDP (US$ bil)	Stock Market (US$ bil)	Bank Assets (US$ bil)
EU 15	373	8,092	5,387	12,387
EU 11	290	6,286	2,999	9,628
USA	268	8,111	12,855	6,203
Japan	126	4,193	2,161	6,034

European establishments. The ECB also lacks the typical French administrative structures of Brussels and Luxembourg institutions. Although the ECB's policy structures are more closely modeled on the Bundesbank, its internal atmosphere could not differ more. It feels more like an Anglo-Saxon than a German central bank."

Here is the timetable for steps already taken that lead to EMU:[12]

- *June 1989.* Delors report on economic and monetary union.
- *July 1990.* Stage one, abolition of capital controls.
- *December 1991.* Maastricht Treaty negotiated.
- *January 1994.* Stage two, European Monetary Institute created.
- *December 1995.* Euro chosen as the name for the single currency.
- *May 1998.* Euro members chosen, bilateral conversion rates fixed. EBC established.
- *December 1998.* Euro conversion rates fixed.
- *January 1999.* Stage three, Euro is launched.
- *January 2002.* Euro notes and coins introduced.
- *July 2002.* National notes and coins withdrawn.

WHY EUROPEAN MONETARY UNION?

EMU was certainly not for economic reasons, but purely for political objectives. The European "cloak" hides the political ambitions of Germany and France. Germans want to protect their competitiveness while projecting corporatism, and are happy to sacrifice monetary policy and the Bundesbank for a single currency. Their sacrifice, however, is conditional, because the ECB must be a clone of the Bundesbank.

Control of the European Central Bank means control of the lives of more than 300 million people, representing 19 percent of global GDP and 18 percent of world trade.[13]

The French elite don't believe money is the economy's lubricant, but instead the most important lever of power.[14] The European Central Bank is their ultimate prize. The French have longed to get their hands on an economic power, such as the Bundesbank and, by capturing the ECB, are willing to tempt the Germans with political union.

France and Germany want a voice on the world stage. The French have an independent nuclear deterrent plus a permanent seat on the U.N. Security Council, but are not taken seriously. Their Nazi past hinders the Germans. Together they could be respected as a superpower and compete directly with the United States.

On December 5, 1998, *The Economist* reported:

> *"The main begetters of EMU a decade ago were President Francois Mitterand of France; Chancellor Helmut Kohl of Germany; and Jacques Delors, president of the European Commission. They saw it as a means to bind Europeans more closely together. They believed that it would strengthen the supranational institutions of the European Union. Indeed, it was precisely this potential for political transformation that made monetary union attractive. Economic gains were a secondary consideration: they appeared relatively small, if they could be calculated reliably at all. Nobody pretended that a system of national currencies was provoking widespread dissatisfaction."*

The economic arguments for EMU are limited, the major benefit being the single currency called the Euro. The Euro will permit a single pricing system throughout member states and signal the end of long-term currency risk management with European member-state trading partners. (Intra-European trade represents 60 percent of their total trade.)[15] These benefits are difficult to quantify, but the costs of becoming an EMU member have been and will continue to be enormous.

Three battles are taking place on the European plains. The first is between corporatism and market forces, which Bernard Connolly calls a struggle

> *". . . between politics and economics, an attempt to stem the tide of market forces that threatened to engulf corporatist Europe in the 1980s and 1990s."*[16]

The second targets the heart of the German Bundesbank, with two armies, composed of French and German politicians, laying siege.

The third battle rages over control of the European Central Bank, Brussels, and the European Super state, "in which French technocrats confront German Federalists, both sides claiming to fight under the banner of Charlemagne."[17]

Bernard Connolly argues that a fourth force, the financial markets, is trying to knock the Bundesbank off its pedestal. But financial markets are not the Bundesbank's enemy. The Bundesbank's monetary policies, monetary targets, and benchmarks are clear, something that cannot be said of French monetary authorities. The truth is that much suspicion surrounds the new European Central Bank, which unfortunately will *not* be a clone of the German Bundesbank with its constitutional and independent commitment to price stability.

The process of European Monetary Union began at The Hague European Summit in December 1969. Luxembourg President Pierre Werner headed a committee to create economic and monetary union in three stages. The first, implemented in 1972, with the currency "snake," a device advocated by the Germans to protect German competition.

The snake's objective was to limit foreign exchange fluctuations to no more than +/- 2.25 percent. Besides Germany, also signing the arrangement were Belgium, Luxembourg, Denmark, Norway, and Sweden. The 2.25 percent range constituted the most any one currency could move or fluctuate against the strongest currency before central bank intervention. The aim: For the currencies of member nations to move together like a snake through a tunnel when matched against an outside currency like the U.S. dollar.

France, Italy, and the U.K. were members briefly, but rising inflation, plus very different economic and business cycles in the various countries, made the snake a sitting duck for currency speculators, an often maligned crowd who, similar to carrions, are only doing their thing. Politicians are to blame for presenting the juicy opportunities to the speculators.

Other, more dangerous, culprits emerged during the next phase of European Monetary Union. In 1978, German Chancellor Helmut Schmidt and French President Valery Giscard d'Estaing initiated the creation of the European Monetary System, the object being monetary stability among members. A member had to label 20 percent of foreign exchange reserves as European Currency Units (ECUs)[18] and, similar to the snake, maintain fluctuation bands of 2.25 percent.

During the early 1980s, a number of strains on the exchange rate mechanism resulted in numerous devaluations and revaluations, culminating in a 1983 French defeat (caused by an inflation rate 300 percent higher than in Germany), and the franc was devalued by 30 percent over the previous 18 months.

The humiliation for the Mitterand administration was absolute. France had to capitulate totally to Germany on budget policy, and agree to targets on their current account. In other words, interest rates had to rise and the budget needed to be tightened to reduce the annual deficit. Such policies were completely contrary to the French way of life, and particularly galling for a socialist government, which spent more than it brought in.

The exchange rate mechanism progressively hardened from 1983 to 1986. Realignments became less frequent as members struggled to emulate German Monetary policy—one requiring higher real interest rates to achieve equality with German inflation results.

CONVERGENCE CRITERIA

On May 1-3, 1988, the European Summit decided which European Union member states would be allowed to join EMU in the first wave, becoming founding members. EC President Jacques Delors was commissioned to devise a blueprint for European Monetary Union. Subsequently, the *Delors Report* culminated in the signing of the1991 Maastricht Treaty, which committed all EU members[19] to join the single currency, providing they met a certain required number of economic "convergence criteria." The two exceptions, or opt-out countries, from EMU are (1) Denmark and (2) the United Kingdom. They negotiated a clause allowing them to "opt-in" or "opt-out" from the single currency.

The convergence criteria required for entry into EMU—the single currency—are the following:

- The annual government deficit must be 3 percent or less of Gross Domestic Product.

- The total outstanding government debt must not exceed 60 percent of GDP.

- The annual inflation rate must be no more than 1.5 percent higher than those of the three best performing member states.

- Long-term interest rates must be within 2 percent of the corresponding average rages in the three countries with the lowest inflation.

- The member state's currency must remain within the exchange rate mechanism for two years.
- The central bank of the member state must be independent from political influences.

Tables 9.2 and 9.3 show (1) the European Union members' currency conversion rates and (2) their standings on "convergence criteria" early in 1998, prior to fixing the currency exchange rates in May 1998.

The Maastricht Treaty requires European member states to meet all the convergence criteria prior to being allowed to become a member of European Monetary Union. According to the European Parliament as of the end of March 1998, 11 member states had qualified for EMU (1) Austria, (2) Germany, (3) Belgium, (4) Spain, (5) Luxembourg, (6) France, (7) Netherlands, (8) Italy, (9) Ireland, (10) Portugal, and (11) Finland. Yet, as of February 1998, only Luxembourg, France (by sleight-of-hand fudging of numbers), and Finland met the convergence criteria for entry into EMU.

Table 9.2: European Union Members—Currency Conversion

Currency	Versus One Euro
Belgian franc	40.3399
German mark	1.95583
Spanish peseta	166.386
French franc	6.55957
Irish pound	0.78756
Italian lire	1936.27
Luxembourg franc	(same as Belgian franc)
Dutch guilder	2.20371
Austrian shilling	13.7603
Portuguese eEscudo	200.482
Finnish markka	5.94573

The final timetable for European Monetary Union was first to fix the exchange rates on May 3, 1998, and then to introduce the Euro and the new European Central Bank on January 1, 1999. Once the official currency and central bank were launched, the introduction of capital markets and a wholesale payments system commenced.

The next major date is no later than January 1, 2002, when the retail systems became operational. All founding members of EMU started to switch from their domestic currencies to Euro notes and coins and withdraw all local notes and coins by July 1, 2002.

And that's it.

REGIONAL EFFECT

When the Maastricht Treaty was signed, astute institutional investors divided up the European Union into three regions. The first were the hardcore countries—Austria, Germany, Netherlands, Ireland, Belgium, Luxembourg, and France. The second region included Spain, Italy, Sweden, Denmark, Finland, and Portugal. The third encompassed the United Kingdom and Greece.

Table 9.3: European Union Members—Standings on "Convergence Criteria" (early 1998)[20]

	Price Stability 2.5% or less	Budget Deficit (3.0)% or less	Gross Debt 60% or less	ERM Membership Yes/No	Long-Term Interest Rates 7.8% or less
Target					
Austria	1.2	(2.5)	66.1	Yes	5.6
Belgium	1.5	(2.1)	122.2	Yes	5.7
Denmark	2.0	0.7	64.1	Yes	6.1
Finland	1.2	(0.9)	55.8	Yes	5.8
France	1.2	(3.0)	58.0	Yes	5.5
Germany	1.5	(2.7)	61.3	Yes	5.6
Greece	5.4	(4.0)	108.7	Yes	10.0
Ireland	1.2	0.9	67.0	Yes	6.1
Italy	1.9	(2.7)	121.6	Yes	6.5
Luxembourg	1.4	1.7	6.7	Yes	5.7
Netherlands	1.9	(1.4)	72.1	Yes	5.5
Portugal	1.9	(2.5)	62.0	Yes	6.1
Spain	1.9	(2.6)	68.3	Yes	6.2
Sweden	1.9	(0.8)	76.6	No	6.5
United Kingdom	1.8	(1.9)	53.4	No	6.9

The first region of hardcore countries represented those who committed themselves to the German Bundesbank's monetary policy at any cost. They were certain to be part of the founding members of the single currency. The hardcore countries had already begun the painful process of convergence with Germany and the Maastricht Treaty convergence criteria.

The second region consisted of potential members that needed a miracle to make the first wave into the single currency, or would be in a position to enter EMU in the second wave.

The third region was an independent (the U.K.) and a country (Greece) with no hope of being in an economic position to enter EMU in either the first or second wave.

As far as European government debt, the benchmark yield curve would be the German government bond market. All sovereign debt values in the European Union would be compared to the German yield curve, the German cost of capital.

The comforting factor about the Maastricht Treaty: It fit well with sound thinking about global real interest rate convergence. Here was a treaty, which politically bound 15 countries to real interest rate convergence with Germany. The worst case a member state could produce in terms of price stability was a German result, with yields on non-German government bonds falling to German levels. Likely France would converge with Germany and, as a result of German reunification, actually see yields fall below German government securities.

Too much political capital was at stake. The Mitterand government had to deliver to the French people. The treaty also promoted deflationary forces, and this aspect of EMU would help yield curves throughout Europe to flatten and fall more rapidly.

Italy seemed weak as an investment, compared to Spain and Sweden. Who can understand Italy's economics or politics with a new government forming every six months?

Spain, on the other hand, had a talented prime minister, Felipe Gonzales, and sound monetary and fiscal policies. Here was a huge investment opportunity and, as long as Gonzales remained in power, it seemed the fiscal deficit would be reduced and high real interest rates maintained. In fact, Gonzales retired, but his replacement, Jose Maria Aznar of the right-of-center Popular Party, continued to forge ahead with enlightened policies, ensuring that Spain become a founding member of EMU. Spanish yields, offering a tremendous investment opportunity, stood 130 basis points (1.3 percent) higher than Italy. Spain had credibility. Italy did not.

Of course, bumps occurred along the way. Denmark voted "no" to the Maastricht Treaty with a 50.7 percent majority, which led to "Black Wednesday" on September 16, 1992, when the European Monetary System's Exchange Rate Mechanism collapsed. Italy and the United Kingdom withdrew from the ERM, with the U.K. never to return.

The events leading up to and including Black Wednesday established a watershed in the life of the Exchange Rate Mechanism, and raised an obvious point, though politicians seemed surprised. In a dynamic, integrated, instantaneous global economy, the currency price will act as a shock absorber, and move with real interest rates that are timed and related to one's business cycle. Conversely, when currencies are fixed to different business cycles, one currency will strengthen and the other weakens.

When East and West Germany reunified, demand for capital to pay for the reunification was enormous, and displaced the cost of capital throughout Europe. Something had to give in those countries that had fixed their monetary policies, and therefore their currency prices, with Germany—either the currency price or a rising unemployment rate, as real interest rates rose in line with Germany's.

THE COST OF CURRENCY PRICE STABILITY

Currency price stability is desirable, but at what cost?

Greater currency stability should emerge in the future as real interest rates and government debt yield converge. No doubt this economic convergence will occur, but it will be market driven, not politically dictated. All-important investors will determine when the economic climate is healthy. They will not accept that everything is stable when they can see a fault-line as volatile as San Andreas.

The competitive devaluation of a currency can have a positive impact on exports while importing inflation, and help ease difficult times during the business cycle. A strengthening currency price slows exports and economic growth. Which brings us to this: European Monetary Union can bring low inflation or stable currencies, but not both.[21]

Much confusion exists about the relationship between a stable currency and low inflation, and a debate rages over the merits of the exchange rate mechanism, and ultimately over European Monetary Union itself. Helmut Werner, president of Mercedes-Benz, warned that exchange rate fluctuations threatened the European single market with disintegration.[22]

Chief Economist of the Bundesbank, Dr. Otmar Issing, took a different tack. He insisted the Deutschemarks revaluation brought only benefit, including low inflation and protection from economic overheating. The fact is, for the Bundesbank, currency instability represented a secondary issue—what mattered was preserving the internal purchasing power of money.[23]

The Exchange Rate Mechanism collapsed again in the summer of 1993 with across-the-board devaluations versus the deutschemark, Belgian franc, and Dutch guilder. Once more the turmoil traced to the differences in the business cycles of the various states.

Public spending in Germany had risen well beyond earlier estimates, prompting real interest rates to climb again. Real economic growth expanded by 5.9 percent and 5.2 percent in 1990 and 1991,[24] at the same time the U.S., U.K., Sweden, Switzerland, and Finland were entering recessions.

Economic growth was robust in Japan, causing interest rates to rise along with Germany's, while rates were falling in the U.S. and U.K. Ominously, annual budget deficits were rising, forcing real interest rates to rise throughout the world. Deficits rose especially in typically slow-growth countries, but also in Germany as the cost of reunification tripled. Competition for global capital was fierce, and the economic financial costs of membership in the exchange rate mechanism grew.

Foreign exchange intervention was enormous. On September 3, 1992, the Bank of England had to borrow $14.5 billion in Deutschemarks to help support Sterling's value.[25]

On July 30, 1993, the *Financial Times* reported:

"The total amount of foreign exchange deployed by the Bank of France to hold the franc's ERM parity is thought to have exceeded French franc 300 billion. Heavy borrowing from the Bundesbank and other central banks wiped out France's foreign exchange reserves, leaving the bank with a net deficit of more than French franc 180 billion."[26]

The 1992 devaluations of sterling, lire, and peseta came home to roost—sterling devalued by 21 percent against the deutschemark, the lire by 33 percent, and the peseta by 25 percent.[27]

What can be stated for certain is that if foreign exchange rates are fixed, the ability to manage an economy and its business cycle is lessened. Without a shock absorber, the economic costs during periods of slow economic growth or financial shocks will be much higher.

CONCLUSION

The convergence criteria defined in the Maastricht Treaty dictated terms for an economic performance or target to a specific point in time. The difficulty will be moving the business cycles of the member states in the same direction at the same time. Every country that joined the single currency in the January 1, 1999—the first wave—needed to parallel business cycles with the anchor currency, the deutschemark.

Then there's the Stability Pact, the agreement which deals with the terms and conditions for each country after European Monetary Union. Said the *Financial Times:*

"Governments must accept—permanently—the constraints that EMU will place on domestic policymaking. No report can predict whether this is going to happen."[28]

The European quoted Milton Friedman:

". . . warning that the Euro will exacerbate political tensions by converting divergent shocks that could have been readily accommodated by exchange-rate changes into divisive political issues. Europe exemplifies a situation unfavorable to a common currency."[29]

EMU is likely to have a difficult time at the outset. Living inside a monetary union imposes a heavy burden of discipline on fiscal behavior, in domestic wage setting, and in many previously sovereign areas of economic policymaking.[30]

Each country has a unique welfare system, standards of living, varying safety nets for workers, and substantially different pension funding. Some nations have huge financial liabilities.

Labor costs vary greatly from country to country. Pension systems will experience a jarring financial impact in those nations with pay-as-you-go schemes. The welfare state, along with corporate capitalism, is in serious trouble as EMU goes forward and if the Social Chapter in the Maastricht Treaty is any indication of political focus in the new millennium. This is not hyperbole. The European continent may need another Marshall Plan in the year 2030.

Where will all the money come from to finance monetary union? Economists talk hopefully about an economic revival for EU, but exceptional times are not likely as things stand now. The EU needs a market-oriented capitalist system with radical liberalization in labor, capital markets, pension systems, tax regimes, and, most important, an attitude change in economic thinking.

This is not what the French and German people want for themselves, but the introduction of monetary union without these changes will either cause unemployment rates to soar or a huge increase in public debt, or both.

Either way, political forces cannot dictate a monetary union. Market forces will push member states in the right direction, and perhaps in years to come the time will be ripe for monetary union.

But the markets must do the work.

The European Commission spends a fortune each year protecting industry from market forces. If the EC scrapped the Common Agricultural Policy, a farce that pays farmers to grow crops that are thrown away and left to rot, up to $90 billion would be released for more productive use.[31]

The welfare system is in lamentable shape and will feed on greater proportions of the annual budget. The social budget in Germany accounts for a third of its domestic product. Contributions to the social budget rose to 42 percent of gross wages in 1997.[32]

Another harsh reality for Europeans is the future of their social security system. In Germany by 2030, there will be one retired person for every individual of working age (not everyone of working age will work and pay taxes).

If the pay-as-you-go pension system is not reformed immediately, pension contributions alone will rise to 30 percent of gross income in 2030.[33]

Now that the single currency has gone ahead as planned, structural reform will be inevitable within the public sector—it will have to shrink. And there's this: The EU held a Jobs Summit in November, 1997, which concluded that job creation is likely to lead to fiscal slippage.

Bottom line: The same old same old. More government rather than less.

ENDNOTES

[1] Dornbush, R. *Foreign Affairs,* September/October 1996.

[2] Connolly, B. 1995. *The Rotten Heart of Europe.* London: Faber & Faber, page 231.

[3] Ibid.

[4] Ibid., page 76.

[5] Ibid., page 31.

[6] *The Economist,* March 15, 1997, page 25.

[7] Ibid., page 39.

[8] Ibid., page 25.

[9] Deutsche Morgan Grenfell. "Global Foreign Exchange Research," February 20, 1998, page 8.

[10] Source: Merrill Lynch, December 31, 1998.

[11] Source: *The Economist,* October 17, 1998.

[12] Connolly, B. 1995. *The Rotten Heart of Europe.* London: Faber & Faber, page 232.

[13] 'Review & Comment,' "The Euro Club." *Wall Street Journal,* March 26, 1998.

[14] Connolly, op. cit., page 4.

[15] "EMU and the World Economy." *World Economic Outlook,* October 1997, page 51. Washington, D.C.: International Monetary Fund.

[16] Connolly, B., op. cit., page xvi.

[17] Ibid.

[18] The European Currency Unit (ECU) is a composite currency based on a basket, with each nation's currency weighted according to each country's share in intra-European trade, its percentage share of European Union gross national product and the relative importance of each country's foreign exchange reserves.

[19] There are 15 members in the European Union: Austria, Belgium, Denmark, Finland, France, Germany, Greece, Ireland, Italy, Luxembourg, Netherlands, Portugal, Spain, Sweden, and the United Kingdom.

[20] 1997 data from Deutsche Bank Research; except long-term interest rate data.

[21] Wolf, M. "Cracks in the Single Market." *Financial Times,* May 5, 1995.

[22] Ibid.

[23] Ibid.

[24] "Global Economic Digest." Barclays Capital.

[25] "World Economic Outlook," October 1992, page 42. Washington, D.C.: International Monetary Fund.

[26] "Faultlines Show in Franco-German Unity." *Financial Times,* December 23, 1993, page 4.

[27] Tett, G., A. Fisher, and A. Hill. "When Strength is a Weakness." *Financial Times,* August 9, 1995.

[28] "The Verdict on EMU Members." *Financial Times,* March 26, 1998.

[29] "Flawed Currency." *The European,* November 20-26, 1997.

[30] "A Harder Currency." *Financial Times,* March 23, 1998.

[31] Roche, D. "EMU Needs a New Social Contract." *Wall Street Journal,* April 6, 1998.

[32] "Euro Joins the Social Whirl." *Financial Times,* December 15, 1997.

[33] Fisher, A. "The Storm on the Horizon." *Financial Times,* April 9, 1996.

Chapter 10
WILL THERE BE LIFE AFTER EMU?

INTRODUCTION

In 1998, many economists predicted EMU would never get off the ground, much less start on time on January 1, 1999. Yet, against all odds—11 founding countries—it happened.

A lot of work awaits EMU members before European super-state status is achieved, but pricing and accounting in a single currency promises to be a big benefit.

The Euro opened trade against the U.S. dollar at approximately $1.17, with the deutschemark trading at DEM 1.67. The price has gone downhill ever since—hardly a surprise, as we shall shortly see.

Crucial to everything, however, was the January 1, 1999, introduction of the European Central Bank (ECB), whose constitution is based on the German model, with a mandate to maintain price stability. A committee of central bankers who stressed the need for independence and downplayed the role of openness and accountability created the constitutional structure.[1]

The ECB is composed of a governing council of up to six member of an executive committee board, plus the governors of each member's central bank. The ECB will conduct monetary policy for members of the EMU. Once domestic currencies disappear, national central banks will have no role in maintaining monetary policy. They will lose all control.

The real test will come at the first signs of trouble. It shouldn't be forgotten that investors need to feel comfortable with the policy *and* the policymakers.

Has the new European Central Bank adopted the Bundesbank's model of price stability? In response to that trillion-dollar question, the answer is no.

Many reasons exist *not* to believe that the ECB will serve as a righteous upholder of true price-stability doctrine. Its constitution states "price-stability," but it also says the ECB should set interest-rate policy accordingly.[2] Investors will remain suspicious unless the new ECB operates like the German Bundesbank, with the same credibility.

THE PRESIDENCY

The first alarm bells tolled when a battle broke out between Germany and France over the presidency of the ECB. How important is this war? The president of ECB will have an impact on the lives of hundreds of millions of people. He will be one of the most power-ful individuals on the planet, ruling over 300 million persons, not one of whom voted for him. Who won this battle? The French.

Can it get worse?

If you live in France, perhaps not. Anywhere else, yes, because the ECB will have a more French-like character than German. As early as November, 1996, Anatole Kaletsky of the *London Times* declared;

> *"The war over Europe's money has been all but won by France."[3]*

Each of the 11 founding members will have a vote on the ECB board, something France pushed from the beginning to dilute Germany's power. With ECB's strong Mediterranean bias, the Germans will not have the votes to control Europe's economic future. What will happen when the German people realize they have been defeated?

The battle for the presidency of ECB was where European Monetary Union got scary, especially if one were British, German, or thinking to invest in Europe in the future. The ECB was to have a president serving an eight-year non-renewable term. The Germans wanted Wim Duisenberg, head of the European Monetary Institute, the precursor of ECB. At first he seemed a shoo-in. But not for long.[4]

On November 4, 1997, French President Jacques Chirac and his socialist Prime Minister Lionel Jospin announced that French Central Bank Governor Jean-Claude Trichet should head the ECB. Jospin said:

> *"France must pursue a policy that preserves its own interest."[5]*

The debate over the two was largely nationalistic, and quickly became personal. Dutch Prime Minister Wim Kok said:

> *"If Duisenberg is blocked, I will not back a Frenchman. That is out of the question."*

During the French general election, Jospin campaigned on four conditions before he would support the Euro (1) membership of Italy and Spain in the first wave was "neces-sary and possible," (2) monetary union must pledge to create jobs, (3) ECB's power must be balanced by political direction of economic policy, and (4) the Euro must not be over-valued against the dollar and yen.[6] Mr. Jospin, to his credit, fulfilled his campaign pledges—he did not have to worry about pledge number (4). The Euro has been in free-fall since its introduction in January 1, 1999.

The story became more frightening.

Trichet, in an interview with *The European,* pointed to a strong framework that would exist post-EMU to ensure the right mix of monetary and fiscal policies within the Euro zone. There would be nothing too brash as the ECB's telling sovereign governments what tax rates to levy, Trichet said. But he maintained that ECB would have a powerful indirect say in national fiscal policies through the manner in which it set monetary policy. *The European* concluded:

> *"This is not just a political union; it is a political union run by a bank."[7]*

Those who yearn for not only monetary union but political union believe the intro-duction of the Euro "has become their Trojan Horse to make political union inevitable."[8]

Attempting to deter Mediterranean countries from entering a single currency and abiding by Maastricht Treaty convergence criteria after EMU, the Germans introduced rules governing the fiscal behavior of member states. Germany wanted only hardcore countries among the founding members to ensure what it considered policies acceptable to itself. Unfortunately, the Germans lost, the French won.

Tension between Chirac and Helmut Kohl of Germany, notable in the past, rose to an even higher level in late April, 1998. The *International Herald Tribune* reported on its front page that with:

> ". . . six days before a summit here [Brussels] at which the EU is to officially name the 11 countries that will adopt the Euro and choose either Wim Duisenberg of the Netherlands or Jean-Claude Trichet of France as president of the new ECB, the mood of the community was described as 'rotten' by a high-ranking diplomat."

This serious EU rift between France and the other 10 members ended in a farce. The French forced Germany to compromise—even Chirac asked of the journalists:

> "Do not laugh."[9]

But others laughed. Instead of making the right decision, the French forced the totally wrong one. In this case, compromise was the worst decision. Mr. Duisenberg would serve the first four years of his eight-year term, then "voluntarily" step down so Trichet could take over the remainder.

Several analysts reported:

> "The impression of political interference could encourage European central bankers to reassert their independence and raise interest rates."[10]

The *Wall Street Journal* commented (May 4, 1998):

> "It's a shame that a brawl between France and its EU partners over who should head the new ECB marred the EU's historic weekend decision to launch the single currency . . . this currency has been shown in laboratory tests to be vulnerable to intense political lobbying."

So who is running the ECB? We know who isn't. The *Financial Times* (May 4, 1998) called the decision and compromise:

> ". . . undignified and disappointing."

The German Bundesbank weighed in, calling it a "lazy compromise." Hans Tietmeyer, president of the Bundesbank, raised his doubts on the deal:

> "Not everything that happened last weekend in Brussels contributed to the necessary expectation that the Euro will be a really supranational depoliticized currency."

To add to the uncertainty of the "timesharing" presidency, *LeMonde* reported:

> "Mr. Duisenberg categorically ruled out retiring after four years of his eight-year term as demanded by President Jacques Chirac of France."[11]

The French clearly won. The German people just haven't realized it yet.

The ECB began life uncertain about who is in charge and for how long, uncertain over the independence of the new ECB. The ECB will primarily use an inflation target as its benchmark, with the harmonized inflation index target of 0-2 percent. The difficulty the ECB faces in the coming years is political interference, and ultimately monetary policy itself. Credibility is everything.

On Thursday February 7, 2002, Mr. Duisenberg announced his retirement on his 68th birthday July 9, 2003, he is retiring a year later than the French demand, although the appearance is meant to preserve ECB independence, but we know better. Jean-Claude Trichet, the Bank of France governor will take over the reins of the ECB now that he has been found not guilty in his role in the financial irregularities at the state-owned Credit Lyonnais Bank.

BENCHMARKS AND ACCOUNTABILITY

A clear, understandable benchmark is necessary, and for this an inflation target is the best measure. In fact, the European Central Bank has adopted a monetary policy, which contains two pillars to its strategy. It has taken a more pragmatic approach, instituting a monetary policy strategy that foresees, "first, a prominent role for money and, second, an analysis of a wide range of other economic and financial indicators in order to form a broadly based assessment of the risks to price stability" (*ECB Monthly Bulletin,* November 2000). The ECB concludes that:

> *"Taken together, the two pillars form a framework which is used to organize the analysis and the presentation of the information relevant for monetary policymaking in order to maintain price stability."*

Above all, the ECB must be accountable, and its decision-making process transparent.[12] Accountability remains the outstanding issue, until policy targets and benchmarks are defined and, more importantly, commitments put to the test.

For example, in the U.S., Alan Greenspan as chairman of the Federal Reserve is responsible to Congress, which *requires public testimony twice yearly* under what is known as Humphrey-Hawkins. He is also called before various congressional committees. The process for institutional reform of the U.S. central bank comes through an Act of Congress. A similar process of accountability exists in Germany for the Bundesbank.

The ECB, on the other hand, is required to provide an *annual* report to the European Parliament, and the president can be called before what are called "competent" committees. The process for ECB institutional reform requires an *unanimous* decision by all members.

So much for accountability and public scrutiny. No wonder the French want control. There is *no* accountability.

GERMANY

The German position represents absolute commitment to low inflation, which should be the backbone and heart of EMU. EMU's ultimate success or failure will depend on the

German population and its belief that trading the deutschemark for the Euro will not compromise price stability. Politics and politicians can, however, upset the foundation of price stability, highlighting the fragility EMU faces if her political guardians decide to move in a contrary direction (i.e., sacrificing price stability for economic growth in an attempt to create jobs).

This is what happened in Germany after the 1998 election made Social Democrat Gerhard Schroder the country's seventh post-war chancellor. With their coalition partners, the Green Party, the Social Democrats (SPD) have 345 of the 669 seats in the Bundestag, the lower house, and control 38 of the 69 votes in the upper house. Chancellor Schroder had firm control over the political machinery.

Schroder's victory emphasized what can happen when a country elects a politician to introduce economic and financial policy that serves the national interests and needs versus the welfare of the Euro or EMU.

Politicians often sacrifice economic principles and beliefs to gain voter support, and ultimately political power. They will, of course, become more practical when reaching their goals, because holding power is not the same as being an opposition party. Gerhard Schroder and his original finance minister, Oskar Lafontaine, are perfect examples. The SPD was elected on the platform of reducing German unemployment, but Schroder and Lafontaine are different people with very different agendas.

Schroder had been chairman of Jusos (the young socialists), but took power as a middle-of-the-road (center left) politician, similar to Bill Clinton and Tony Blair, trying to unite both sides of the economic equation, individuals and business.

Finance Minister Lafontaine had other ideas. Dubbed "Europe's most dangerous man" by the U.K. *Sun* newspaper, he advocated the following wrong-headed policies:

- Keynesian economics as the key to success for the German economy, especially reducing the unemployment rate.

- Closer coordination among fiscal, monetary and incomes policy to achieve an optimal economic mix, rather than the goal of low inflation.

- Monetary policy to support growth and to eliminate what *he* deemed unfair tax competition in the EU, *raising* tax burdens to the high German levels.

- A demand that the system within the EU be changed to majority voting on EU tax policy, instead of the unanimous system presently in place.

- Stabilizing the Euro exchange rate against the U.S. dollar and Japanese Yen.[13]

Mr. Lafontaine obviously is an interventionist. He wants to reduce interest rates, expand fiscal spending, control exchange rates, and harmonize tax rates across the EU to ensure there are no competitive advantages versus Germany. One difference between today's and Hitler's Germany is that Hitler used bullets to protect German industry and her exports, while Lafontaine employs the Maastricht Treaty to achieve the same end.

The Euro is growing up in uncertain times. Lafontaine's political agenda in Germany flies in the face of the ECB constitution's primary objective of price stability. Plus the committee of the EU finance and economic ministers is responsible for exchange rate policy, providing that exchange rate policy does not conflict with monetary policy.

Mr. Lafontaine found sympathy from French finance Minister Dominique Strauss-Kahn, who was also keen on managing exchange rates—currency fluctuations. If they had been ambitious enough, their policies might have destroyed EMU in its infancy.

Professor Rudi Dornbush of MIT wrote in the *Wall Street Journal,* "The Trouble with Oskar" (November 25, 1998):

> *"The finance minister can be characterized as neither center left, nor even new left, but, rather, unreconstructed left. He is bright. He is a schemer. And if he gets his way he will shape the future of Europe for the worse. . . . Sometimes it seems that Mr. Lafontaine has spent the past 20 years in some distant gulag. . . . In terms of economic thinking and style, Mr. Lafontaine is to U.S. Federal Reserve Chairman Alan Greenspan and U.S. Treasury Secretary Bob Rubin what Attila the Hun was to western civilization."*

The conflict between Schroder and Lafontaine with central bankers and business continued to build at the close of 1998. Schroder clashed with the Bundesbank and the ECB when he spoke to trade unionists in October:

> *"My request is that all instruments be used to allow the economy to grow. These institutions should understand their responsibility not only for monetary stability but also for reasonably managed economic growth."*[14]

Translation: Price stability should be sacrificed for economic growth—jobs.

Schroder and Lafontaine then went after the EU voting system in an effort to change the tax system in the EU. They wanted the EU to abandon unanimity to decisions on taxation in favor of majority voting on tax matters. That didn't go down well in London, which understood that taxes would rise to German levels, not fall to somebody else's (see Table 10.1).

Lafontaine had a potentially devastating political agenda. Between the alienation of German business and the desire to force EU members to raise taxes and control exchange rate movements, he soon found himself in trouble. Thank goodness. The widest rift occurred with Mr. Schroder on policy.

The policy differences between the two men became more public and ended on Thursday, March 11, 1999, when Lafontaine was forced to resign from government and from the leadership of the SDP, saying he was quitting politics. His replacement, Hans Eichel, was a pro-business Social Democrat.

The German stock market index, the DAX, rose by 5 percent on Friday, March 12, with several Lafontaine-targeted companies seeing their share prices rise by double-digit percentages.

The point of this story is to emphasize the nature of European politicians and their search to protect national interests. If EMU is fragile at this stage, imagine what happens when the next recession hits. The Euro, like any newborn child, needs absolute support, but may not get it, let alone be allowed to mature. The Euro is thrown around like a new toy, which leads to little credibility—at least little political credibility. Investors should continue to be suspicious particularly after domestic currencies are abolished.

Table 10.1: Corporate Tax Rates by International Comparison[15]

Country	Corporate Tax Rate (%)
Germany	43.6-56.7
Japan	51.6
France	41.7
Italy	41.3
Belgium	40.2
USA	40.0
Greece	35.0-40.0
Portugal	39.6
Luxembourg	37.5
Netherlands	35.0
Spain	35.0
Austria	34.0
Denmark	34.0
Ireland	32.0
U.K.	31.0
Sweden	28.0
Finland	28.0

In fact, the Euro has dropped unimpeded against the U.S. dollar since its birth at $1.17 to one Euro to $0.87 per one Euro (as of March 24, 2002), a fall of more than 20 percent in its value against the U.S. dollar. Uncertainty sends prices one way—down. So far, Europe is not attracting enough investors because of uncertainty and its economic and financial unattractiveness.

STABILITY PACT

In an attempt to influence fiscal behavior after the Euro was introduced, the Germans presented a policy proposal called the Stability Pact. Before the Stability Pact is described, however, the reader should know how the U.S. economy deals with regional economic disturbances. The safety valve is a flexible and mobile U.S. labor market, and the federal government provides tax transfers, which inject funds into distressed regions.

There will, of course, be regional economic differences from one country to another in the European Union. Each member state will be moving at varying economic speeds with non-matching business cycles. *The Economist* notes:

> *"A tricky task of setting monetary policy will be the fact that the ECB policies will affect each country differently."*[16]

The peripheral countries such as Italy, Spain, Portugal, and Finland may experience boom/bust cycles in relation to stable economic growth within the core member states. This is precisely the event that faced the ECB during the summer of 2000. J. P. Morgan reported in its weekly "Global Data Watch," (August 25, 2000):

> *"For the first time since EMU began, all of the Euro area economies now have inflation above the ECB ceiling of 2 percent. . . . The growing divergence of*

inflation rates raises the possibility that some economies of the region might be overheating. This concern is reinforced by an analysis of cross-country developments in growth and inflation. This clearly shows that those countries with the fastest pace of growth over the past three years, and the steepest decline in unemployment, have seen the greatest increase in core inflation. The close link between the maturity cycle and inflation developments raises the question whether those economies—Spain, the Netherlands, Finland, Portugal, and Ireland—are overheating"

This is the type of problem, and symptoms of a much greater problem, soon to face the Euro countries as economic and business cycles shift one direction or another—how to keep it all together. Without political union or an ability to control fiscal transfers from one member state to another, the job of the European Central Bank will be much more difficult, if not impossible.

The Stability Pact dealt with terms and conditions of fiscal behavior after the introduction of the Euro on January 1, 1999. Economic convergence at a given point in time—when certain economic statistics merge/converge from different countries at a defined date—is one thing. Eleven countries moving together, ensuring that all the specified economic statistics remain converged as eleven countries move economically together as one, is quite another.

Theo Waigel, Germany's Finance Minister, introduced the Stability Pact in 1995. Using automatic fines to ensure fiscal responsibility, Waigel's proposals included an annual budget deficit target of no more than 1 percent of gross domestic product under normal economic conditions. If the Maastricht Treaty's annual budget deficit target of 3 percent were broken, then an interest-free deposit or fine would be levied. The fine would be the equivalent of 0.25 percent of GDP for every 1 percent of the debt over-run, with no limit. The fine would be forfeited if the annual excess budget deficit was no eliminated within two years. In 1999 terms, if Italy allowed its budget deficit to rise to 6 percent, a devastating fine would be levied equating to $152 for every man, woman, and child.

A European Commission counter-proposal failed to introduce automatic fines. The proposal suggested that the EC would deal with each member state on a case-by-case basis if the annual budget deficit target were breached or if any of the Maastricht Treaty convergence criteria were not met after the introduction of the single currency.

The difficulty with European Monetary Union, particularly after the introduction of the Euro, is not the annual budget deficit but the total debt to gross domestic product ratio.

The total debt to GDP ratio differs dramatically from country to country, and these member states must reduce these debts. But how can they achieve that goal after the introduction of the Euro? There are only two answers. The fist allows each country to maintain autonomy over fiscal policy. The second is through political union, in which a European government in Brussels would have tax-raising powers and an ability to transfer tax revenues from one member state to another. The European government would also have to assume all domestic debts outstanding by all the member states. If this method is adopted, expect outrage from the fiscally prudent member states. The member states with total debt to GDP ratios less than 60 percent get penalized because they will have to repay the outstanding sovereign debts of those countries with ratios in excess of 60 percent, particularly the Belgians and Italians with ratios well above 100 percent.

Member states that have relied on inflation to reduce debt burden will no longer have a domestic central bank to print money. The European Central Bank will control monetary policy and member states' fiscal authorities will not have access to their own central banks to finance debts of any kind (unemployment, health, financial crises, or military conflict).

The quickest way to destroy EMU is to tell German or British taxpayers that they have to service the accumulated debts of the Italians. That won't fly. On top of all this, most countries did not really reduce their annual fiscal deficits in 1997. In 1997, they used one-off measures (selling state assets whose value will never be recovered) to reduce their annual budget deficit downward in an attempt to meet the annual deficit target of the Maastricht Treaty convergence criteria. Table 10.2 shows the impact of the one-off measures in 1997.

Table 10.2: One-Off Fiscal Measures in 1997[17]

Country	Adjusted Balance	One-Off Measures	Real Balance[18]
Germany	(2.7)	0.2	(2.9)
France	(3.0)	0.6	(3.6)
Italy	(2.7)	1.0	(3.7)
Spain	(2.6)	0.1	(2.7)
Netherlands	(1.4)	0.0	(1.4)
Belgium	(2.1)	0.3	(2.4)
Portugal	(2.5)	0.2	(2.7)
Finland	(0.9)	0.6	(1.5)
Ireland	0.9	0.0	0.9

If Italy and Belgium want to meet the total debt to GDP ratio, they must run budget surpluses of 2.5 and 2.7 percent respectively on an annual basis until the year 2007, when they meet the 60 percent debt to GDP level.[19] It's not clear how the politicians will sort through these particular issues, but we know how markets deal with indiscretions. Those member states that stray from market-acceptable behavior will be penalized by having to borrow money at a higher real interest rate than their fellow EU members.

Credit analysis and sovereign yield spreads will be the best way to punish member states that do not demonstrate fiscal prudence. Expect those member states that do not, in the view of the markets, meet the Maastricht Treaty convergence criteria to pay higher real interest rates on their government debt securities than those countries that do meet the criteria.

Unfortunately, the original stability pact agreement in 1995 surrendered to French demands that it be called a "stability and growth pact." The German emphasis on budgetary discipline gave way to France's demand to promote economic growth and create more jobs. In the end, the thrust of the "stability and growth pact" agreed on at the European summit on May 2, 1998, was greatly watered down.

In a further embarrassment for the Stability Pact, European Union finance ministers fudged—an already watered-down version of the stability pact—an agreement on February 12, 2002, as Germany and Portugal approached the top limits of their annual three percent budget deficit target limit. The real issue and confrontation took place between Germany and the European Commission, specifically, Hans Eichel, German finance minister and Pedro Solbes, European economic and monetary affairs commissioner. In essence the agreement forged was a face-saving formula to keep the stability pact alive—albeit just. The *Financial Times* reported (February 13, 2002):

> *"To some cynical chuckles from German journalists . . . ."*

Hans Eichel announced the terms of the EU's unanimous agreement.
The Economist offered it opinion in it 'Leaders' column:

> *"Europe knows its fiscal rules have failed. Instead of fixing them, it fudged."*

One thing we can count on is that politicians will be unable to fool the markets, and if they do not police EMU properly, the markets will do it for them.

MARKET REFORMS

A number of positive aspects will no doubt emerge from EMU. The development of transparent marketplaces for local government debt, similar to the tax-exempt municipal bond market in the United States, will benefit borrowers and savers in Europe. Corporate debt and equity markets will help less creditworthy companies to raise capital. Venture capital will be dramatically more available for lenders and ultimately budding entrepreneurs throughout the European Union. In an Anglo-Saxon system, those who are fiscally prudent will be rewarded, and those who are not will be severely punished by the market.

Competition within the European Union will surely be more intense, a huge benefit for consumers. Ultimately, labor market reforms, allowing people easily to seek employment throughout the European Union, and removing the safety nets required of companies to protect employees, will occur naturally.

Politicians won't solve labor market reforms, and it remains to be seen whether Brussels will stop the market from reforming and liberalizing itself. Businesses will move to those member states that offer the most attractive long-term investment environment, similar to the individual states in the U.S.

Probably global economic Darwinism will be more intense in the European Union than anywhere else in the world. Even the French politicians will be unable to stop the tidal wave of the coming market.

To a large extent, the future of EMU and the Euro will depend on luck, chance. The success or failure in the early years will be determined by the condition of the business cycle in each member state, unemployment rates, and on the condition of the global economy. The future of Corporatist Capitalism remains a mystery, because without market reforms we do not know how EMU can possibly work.

The chicken and egg problem for politicians relates to market reforms and their impact on unemployment rates. The United States and United Kingdom have added millions of new jobs to their respective economies. Unfortunately for the European Union, they begin with double-digit unemployment rates before starting the reformation process. The electorate may not allow present political administrations to survive if unemployment rises substantially. But without market reformation, jobs will be scarce over the longer term. To the chicken and egg problem, market reformation must come first.

A significant disappointment with the EMU process has been the failing of member countries to achieve their deficit and debt goals through reforms, which could have produced durable central government spending reductions. This has been a missed opportunity, and the use of one-off deficit reduction programs is fudge and does not prove there is a commitment for fiscal discipline, let alone fiscal improvement. The fudge factor will come back to haunt those countries that used it to meet the convergence criteria, because the economic pain to achieve the deficit and debt limits will become even more difficult to bear.

Hans Tietmeyer, President of the German Bundesbank, pointed out:

". . . that Maastricht is not merely the extrapolation of an historical trend. Monetary union is a qualitative leap."

He went on to say:

"According to the treaty, no country will have, any longer, the option of trying out another route. And each of the participating countries will, forever, face intra-European competition—without being able to adjust an exchange rate or to alter central bank interest rates to suit its own economic situation."[20]

There will eventually be a confrontation between monetary and fiscal policy. Unemployment rates remain historically high. The positive impetus from the present business cycle will not be enough to create jobs in Europe. Table 10.3 shows recent unemployment percentages in Europe.[21] The interesting conclusion to draw from these statistics, of course, is the fact that they have fallen, but unfortunately the global economy is slowing, and therefore the ability to reduce unemployment rates further will be difficult should they start to rise. The lack of economic and financial reformation is to blame for most of this problem.

Table 10.3: European Unemployment

Country	Unemployed % (early 1999)	Unemployed % (2002)
Austria	4.4	6.9
Belgium	13.3	8.5*
Denmark	7.9	5.1
EMU-11	12.3	8.3
EU-15	10.9	9.0*
Finland	14.5	9.0*
France	12.5	9.0
Germany	11.4	9.8
Greece	9.8	8.9*
Ireland	10.2	4.5*
Italy	12.2	9.1
Luxembourg	3.7	2.7*
Netherlands	5.5	2.6*
Portugal	6.8	4.1*
Spain	20.9	11.3
Sweden	8.0	3.9
United Kingdom	5.6	3.2

*As of 2001. These European countries have merged their numbers into the Euro market.

The United States has a single currency, and there are asymmetric shocks from time to time—recall New England's recession in the mid-1980s when the rest of the country was booming. But Americans move to where the jobs have shifted, even if it means crossing state lines. And the federal government also makes stabilizing resource transfers. According to one 1980s estimate, up to 40 percent of any fall in gross state product is offset by, and lower taxes paid to, the federal government.[22]

Wage flexibility is a major adjustment mechanism in the modern world. Labor markets are reforming and, if Europe is going to compete, that is a priority. Deutsche Bank analysts stress the point that wage policy must be compatible with stability. Moderate pay settlements and structural reforms in the labor and goods markets are necessary if unemployment is to be reduced.[23] Unfortunately, so far the reform process in Europe is not occurring nor are labor reform policies expected to be implemented in the near future.

POLITICAL SHIFTS

Fundamental difficulties for labor and tax reform are high unemployment rates, along with the general election results throughout the EU sweeping center-left parties into power. A leftward shift has occurred in Germany, the backbone for conservative policy in Europe. European society may very well decide that EMU is not worth its costs.

The Stability Pact got sacrificed for the political need to create more jobs. No judgment needs to be passed about that, but investors can expect inflation to rise as fiscal policy expands, a scenario which may overwhelm EMU.

After the German elections in September 1998, 13 of the 15 governments in the EU are left-of-center parties, the first time since 1929 that the three main EU governments—France, Germany, and U.K.—have been left wing, adding to the uncertainty and contradictions about the future of fiscal and monetary policymaking in Europe.

LABORS LAWS

Reforming the individual European countries has been extremely slow and arduous, moving along at a turtle's pace. The reformation of the European Community has been even slower—at a snail's pace. Economic and financial reforms in each member of the European Union and the European Union itself are needed to shrink the size of central government and teach people to become self-sufficient in a variety of areas. These include labor laws to benefit the employer and employees, but allowing employers to fire or reduce their staff numbers, and providing the necessary incentives for the individual to be self-sufficient and more able to move freely between jobs. The United States has proven that jobs are created by small businesses within an economic environment where capital markets and entrepreneurs flourish. The old labor laws of the European continent are based on large industrial complexes, protecting the working class from the brutal employer class, but those days are long gone. Labor laws in Europe are still based on the ideology of centrally managed capitalist systems, where central government knows better about the economic welfare, rather than citizens knowing what is better for themselves. Those days are also long gone. But the European community is not reinventing its labor laws to give people the ability to start companies and employ people under less stringent rules and regulations.

THE PENSION SYSTEM

Reformation of the pension industry is vital, and if not completed soon, will pose a huge liability for future generations, which could quite possibly be our children. National pension systems in Europe are predominately pay-as-you-go schemes, discussed in Chapter 2. As the average age of our global population increases, so too will the liability for caring for pensioners. If pension liabilities are paid out of the annual tax receipts, then, as pointed out in Chapter 2, they will command a greater proportion of central government expenditure. Remember that part of the problem in creating a flexible labor market has to do with reforming the pay-as-you-go pension system into a fully funded and private pension system.

There has been progress toward reforming Germany's pension system, but on the whole very little has been accomplished. And if the pension system in Europe is not dealt with in fairly short order, Table 10.4 (*Financial Times,* November 10, 2000, entitled "Defusing the Demographic Time Bomb") will become a horror story for the next generation of workers—our children.

Table 10.4: Public Pension Expenditures as a Percent of GDP (in 1994 prices)

Country	1995	2020	2040
Austria	8.8	12.1	15.0
Belgium	10.4	10.7	15.0
Denmark	6.8	9.3	11.6
Finland	10.1	15.2	18.0
France	10.6	11.6	14.3
Germany	11.1	12.3	18.4
Italy	13.3	15.3	21.4
The Netherlands	6.0	8.4	12.1
Portugal	5.2	9.6	15.2
Spain	10.0	11.3	16.8
Sweden	11.8	13.9	14.9

TAXES

One of the only bright spots on the economic and financial landscape is the fact that European tax rates are falling. But do not be confused. One of the only reasons that tax rates are falling is the fact that they are falling in many of the Euro member competitors, such as the United States and United Kingdom. They have had no choice but to lower their tax burdens, but it is for the wrong reasons. The Europeans are not reducing their fiscal policies to offset the tax reductions. Without fiscal reform, tax reform is for nothing, and taxes and interest rates in the Euro area will have to rise into the future. The Germans started the process, and needless to say the rest followed. Hardly a surprise.

As the U.S. budget starts to balance, I continually ask clients in European and emerging market countries to think where taxes are going in the U.S., and where they are going in their own country. Then I ask in which country they want to set up their new company or go to work in. Hands down everyone from South Africa to Israel, Western and Eastern Europe to Latin America, all want to come to America. Is that a surprise? As corporate and individual tax rates fall in the United States, the Europeans must keep pace, but they are not. Table 10.5 (J. P. Morgan, September 29, 2000) shows the present and recent past tax rates for corporations and individuals. They do not compare well with U.S. tax rates.

Table 10.5: Evolution of Statutory Tax Rates, 1985-2001

Corporate

	1985	1994	1998	2000	2001
Germany	61.7	54.9	56.7	51.6	25.0
France	50.0	33.3	41.7	36.7	33.3
Denmark	50.0	34.0	34.0	32.0	30.0
Sweden	52.0	28.0	28.0	28.0	28.0
Belgium	45.0	39.0	40.2	39.0	35.0
The Netherlands	48.0	35.0	35.0	35.0	35.0
Spain	N/A	35.0	35.0	35.0	35.0
Italy	41.0	53.2	41.25	41.25	40.25
U.K.	40.0	33.0	31.0	30.0	30.0

Individual

	1985	1994	1998	2000	2001
Germany	56.0	53.0	53.0	51.0	48.5
France	65.0	56.8	54.0	54.0	53.3
Denmark	73.2	68.7	58.7	59.7	59.7
Sweden	54.0	52.0	59.7	56.0	56.0
Belgium	72.0	55.0	55.0	55.0	52.5
The Netherlands	72.0	60.0	60.0	60.0	52.0
Spain	66.0	53.0	56.0	48.0	48.0
Italy	62.0	51.0	46.2	46.2	46.2
U.K.	60.0	40.0	40.0	40.0	40.0

THE CAPITAL MARKETS

Another aspect, which requires reform yesterday, is the integration of Europe's capital markets. Proposing economic reform is needed, but without reform of the financial sector, any economic reform would be limited. For example, if pension funds were able to operate across borders, Ford Motor calculates that it could save nearly $40 million per annum if their employees participated in a unified corporate pension scheme throughout Europe. European financial institutions do not offer the same facilities and services Europe-wide as they might in one country or another. The integration and adoption of a single capital market throughout the Euro area would yield greater liquidity, perhaps greater returns, and certainly lower borrowing costs.

Many domestic idiosyncrasies remain in place, and business suffers—especially cross-border business. The need for legal harmonization, accounting harmonization, corporate law, the rules of conduct such as bankruptcy law and procedures is long overdue; and a long way from being considered, let alone implemented. Without it, economic reform is really futile.

Without economic and financial reforms, the long-term viability and credibility of the Euro is held hostage to short-term-ism.

The word *credibility* in relation to the Euro confuses market commentators. Credibility of a currency does not predicate itself on the basis of short-term strength and weakness. It relies on long-term currency strength. But over the short term, the Euro will be a hostage of the business cycle at the time of its introduction.

The Euro may become a major reserve currency, but the long-term viability and credibility will depend on the monetary and fiscal policymakers.

Remember, a currency price is a means to an end. Euro-dominated assets have to offer value among its member states and relative to global assets denominated in U.S. dollars or Japanese yen.

Short-term movements of the Euro should not matter, because the price can be hedged inexpensively relative to U.S. dollars. Of more concern are the long-term movement and the uncertainty of the Euro.

Said *Euromoney* magazine (August 2000):

> *"Even a whiff of a country's likely exit from eurozone membership could cause a run on that country's banks and become a self-fulfilling prophecy. This is the logical conclusion that few within the eurozone, or even outside it, dare to rehearse. It could destroy the euroland banking system."*

My advice is, start rehearsing, folks. The euroland economy is slowing the patterns in business cycles, which are very different and moving in very different directions, and since we know about politicians, particularly European politicians, the risk of countries such as Italy pulling out of the Euro becomes a probable reality.

The president of the European Union and ex-Prime Minister of Italy has already stated:

> *"Losing one percentage point of competitiveness per year, if it goes on in time for a number of years, would become a condemnation for Italy and it would be difficult for us to stay in the single currency."*

There are interesting assumptions to draw from this comment. First, Mr. Prodi has already, in his own mind, found it acceptable for Italy to pull out of the Euro. Second, Mr. Prodi made this comment as he was being confirmed as European Commission President. His loyalties are with Italy.

The International Monetary Fund recently produced an interesting economic simulation of the two directions the EC can take their economy.[24] The IMF used a version of their multi-currency econometric model (MULTIMOD) in the assessment, creating two predictions of EMU's effect on Europe's economy.

In the IMF's first scenario (see Table 10.6), EMU is assumed to serve as a catalyst for fiscal and restructuring policies. Budget consolidation goes beyond expectations with additional reducion of government expenditure equivalent to 2 percent of GDP on the fiscal policy side. On structural reforms, the product market liberalization adds 0.5 percent in total factory productivity, accompanied with labor market reforms, which reduces the natural rate of unemployment[25] by 2 percent.

Table 10.6: First Scenario

EMU members	2000	2001	2002	2003	2010
Real GDP	0.3	0.9	1.0	1.1	2.9
GDP deflator	-0.3	-0.7	-1.1	-1.4	-1.9
Long-term real interest rate	0.1	-0.1	-0.3	-0.4	—
Unemployment rate	-0.2	-0.4	-0.6	-0.8	-2.0
General gov. balance (GNP %)	0.4	0.9	1.5	2.1	0.8
General gov. debt (GNP %)	-0.4	-1.4	-2.7	-4.5	-12.6
Trade balance (U.S. billions)	-3.5	13.8	22.8	31.6	27.9

The second scenario, called "reform fatigue," offers a picture of what may happen if real wage flexibility remains low with the natural unemployment rate increasing. Although member states are constrained by the stability and growth pact, national governments will attempt to offset the effects of rising unemployment and falling factory output with additional fiscal spending (see Table 10.7).

Table10.7: Second Scenario

EMU members	2000	2001	2002	2003	2010
Real GDP	0.1	-0.3	-0.6	-0.9	-2.5
GDP deflator	0.1	0.3	0.6	0.9	2.3
Long-term real interest rate	0.2	0.3	0.4	0.5	0.5
Unemployment rate	0.2	0.4	0.7	0.9	2.0
General gov. balance (GNP%)	-0.2	-0.5	-0.7	-0.9	-1.3
General gov. debt (GNP%)	0.1	0.7	1.4	2.3	9.8
Trade balance (U.S. billions)	-1.7	22.1	31.7	38.8	67.3

The two scenarios outline dramatic pictures for the European economy under EMU. The differences of each policy direction are clear. Without reform, the European member states that found EMU will suffer tremendously if new policy initiatives to liberalize their markets are not undertaken. The welfare of hundreds of millions of lives is at stake, and the politicians must rise above their ideologies. Policymakers in Europe must be prepared to give up today for a bitter tomorrow.

MEMBER COUNTRY SUPPORT

The final word, as always in democratic societies, will be public opinion. In 1992 the electorate was given the opportunity to express its opinion for EMU by voting in a referendum on the Maastricht Treaty, first in Denmark and later that year in France. On June 2, the Danes rejected the Maastricht Treaty by a 50.7 percent majority. On September 20, the French voted in favor of the treaty by 51.1 percent.

Denmark has an opt-out clause to EMU and could therefore adopt its own policies necessary to help its economic circumstances. At the time of the referendum vote, the Danish unemployment rate was 10.5 percent, but it fell below 8 percent by the time EMU commenced in 1999, because the Danes could ignore EMU structures.

France, on the other hand, had an unemployment rate of 10.4 percent in 1992, and it went higher, with no hope in sight. The French people voted out the Juppe government on June 1, 1997, electing Socialist Lionel Jospin as Prime Minister.

In Germany, the unemployment rate in 1992 stood at 8.5 percent and rising. No wonder a majority of Germans are opposed to EMU. Fifty-eight percent of those questioned in a Handelsblatt Survey in January 1998 were against monetary union.[26] The Germans never put the single currency to a formal vote.

In early February 1998, more than 150 economics professors in Germany called for an "orderly postponement."[27]

Professor Hurst Siebert of the Kiel Institute of World Economics reported an increase in European unemployment is inevitable under the planned single currency unless steps are taken to free labor markets. The years of obsession with price stability (if it is an obsession, it is a good one) may come to an end. A more flexible German attitude, especially over a trade-off between inflation and employment, could narrow the political gulf between France and Germany over the conduct of monetary and fiscal policy under EMU.[28]

With immigration at record levels throughout the European Union, coupled with proposed future EU expansion to include Poland, Czech Republic, Hungary, Slovenia, and Estonia, the European Commission and European Central Bank will have their hands full. And immigration and EU expansion will make the employment pool rich pickings. The black market economy will spread without formal political labor reforms and the best and brightest will move on to new markets. The expanded EU will be a huge trading power and a marketplace with more than 500 million people—a powerful force. But so was the Soviet Union until the money ran out.

The crux of the problem is the individual countries themselves and the desire of citizens to remain nationals and preserve their identities. Everything else is secondary, particularly the merits of having a single currency, which is questionable in itself. Therefore, the idea of sacrificing one's national identity for a single currency and a European bureaucracy in Brussels is a no-brainer to voters in Denmark, the United Kingdom, and Switzerland—an emphatic *no* to the Euro.

On September 28, 2000, Danish voters delivered an emphatic no to joining the single currency, with 53.1 percent of the vote. On the day after the vote, the *Financial Times* editorial reported:

"The Danish people's decisive NO to the euro is bad news for the EU."

However, the Danes felt that they re-established their nationhood and did not want to be pushed around by Europe. The Danish no vote added another risk to the single currency, the concept of a two-track integration. The *Financial Times* (September 30, 2000) reported that the German foreign minister, Joschka Fischer, declared that the Danish vote provided incentive for Germany and France to move ahead with integration, and the French finance minister, Laurent Fabius, suggested a "two-speed Europe."

In addition to the Danes, the Swiss people voted on March 4, 2001, against joining the European Union, an overwhelming 76.7 percent saying no! The United Kingdom is planning a referendum on joining the euro, but as of today it is still in the planning stage. However, public opinion polls indicate voters in the U.K. will say no as well. These individual countries in themselves do not impact the development of the euro, but all three as a whole send a very strong signal to the future of the euro. The people of Europe are questioning the merits of the survival of the euro.

ENLARGEMENT

During the last six months of 2000, the French assumed the presidency of the European Union, culminating in the European summit in Nice starting December 7, 2000. The meeting in Nice was to discuss policy for enlarging the European Union and for determining the members for the euro. France (not surprisingly, and symptomatic of the problems leading to further European integration, let alone the survival of the euro) wore its European presidential hat in an effort to bully its EU partners into adopting policies in French national interests. Of course, as the French insisted on their national interests, the rest of the EU weighed in to protect *their* individual interests—self-perpetuating the problems. The French shot themselves in the foot. The *Financial Times* reported (December 29, 2000) that the French presidency:

> *". . . could mark a turning point in EU affairs after which France will no longer be able to assume power and influence greater than its status"* [as a simple member of the EU].

The *Financial Times* also said:

> *"Rarely has a European Union presidency been so keenly awaited as that of Sweden."*

The Swedish presidency will be focused on enlargement, the environment, and employment, although EU members differ dramatically over the reform plans to accomplish enlargement, the environment, and employment.

No doubt, EU enlargement proposes the greatest fundamental difficulties for EU leaders. And enlargement will start to evolve before economic and financial reforms have been decided, let alone implemented. The deal in Nice determined the structure of the EU prior to enlargement. It was a battle between the big countries of the EU against the small ones. The key points of the Treaty of Nice are as follows (*Financial Times,* December 12, 2000):

- *More majority voting.*
  More decisions will be taken by majority voting. Unanimous voting is retained in areas such as taxation, social security, and immigration.

- *Reweighting of votes.*
  Number of votes allocated to each nation reweighted in favor of larger nations. Threshold required to win majority votes raised.

- *European commission trimmed.*
  Big nations lose their second commissioner in 2005.

- *Closer cooperation.*
  Some countries will be able to move ahead with closer integration faster than the rest.

EU enlargement will add as many as 13 countries to the EU, which will raise the total national membership to 28. The front-runners for membership are Cyprus, Estonia, Poland, The Czech Republic, and Slovenia. The additional applications include Bulgaria, Hungary, Latvia, Lithuania, Romania, Malta, and Turkey. Enlargement seems to make sense in terms of bringing Eastern and Central European countries into the community to provide a trading bloc of over 500 million people. It would be a tremendous opportunity for the new countries, but it will also offer many of the present member's very difficult economic and financial competition. I suspect the Eastern and Central European countries will win market share handsomely.

Enlargement is being seen in EU official circles as the opportunity to put the EU right. I do not think so. If the EU and euro issues are not put right very soon, enlargement will add to the chaos, because the younger, hungry, and entrepreneurial Eastern and Central European countries will cause more displacement, rather than greater European harmonization.

European Union enlargement may include up to 10 countries according to a European Commission report:

- Estonia.

- Latvia.

- Lithuania.

- Poland.

- Czech Republic.

- Slovakia.

- Slovenia.

- Hungary.

- Cyprus.

- Malta.

However, the EU concluded negotiation with 10 new members allowing them to join on May 1, 2004, in time for the European elections.

One of the key and sensitive issues with the European Union is money; financing enlargement. The financial issues are a double-edged sword. For the countries who are net contributors to the EU budget and those countries who the net recipients of the EU budget. Needless to say, the net contributors do not want to contribute any more money than they are at present for the 10 new members and the net recipients do not want their money cut off in favor of the 10 new member nations. The net contributors are Germany, The Netherlands, United Kingdom, Sweden, and Finland who provide the bulk of the annual

$80 billion for the EU budget. This is distributed to countries such as Ireland, Greece, Spain, Portugal, and Italy.

I discussed earlier that the time would come for a country such as Portugal, who receives an annual payment of nearly 3 percent of their GDP from the EU, to have to rustle up for themselves as these funds are now provided to those countries who are joining the EU. The strain is intensified when countries such as Poland, the largest candidate country, with 27 percent of the total labor force living on self-subsistent farms, wants money from the EU immediately so they can start catching up economically with the rest of the EU. This is going to be a very interesting process and as discussed a few paragraphs earlier, EMU countries such as Germany and Portugal are finding times difficult to maintain their annual budget deficit target ceiling, at a time when the economic slowdown has been fairly mild. So what is going to happen if Germany must increase it contributions, the Portuguese lose their contributions and the new EU members overwhelm the economy of the present European Union. The last difficult issue outstanding from European budget negotiations was resolved in late October 2002. The EU agreed on the Common Agriculture Policy (CAP) budget measures and direct aid in the EU-25 during the years from 2007 to 2013. CAP payments will be frozen at 2006 levels, with a 1 percent annual inflation adjustment. In addition to these issues regarding EU enlargement, is the process of creating a European constitution in preparation with enlargement.

EU CONSTITUTION

An EU constitutional convention started on February 28, 2002 in the European Parliament building in Brussels, Belgium. They will meet about 20 times per year and the convention will consider the future of Europe that will produce a report by 2003 which will either offer options or recommendations for the necessary reforms required as the EU enters enlargement in 2004. The chairman of the convention is the 76 year-old ex-President of France, Valery Giscard d'Estaing, with the vice-chairmen coming from Italy, Guillo Amato, and Belgium, Jean-Luc Dehaene. In addition, there will be 15 representatives of member state governments, 30 members of EU national Parliaments, 16 members of the European Parliament, 2 representatives from the European Union, along with 30 representatives of 13 accession countries, 1 from each government and 2 national parliament members, who have a voice in the proceedings but cannot block any consensus decisions made by the presiding members states of the EU.

The constitutional convention will be focusing on several areas in an attempt to start framing a constitution for the European Union. One of the fundamental issues is the broad division between the federalists and anti-federalists. The same old issues that every nation-state faces—big central government versus states rights and the rights of the individual. The federalists want big erosion in the power of individual states, which includes the way in which individual countries handle their own domestic issues as well as the way national parliaments will behave, particularly in the U.K. where a two-chamber system exists. The convention will also deal with human rights by creating a charter of rights, which will add the present EU rights. The other contentious issues include minority voting, the direct election of a European President, direct taxation along with foreign policy and judicial affairs. The new European constitution will begin the formal process of fiscal and political unity in conjunction with European Monetary Union. If the European Union's past decisions and literal following of present rules surrounding EMU are any indication, the constitutional convention will be fudged and doctored to ensure that EU enlargement and EMU will continued to be questioned by the market players—investors into the EU cannot be fooled.

CONCLUSION

The financial demands on those EU members who must fund EU enlargement and those countries who want to enter the EU will be financially burdened. The financial burdens will be much greater than anticipated in 2003 and forecasted for 2004. In addition, without electoral legitimacy by the population of the EU members, EU leaders and its parliament will not command the respect and legitimacy required for any central government organization.

The debate for the future of the EU and EMU rests to a large extent on the way each capitalist system operates, particularly the difference between Germany, centralist capitalism, and the United Kingdom, market-driven capitalist system. The way unemployment is handled, the corporate takeover rules and regulations are very different between the two differing capitalist systems. The way capital is filtered through the economic systems will also have a huge impact on how the European constitution is negotiated and ultimately implemented. I believe that most European countries must change their economic models in an attempt to compete with the United States.

The whole crux of this book is about the global financial economic convergence that is taking place throughout the world as institutional investment capital seeks the best home for returns on investment. As the United States continues to enjoy productivity growth and increasing standards of living with a free-market capitalist system, which continues to show resilience and investment opportunities, the EU members must not ignore the U.S. whilst considering their future. In a *Financial Times* editorial "The Best US Export," (January 26, 2002) stated:

"Creative destruction is alive and well in the US . . . ."

Coming right after the Enron collapse that the U.S. government and the capital markets allowed one of its largest companies to go bankrupt without any aid from the government or the capital markets. The *Financial Times* adds that in Enron's aftermath it is still

". . . impossible to think of a European Amazon, or for that matter, large bankruptcies or corporate restructuring in Europe that has occurred without serious stink."

The editorial continues that:

"This difference has allowed the US to be more successful over time: not in all respects, but in the most important measures of economic performance and prosperity."

Time will be the final judge of EU enlargement, the new constitution, and EMU. The debate will no doubt be lively with the future of the EU and EMU at stake. The real investment potential is in those countries that join the EU in 2004. The risk will be the countries along the southern half of the European continent who must forego their EU financial support in favor of those joining the EU.

ENDNOTES

[1] "EMU: A User's Guide." J. P. Morgan, October 17, 1997, page 22.

[2] Ibid.

[3] Kaletsky, A. "Kohl Loses Battle Over Euro." *London Times,* November 19, 1996.

[4] Graham, R. "Masters of the Grand Gesture." *Financial Times,* November 6, 1997.

[5] Ibid.

[6] Ibid.

[7] "An Honest Banker." *The European,* February 23-March 1, 2000.

[8] Ibid.

[9] "Chirac Laughs off Suggestions of Farce." *Financial Times,* May 4, 1998.

[10] "EU Deal Puts Single Currency to Test." *Financial Times,* May 4, 1998.

[11] "Duisenberg 'Will Not Quit' Mid-Term as ECB President." *Financial Times,* December 31, 1998.

[12] *ECB Monthly Bulletin,* November 2000.

[13] "Germany's Agenda." *Financial Times,* December 7, 1998.

[14] "Schroder Clashes with Bundesbank over Growth." *Financial Times,* November 2, 1998.

[15] "Lafontaine Fights a Rearguard Action to Defend Tax Ambitions." *Financial Times,* March 3, 1999.

[16] "Can One Size Fit All." *The Economist,* March 28, 1998.

[17] "Global Data Watch." J. P. Morgan, March 27, 1998, page 3.

[18] Budget positions excluding the one-off measures.

[19] "Global Data Watch." J. P. Morgan, March 27, 1998, page 3.

[20] Tietmeyer, H. "Der Euro—Ein Entnationalisiertes Geld." *Die Zeit,* December 12, 1997, EMU Watch, Number 48, Deutsche Bank Research, March 17, 1998, page 6.

[21] Ibid.

[22] "The Merits of One Money." *The Economist,* October 24, 1998.

[23] Ibid., page 1.

[24] "EMU and the World Economy." *World Economic Outlook,* October 1997, Chapter III, page 75. Washington, D.C.: International Monetary Fund.

[25] The natural rate of unemployment is the rate at which pressures on wages are in balance, tending to neither increase nor decrease the rate of inflation.

[26] EMU Watch, Number 48, Deutsche Bank Research, March17, 1998, page 4, Handelsblatt, February 13, 1998.

[27] "German Economics Professors in Call to Postpone EMU." *Financial Times,* February 9, 1998, page 1.

[28] Munchau, W. "Could Germany Soften." *Financial Times,* March 30, 1998.

Chapter 11
DEBT CRISES

INTRODUCTION

Currency crises are economic and financial equivalents to a tornado. A debt crisis more resembles a hurricane. A sovereign debt crisis occurs when countries cannot make their interest and principal repayments.

A major cause of these difficulties is borrowers pyramiding debt on top of itself to hold off default, like an individual borrowing on one credit card to pay off another—a destructive course. At other times, borrowed money is based on unrealistic asset valuations (i.e., when a property owner values his holdings at far more than their actual worth, and the lender accepts the valuation). Once the rug is pulled from under those valuations, the pyramid comes crashing down under its own weight.

The way countries solve debt crises depends on their type of capitalist system, whether corporate or Anglo-Saxon. A common denominator between the two is for authorities to deny it is happening. They attempt to keep investor confidence high and maintain the reputation of the domestic banking system. In short, they tell people what they want to hear. But after that, *solving* the debt crisis is another matter, which differentiates the two capitalist systems.

Debt crises are very different from currency crises, although a currency crisis can lead to a debt crisis with similar economic and financial problems. Debt crises are more severe in terms of economic and financial damage and the amount of time it takes to repair the damage.

Debt crises are more difficult to identify. Investors must be aware of the valuation of a banking institution's loan portfolio or assets—this falls into the category of transparency and credibility. Are we aware of a bank's portfolio value and, if so, do we believe what it is telling us? That's the problem in anticipating debt crises in emerging, developing, and industrial markets. The end game of debt crisis is government intervention, because taxpayer money is the last resort for any sovereign debt crisis.

THE BANKING SYSTEM

A banking crisis is not the failure of a single banking institution, but when large portions of deposits in a national banking system are at risk. Quite naturally, once a business cycle peaks and starts to head downward, the banking system, along with credit insurance companies, are the first to see and feel the effects of an impending economic downturn, and therefore a risk to loan portfolios.

If the banks have lent prudently, their losses will rise but remain manageable. However, if they have not lent wisely, a bank will have to write off large proportions of its loan portfolio, which causes the bank to repair its balance sheet before it can start to lend money again. Thus, the economy takes a longer time to recover.

To reduce the amount of time for the economy to recover, so banks can start to lend money sooner, a public injection of taxpayer money helps ease the credit shortage from banks' writing off bad loans.

However, the government may decide to intervene in the markets in a staged way, because monetary policy can also be used to ease a debt or banking crisis in its initial stages. The monetary policymakers can decide to lower interest rates, and also ease reserve restrictions to allow banks to increase their credit lines. The risk for public policy is inflation, reducing taxpayer standards of living.

Government intervention can also take the form of changing banking regulations, such as reporting requirements, capital requirements, a better mechanism for calculating, measuring and reporting risk, and the way in which the industry operates domestically and uses international markets.

In addition, a government might allow foreign banks—previously excluded from doing business in the country—to step in and purchase the ailing lending institution.

An IMF study on systemic bank restructuring in April 1998, found that:

". . . the resumption of bank lending and a return to profitability require prompt corrective action and a comprehensive approach. Policymakers must address the immediate problems of weak and insolvent banks; shortcomings in accounting, legal, and regulatory frameworks; lax supervision and compliance. During restructuring, the central bank must also stand ready to provide liquidity support to viable banks. The central bank should not, however, provide long-term financing to banks, nor should it be involved in commercial banking activities—this leads to increased costs and creates conflicts with the central bank's monetary policy objectives." [1]

Since the Latin American debt crisis in the 1980s, debate has been building as who is financially responsible for a banking crisis caused within and by the private sector. Should public monies be used to bail them out, or should banks themselves and their shareholders finance the bail out?

Ultimately, a bank and its banking system must start to take responsibility for its behavior and losses. The taxpayer cannot be expected to finance a bail out when something goes wrong or a bank's management behaves badly.

This includes the global system as well, where the IMF has suddenly become the lender of last resort to every debt crisis around the world. The money has to come from somewhere when a bank's balance sheet falls into disrepair, and it is too often the taxpayer who picks up the tab. When countries such as Russia refuse or default on interest and principal repayments on loans made by the IMF, the Russians are in fact defaulting on repayments to American, Japanese, and German taxpayers who gave the money to the IMF.

If our tax money is going to be used to bail out countries which have gotten themselves into trouble, it is reasonable to expect proper banking reforms to ensure that the system returns to health as quickly as possible, and to prevent future banking system weaknesses.

Over the past 10 years, since their debt crises, the Latin American countries have undergone a huge transformation for the better. *Forbes* magazine reported on June 1, 1998:

> *"In a little over 10 years, Latin America has gone from isolation, state owner-ship and military government to trade liberalization, privatization and democra-cy; from recession, hyperinflation, tumbling wages and capital flight to GDP growth of 5.2 percent in 1997, regional budget deficits averaging 1.9 percent (and estimated at 1.8 percent for 1998) and inflation down to an OECD-like 3.8 percent. And in 1997, foreign direct investment in the region was $50 billion."*

And the economic environment in Latin America has continued to improve, which shows that if countries take the right corrective action, they'll find their way out of the economic wilderness and become important players in the global economy, creating an educated, busy-as-a-bee middle class, the *sine qua non* of a successful capitalist society.

What did the Latin American countries do right? They robustly attacked inflation (the cruelest enemy of wealth creation and standards of living), introduced policies (most important, bringing the federal budget under control) that attracted foreign and domestic investment (reversing capital flight), and passed effective regulatory legislation for the banking industry.

But we all can make mistakes. The problems arise when we keep repeating them. Nations need to develop a transparent, credible, standardized banking system if they want the global financial system to work.

LESSONS FROM THE PAST

Resolving a debt crisis or banking crisis is not an easy job. It does not happen overnight. Table 11.1 lists the more recent bank bailouts and cost to the economy in terms of percentage of gross domestic product:

Table 11.1: Cost of Recent Bank Bailouts (% GDP)[2]

Country	Date	Cost (%)
Argentina	1980-82	54
Chile	1981-83	42
Uruguay	1981-81	32
Israel	1977-84	30
Spain	1977-85	17
Bulgaria	1990s	14
Mexico	1995	13
Japan	1990s	12 *
Hungary	1991-95	10
Finland	1991-93	8
Sweden	1991	7
Malaysia	1985-88	5
Norway	1987-89	4
United States	1984-91	3

*The Japanese banking crisis, which started in the 1990s continues until today.

UNITED STATES

The one closest to our hearts was the savings and loan debt crisis in the United States in the 1980s. American authorities procrastinated for years as savings and loan institutions throughout the country struggled—property prices fell and outright fraud proliferated. Skullduggery—now-you-see-'em, now-you-don't scams. Even outright theft spread rapidly, ultimately sending many of the operators to prison. They had the chutzpah of a Jesse James, but stole from the *inside.*

Government authorities hoped that the depressed real estate prices would bounce back, allowing the problem to resolve itself, demonstrating that even Anglo-Saxon capitalism can be guilty of "wishful thinking" to resolve a debt crisis.

However, as the 1980s ended, the U.S. government was compelled to do something.

In the summer of 1989, Congress created the Resolution Trust Corporation (RTC) that became responsible for all the repossessed office buildings, shopping centers and malls, and houses financed by savings and loan institutions. The basic thinking and the way to solve the S&L crisis were to take a quick and painful hit within a short time frame. The federal government closed 747 savings and loan institutions, many with numerous branches, a staggering number, with assets of $455 billion. Once the assets were sold off, the total bill for the U.S. taxpayer was around $155 billion. The lesson learned: Take your medicine, the sooner the better.

Dilly-dallying on the S&L crisis made the problem worse, but decisive measures arrived on time, and now the episode has been relegated to financial history. The RTC ceased operations in 1995. What must be asked now is, what did we learn from the S&L experience?

From the perspective of the Japanese, not much.

JAPAN

Japan is a classic case study for banking and debt crises—more along the lines of what not to do rather than a successful formula for solving the problem. The Japanese story of success and failure will be studied for years to come.

People had stood in awe of Japanese achievement, wondering what they did that Americans did not. Japan was able to constantly refashion, to reinvent itself, and to create and gain market share resulting in phenomenal rates of economic growth from post-World War II until the 1980s.

At the heart of the debate about how Japan must solve its present debt crisis is its philosophy of controlled capitalism, corporate capitalism. A recent *Foreign Affairs* article by Michael Porter and Hirotaka Takeuchi summarized the Japanese model:

> *"The underlying rationale for the Japanese government's activist role is that no corporation can have the proper perspective and information to guide the economy. Some industries should be targeted because their growth prospects and opportunities to support a higher standard of living are inherently better than others are; other industries should be sheltered to gain scale to compete internationally. Intervention in general avoids the wasteful and destructive aspects of competition and allows a country to conserve its resources. At the center of this thinking lies an export-led growth policy promoted by the central*

government and guided by a stable bureaucracy, with government-sponsored cooperative research and development, lax antitrust policies, officially sanctioned cartels, subsidized activities, and intervention in declining industries. Restrictions on trade and foreign investment, which have been reduced only grudgingly, also fit this view, since they allow Japanese companies to gain strength at home in order to penetrate markets abroad."[3]

The article continues:

"The model of Japanese corporate success centers on the notion that a company can achieve both high quality and low cost by employing—and continuously improving—fundamentally better managerial practices. The idea is that companies compete by relentlessly staying at the frontier of best practice. This model is not an abstract theory but stems from extraordinary advances made by the Japanese companies after the introduction of now well-known managerial practices, such as total quality management (TQM), lean production, and close supplier relationships."[4]

Japan was the envy of the world. The Asian continent adapted Japanese principles as their model and for their own benefit, creating the environment for the Asian economic miracle.

What happened? Why is Japan in so much economic trouble?

The economic difficulties in Japan have to do with its fundamental model—government intervention rather than allowing market forces to prevail. The Japanese system today is a product of post-World War II when there was a need for government authorities to promote manufacturing companies, large industrial companies, and to focus efforts on helping exports while inducing domestic consumers to save their money.

From 1989 to 1990, when the Nikkei Dow stock index rose to 39,000, the Japanese economy was bubbling at the top of its economic cycle.

A dramatic fall in Japan's real interest rates occurred in 1988. The real interest rates were moving in an opposite direction from the United States and German markets. They were falling as U.S. and German rates were rising, making them unattractive in Japan. This caused greater risks for foreign investors and investors stayed well clear of Japanese Government bonds (JGB).

During the bubble economy period in Japan, government authorities remained committed to their export-led economic growth drive, while protecting the domestic economy, and squeezing the domestic consumer by raising taxes rather than listening to warnings from the markets.

A reason for the economic, financial, and property bubble was cheap money, low real interest rates. Domestic projects do not have to yield a high real rate of return because the real and nominal cost is fractional. Japanese companies, called Keiretsu, are interrelated companies in all areas of industry owned by banking conglomerates, which provided the cheap money.

Corporate capitalism created the huge conglomerates, which were owned by banks, providing the necessary finance for their subsidiaries at low nominal and real interest rates, an incestuous relationship, rather than the system used by the Anglo-Saxon model, which employs open market means for raising capital, such as stock flotation and bond issues.

The Keiretsu system, based on the prewar Zaibatsu system, was powerful industrial conglomerates. In this regard, the Japanese system is very similar to the German "Rhineland" system discussed in an earlier chapter. When the price for money (the cost of borrowing) became too cheap, borrowers in Japan settled for poor projects offering low rates of return, rather than seeking more attractive opportunities in the global marketplace. The bubble had to burst when ridiculously low interest rates created a situation similar to the tulip price nose-dive in 1637.

The banking crisis occurred for three reasons (1) bad loans, (2) the faulty process of loan-loss recognition and disposal of bad loans, and (3) the exposure of banking institutions' capital base to market risks.

Banks in Japan invest a portion of their regulatory capital in the stock market. As the value of the stock market falls, so too does the value of a bank's regulatory capital base. When the Nikkei Dow plunged from 39,000 in January 1990 to 14,000 in August 1992, the value of bank capital invested in stocks fell with it.

The debt and banking crisis arose when banks lent cheap money to high-risk property development projects. Citizens believed the federal government would never allow a bank in Japan to fail. Therefore, depositors did not care to whom the bank lent.

They lent on risky property deals, without a care in the world. Keen observers were floored, shocked by the scale and size of the speculative bubble, along with the poor lending practices of the Japanese.

As with many speculative bubbles and subsequent economic and financial crises, the true problems did not surface until interest rates started to rise in 1990. *Moody's Investor Services* reported that commercial real estate loans

> *". . . were booked with very little regard as to how they would be repaid, other than reliance upon the belief that (1) they were collateralized and (2) that Japanese commercial real estate could only appreciate in value."*[5]

Those loans were made on what proved to be three fallacies (1) that the loans were, in fact, collateralized in a practical sense, (2) that such collateral would retain its value, and (3) that, because such collateralized loans were virtually risk free, there was no need for any relationship to exist between the amount of the bank's commercial real estate loans and its capital. Instead of having commercial real estate concentration limits, many banks had commercial real estate loan growth targets. Bankers, in their rush to loan money, more often resembled Old West patent medicine hustlers than the sober, serious pillars-of- the-community-type men of popular conception.

The Bank of Japan raised interest rates in March 1990 by lifting the Official Discount Rate (ODR)—what the Central Bank charges other Japanese banks for money. When rates rose by a full one percentage point from 4.5 percent to 5.5 percent, the stock market fell like a ton of bricks.

The problems with the Japanese economy that led to a prolonged debt and banking crisis were based on the "old" government policies of interventionist or controlled capitalism. The Japanese economy needed to be restructured and brought into the next millenium. Reforms were required on a scale of President Reagan's and Prime Minister Thatcher's supply side policies of the 1980s. Instead of tax reform, developing smaller service companies, reducing manufacturing overcapacity, promoting general structural reform between the public and private sector, the Japanese attempted to stimulate consumer demand through classic and outdated Keynesian fiscal policy—so successful post-World War II—by injecting huge public spending packages into the economy.

The Japanese attempt to stimulate and control the economy from a centralized capitalist system failed, and caused growth to spiral downward.

A *Wall Street Journal* article by Michael Porter (March 21, 2001), "Japan: What Went Wrong," points out that:

> *"The reality is that Japan's activist government policies explain Japan's failures much better than its successes. Government had a surprisingly small role in many of Japan's most impressive export successes, such as cars, robotics, cameras and video games. It was in uncompetitive sectors, such as chemicals, aircraft, software and financial services, that there was extensive government regulation and subsidies, legal cartels, government-sponsored collaborative activity and sustained protection."*

Porter concludes that Japan's past of

> *". . . government intervention and protection not only made the cost of living for Japanese consumers extremely high, but drove up the cost of doing business for Japanese companies. Policy-makers thought they could create an efficient export sector while at the same time protecting and subsidizing domestic industries."*

The Japanese government thought wrong.

The really interesting and educational aspect of the Japanese banking crisis involved the classic liquidity trap created in its financial system. A liquidity trap occurs when monetary policy becomes ineffective because interest rates cannot go any lower than 0 percent. Keynes described it as a situation when the nominal interest rate falls to zero, and investors prefer to hold on to cash rather than interest-bearing assets—which implies that the amount of loanable funds falls to zero.

A liquidity trap is one of those good news/bad news situations. The good news is that interest rates and real interest rates are very low and make borrowing money financially attractive. The bad news is that banks are not going to lend money because they do not have any to lend.

As the Nikkei Dow stock index approached 14,000, in an effort to maintain their policy of "riding out the recession," the Ministry of Finance announced that Japanese domestic banks could value their equity holdings at book cost value rather than at prevailing market value for purposes of reporting their regulatory capital for the calendar quarter ending September 1992.

Now there's an original idea—doctor the books! And since property prices were in free-fall, with a majority of banks lending to commercial real estate, the government also announced an enormous yen 10,700 billion ($89 billion) fiscal spending program through public construction projects and government purchases of land.

Another brilliant idea—build more!

Would this solve the banking crisis? Absolutely not!

The problem was prolonged and, as we will soon see, these policies worsened Japan's economic future for many years.

Until the announcement of this particular fiscal spending package, investors hoped Japanese authorities would come out fighting, with revolutionary ideas on ways to solve their economic and financial difficulties.

They were wrong. The fiscal policies indicated that Japan headed for a *generational* economic fall. Tampering with market forces to prop up a failing system only leads to disaster. Japan was in serious financial trouble, and the longer the government authorities waited to write off bad debts, the longer and bigger the mess—particularly as public funds were pumped into the system for no good reason. They were throwing good money after bad. My newsletter reported in March 1993 that:

"Japan's job-for-life culture is now under threat."

The Japanese government introduced two more fiscal packages in 1993 (1) in April, yen 13.2 trillion ($105.6 billion) and (2) in September, yen 62 trillion ($496 billion). The first three stimulus (dig your own grave) packages were spent on dubious one-shot public works projects—like unneeded bridges and parking garages—instead of injecting the same amount of money into the banking system, repairing bank balance sheets, to enabling banks to get back into the business of loaning money, albeit in a banking industry radically reformed and restructured (e.g., no more incestuous loans to subsidiaries and friends).

In February 1994, another fiscal stimulus package worth yen 15.2 trillion was announced. Yes, more public works projects.

To make matters worse, the Kobe earthquake hit early in 1995, at the heart of Japan's industrial powerhouse, accounting for 12 percent of total production. It would cost an estimated $60 billion to rebuild.

A further supplementary budget was announced in April 1995, for yen 7 trillion for the reconstruction of Kobe. This was followed by another fiscal stimulus package of yen 14.2 trillion in September 1995, followed by a Bank of Japan Official Discount Rate reduction by 0.5 percent to a record low of 0.5 percent. Virtually free money—a borrower's dearest dream come true, except when he learns there is no money to borrow.

In other words, one reason the Bank of Japan reduced interest rates was that taxpayers' monies finally began going toward writing off the banking system's bad debts. Because the Japanese authorities waited to start writing off their debts, the total had risen to more than $1 trillion.

The low interest rates in Japan did not have a positive impact on economic growth. Conversely, the liquidity trap was so entrenched that savers were saving even more at the very low interest rates rather than spending the money, because of their fears of further economic trouble. The impending demise of the "old" economy seemed fairly obvious to Japanese citizens and the "new" economy meant rising unemployment, causing Japanese people to save even more as a hedge against expected bad times.

The Japanese government announced four additional fiscal stimulus packages. The first, in April, 1998 of yen 16.7 trillion. The second, in November 1998 of yen 23.9 trillion. The third, in November 1999 of yen 18 trillion. The fourth, in 2001 yen 9.9 trillion, and in December 2002, yen 4.4 trillion. A total of 10 fiscal stimulus packages spanning nearly 11 years in which the central government intervened in a capitalist economy and tried to prevent the course of market forces—which, of course, carried the day.

The Japanese government threw good money after bad and achieved nothing in terms of promoting economic growth, and, in fact, made the situation much worse. Instead of restructuring and reinventing themselves, as every country or person must do throughout their lives, the government in Japan tried to hold on to their past, thinking they knew better than the market.

Michael Porter continued to add to his *Wall Street Journal* article (March 21, 2001) that Japan's reforms

> ". . . were hardly reforms, and mostly targeted at the wrong problem. The cornerstone of Tokyo's response has been massive government spending—intended to pump up domestic demand and bail out companies—to the tune of more than $1.1 trillion. Structural reforms have been marginal, so that stifled competition, a regulatory morass, weak corporate governance, and a high cost of doing business still remain. Couple this with increased taxes on consumption, capital gains and property transfers, and Japanese economic growth has gone nowhere."

In 2001, the stock market's capitalization had fallen by 52 percent to $2.059 trillion, to number three in the world,[6] down from number one in 1989.

The Japanese economy started the 1990s with an annual budget surplus, but by 1998 the budget deficit approached 10 percent of GDP, making the national accounts of some third world countries look attractive. The annual budget deficit has since been falling, a deficit of 6.4 percent in 2002, expecting a 6.0 percent deficit in 2003. According to many forecasts, the Japanese public GDP deficit will rise to 150 percent by 2004. Japanese government bonds are being issued in massive quantity to finance the fiscal stimulus packages, and, unfortunately, the public sector has to absorb the bulk of the issuance with nearly 60 percent ownership.

The Bank of Japan's Official Discount Rate stood at 4.5 percent in January 1990, falling to 0.25 percent in 1998, with the 3-month Euro deposit interest rate holding steady at 0.1 percent—one-tenth of one percent—for the past four years and expected to be there in 2004. The unemployment rate was 2 percent in March 1990 and rose to 4.1 percent in April 1998. Because of statistical quirks, a similar number in U.S. terms would place the actual unemployment rate closer to 10 percent. After more than a decade of their zero interest rate policy, life in Japan is awful. The zero interest rate policy is doing no good at this point, and the real need is for complete restructuring of the Japanese financial system.

A square meter of real estate in Tokyo's Ginza District, costing yen 33.5 million in 1991, dropped to yen 1.10 million. Automobile production fell from 13.5 million cars in 1990 to 11 million in 1997. VCR production was 28.2 million in 1989, 9.6 million in 1997.

A more telling statistic between Japan and the United States over this period shows how the U.S. has moved forward as Japan moved backward. The market capitalization of the top 10 Japanese information technology companies, which stood at $380 billion in 1990, fell to $362 billion by 1997, while in the United States the same number rose from $230 billion in 1990 to $915 billion in 1997.

Lastly, amusing but telling, the cost of golf club membership (at Koganei Golf Club) was yen 440 million in 1989, falling to yen 61 million in 1998. And Rolls Royce sold 518 cars in Japan in 1990, but only 51 in 1997.[7]

What did the government accomplish with its policy of "wishful thinking"? After nearly nine years, *The Economist* reported (January 1998):

". . . if they [Japanese government authorities] honestly admitted the market value of the loans, shares and property they [the banking institutions] hold, many would be insolvent. The size of the hole staggers the imagination. The latest official estimate for the banking system's bad loans, yen 77 trillion ($600 billion), may still be an underestimate, and the gap in life insurance companies' accounting may be yen 60 trillion more."[8]

So after nine miserable years the Japanese still had more than $1 trillion of bad debts. *The Economist* suggested that the

". . . cure it is considering makes leeches look good."[9]

The Japanese model for dealing with the banking and debt crisis introduced a new term into the global economic vocabulary, "package fatigue," which referred to the bored reaction of investors to the same old same old failed stale policies offered before by the Japanese.

The Japanese waited too long to learn from historic experiences, like the Latin American debt crisis of the early 1980s, the United States in the mid-1980s, the Scandinavian banking crisis, or the re-structuring of the U.S. and British economies. The Japanese thought they were different.

When the new financial year commenced on April 1, 1998, the Japanese government had spent $692 billion in an attempt to jump-start its economy. Then what was called the "big bang" occurred, when, *overnight,* the Japanese tore up their own rules and opened the marketplace to the world, the idea being to bring in capital from other countries—to become more like the U.S. and U.K.

The "big bang" more resembled a whimper—too little too late—because it occurred in stages. Also, unlike what happened in London, where the English dealt from strength, the Japanese introduced changes from a position of weakness.

Watching Japan was like seeing a massive train wreck in slow motion. For nearly 10 years, it had been clear that until they took their medicine—losses on non-performing loans, restructuring the entire system—Japan lay dead in the water.

Japan had dug itself into a huge debt crisis, for no rational reason, for perhaps a generation to come. Historically, the Japanese people have been savers. These saving provided a lifeboat of sorts to the debt problems over 10 years. But those savings dwindled and, in addition to the $1 trillion of bad debts, a different financial crisis will affect those savers.

There is another pool of money, which the Japanese government uses to finance public works projects, announced in each fiscal stimulus package. The government has on hand a fiscal investment and loan program known as Zaito. These funds do not come from tax revenues or from issuing government bonds, but from the savings of the Japanese people.

These savings are drawn from the postal-saving system, similar to the old savings bonds in the U.S., run by the Finance Ministry. All deposits held by the postal-saving system had to be deposited with Zaito. By early 1998, Zaito had borrowed yen 395 trillion from the fund it ran, an amount equal to about 70 percent of Japan's gross domestic product.

It was bad. Savers had to be repaid with interest, but all this money was invested in non-performing infrastructure projects.

Who would invest in this company?

The Japanese government guarantees the deposits within the postal-saving system, and the time has long since come to include the liabilities owed to the postal-saving system within the total debt to GDP, already the highest in the industrial world.

Was there near-term hope? No. Japan entered 2000 mired in recession.

What happens when Japanese savers remove their funds from the postal-saving system?

In early 2000, GDP, the world's most important economic measurement, was falling. In fact, seven of the last nine quarters had witnessed contractions in the GDP.

Japan has an aging population, which means pension liabilities will soar. According to Goldman Sachs, corporate pension fund under funding has reached yen 80 trillion. If Nissan Motor today filled in the hole of its pension funding liability, it would cost 54.8 percent of total shareholder equity. Overall, corporate pension funds are approximately 40 percent under funded.

The pension fund system will have to pay an estimated 14.3 percent of annual GDP by 2020, versus 5.2 percent in the United States and 5.1 percent in the U.K.

A Japanese economic historian, Taichi Sakaiya, wrote in a recent best-selling book that, by the year 2018, Japan's sales tax would reach 20 percent, up from the present 5 percent! But what choices will Japan have for its future other than to raise taxes?

Frankly, any foreign investor who owns Japanese Government bonds (JGB) during the next 10 years should have his head examined. Not only will the Japanese government be issuing a record volume of bonds to raise capital, but Japanese companies have also been issuing debt instruments in record amounts. The Japanese economy needs money, whether it comes from their savings surplus invested overseas (which used to be the envy of the world, representing 15 percent of GDP in 1994) or from domestic savers and taxpayers. But it has to come from somewhere.

And the U.S. should be concerned with Japanese savers holding billions in U.S. Treasury bonds. Thank goodness the U.S. had balanced its budget for a few years because the reliance on Japanese investors to fund the deficit could have backfired with an all-out repatriation of Japanese investments. According to Merrill Lynch the Japanese exposure to U.S. markets and investments has been falling. However, there is a double-edged sword when the Japanese consider repatriation of their foreign investments in either the U.S. dollar or euro-denominated instruments. If they sell their foreign holdings they can use the money to write off their bad debts but, on the other hand, with a zero interest rate policy extending over 10 years and a stock market index which has gone nowhere in over 10 years, the only return on investment Japanese investors can hope to attain is overseas.

In November 1998, *Moody's Investor Service* downgraded the credit rating of Japan's debt. The *Financial Times* reported on November 18, 1998, that:

> *"Moody's downgrade was a warning to the government that its attempt to spend its way out of recession might fail, but worse, that it could damage both the Japanese economy and global markets. The danger is that the huge volume of additional net Japanese bond issues—by one estimate yen 52,000 billion ($436 billion) will be issued this year and next—could prick the bubble in bond*

prices that has appeared to defy economic logic. Such a correction would have
calamitous consequences for Japan's already troubled banks, which are big
holders of bonds, and could send shock waves through the world's financial
markets."[10]

The new millennium has brought no improvement, and until JGB's offer a real interest rate above U.S. Treasury bonds or German euro-denominated bonds, no one should buy.
The longer the economic recession, the larger the budget deficit and the greater the supply
of bond issues. The truth is, sometimes economic growth is good for the bond markets, and
Japan needs growth to reduce the budget deficit and therefore the supply of bonds. Foreign
investors represented only 5 percent of the total JGB holdings.

J. P. Morgan reported the astonishing fact that of all the money needed *in the world*
to finance government budget deficits, 90 percent would be required by Japan.

An *International Herald Tribune* article, February 10, 1999, revealed that the
Japanese government had urged the U.S. to buy its bonds. Chief Cabinet Secretary
Hiromu Nonaka argued:

"Japan bought U.S. Treasuries in the 1980s when the U.S. economy was in a
difficult state, which more or less contributed to the economic recovery in the
United States."

Hence, Nonaka reasoned, the U.S.

". . . should take steps to maintain the balance when our country's financial
condition is bad."[11]

They were getting desperate. But no one in his right mind would invest in Japanese
government bonds, given the state of Japan's economy. In the 1980s, the U.S. was not
floating near dead in the water. Buying Japanese bonds would be the equivalent of
throwing taxpayer money into a burning pit.

If you ever wonder whether debt is a good or bad thing, the situation in Japan should
put the question to rest.

The *Financial Times* reported that in one year:

". . . the number of suicides surged 18 percent. . . . It is sometimes considered an
honorable way to express shame or atone for problems, such as unpaid debt."[12]

The solution to Japan's woes gets more difficult with each passing day. Japan can
either let the problems run their course, or start solving them by restructuring the service
sector and reducing overcapacity in the manufacturing industry. Government officials
might even try to reflate the economy, drive real interest rates into negative and, more
importantly, create inflationary expectations so depositors will withdraw and spend their
savings, as suggested by Professor Paul Krugman.

One dizzying brainstorm from the policymakers was the issuance of $6 billion of
shopping coupons that had to be spent in a short time. That's how dire things had become,
yet perhaps the worst news is the best news for Japan, as *Euromoney* magazine explained:

"Japan will avoid restructuring until it is forced by circumstances to abandon
its flawed political and financial system. Only when the numbers get enormous,
only when ordinary Japanese people feel insecure and even poor, only when

there are runs on banks and the pension system is demonstrably bankrupt will Japan change."[13]

Japan missed the economic changes taking place in the Anglo-Saxon economies—the creation of small, flexible entrepreneurial companies. The way in which centralist capitalist countries distribute money to the private sector needs to be completely liberalized. Unfortunately, an open distribution of capital in Japan destroys the old-economy way of doing business. Japan has never actually committed itself to economic and financial restructuring through a proper process and, until it does, there is no hope.

The mood in Japan was gloomy in April 2001, to say the most. Japanese housewives were going back to work as their husbands' businesses failed. Companies could not take advantage of the zero interest rate policy because they have nothing to invest in. In a *Financial Times* article (March 23, 2001), "Japanese Plans for Investment Take a Hit," one company executive is quoted as saying:

> *"We are reducing investment because there is nothing to invest in. Even if we were to build a new factory, there is no prospect of seeing addition demand, so we can't be bold."*

The Japanese people are keeping their savings in cash—more than 54 percent is held in cash. Therefore, the prospect of a stock market rally in the near future is slim.

Japanese trade is collapsing and, as the United States economy slows, the prospect that the U.S. consumer can help Japanese exports is limited. The Japanese banks are not lending to Asian neighbors. The entire region, as in 1997, is at risk because of Japan. The Japanese economic crisis—which is also now a debt crisis—has experts calling the period "The Lost Decade."

The lost decade is rapidly becoming the "lost decades" as Japan sits on the precipice of an economic and financial black hole. In nearly a decade the banking system has written off approximately $600 billion dollars of bad loans since 1992, with the remaining problem loans ongoing into 2003 exceeding the total equity of the entire banking system. Gillian Tett comments in the *Financial Times* (August 31, 2001):

> *"Anglo-Saxon logic suggests that the best way for banks to tackle this kind of loan is to demand corporate 'restructuring'—separating out the viable and non-viable parts of a business, then writing off part of the debt to create a healthy company. Yet in Japan there is a deep cultural dislike of separating winners and losers—banks are reluctant to "offend" traditional borrowers. Bankruptcy has been considered so shameful; in Japan—in contrast to the US—that executives almost never voluntarily seek restructuring."*

A very important point which has been a theme throughout this book—the Japanese people have their financial and economic system to blame for their ongoing financial and economic problems, which will get dramatically worse in the years to come if left in its present state. According to another *Financial Times* comment by Martin Wolf (November 14, 2002) "Japan on the Brink":

> *"Between 1991 and 2001, the ratio of gross public debt to GDP rose from 61 percent to 131 percent . . . ."*

The article continues and suggests that the gross public debt ratio to GDP will rise to 185 percent in 2007 and 310 percent in 2015 if the situation in Japan remains the same.

According to the *Wall Street Journal* (November 21, 2001), "Investors Seek Profits in Japan's Debt-Laden Golf Courses," golf courses built in the 1980s for $150 million are now being purchased for $10 million or less. Japanese life insurers are starting to feel the affects of the rising liabilities for their retired life insurance contracts versus the falling returns that they are achieving through their investments. In fact, the investment portfolios of the top ten life insurance companies in Japan have seen their values collapse raising the gap between their assets to liabilities by more than $10 billion. The unemployment rate in Japan has reached a post-World War II high of 5.6 percent, as the Nikkei Dow closed below the U.S. Dow Jones index for the first time in 45 year. It closed at 9,791 on February 1, 2002, from its high (just to remind you) of 23,915 in 1989. As the Nikkei fell by 75 percent, the Dow Jones index had risen by 260 percent over this same time period.

The Japanese government needs a Margaret Thatcher to accomplish with Japan what she did in the United Kingdom in the 1980s. Japan is now undergoing its third restructuring since the beginning of their economic crisis in 1989. The first attempt was from 1992-1994 when the effort was on streamlining costs and white collar head counts. The second policy attempt to restructure Japan's economy took place between 1998-1999 when the attention focused on cutting the total work force and production capacity, reforming boards of directors. The third scheme came in 2002, which involved nothing more than revamping the traditional business relationships prevalent in a centralist capitalist system. In their latest idea, nothing new—as *The Economist* summed it all up in their February 16, 2002 editorial entitled "The Sadness of Japan:

> "*Japan looks to be an irrelevance. Alas, it could well become a liability.*"

ASIA

Kevin Muehring wrote, without exaggeration, in the September 1998, *Institutional Investor:*

> "*Thailand, Indonesia, the Philippines, South Korea. Over the past year the Asian financial crisis has swept through one country after another, sucking some 400 million people into its vortex. Add to that nearly 2 billion more people or so as the contagion has spread this year to Russia and Ukraine and continues to pound Malaysia, Hong Kong, South Africa, Brazil, Venezuela, China and Japan. As the crisis has deepened, once-mighty banks have collapsed, conglomerates have crumbled, and communities have been destroyed.*"

The Asian liquidity and debt crisis was a very different tale from Japan's, though once again the problem starts with a fixed exchange rate regime. What should have been a simple currency crisis, easily repaired, turned into a full-blown debt crisis.

Sadly, many Asian countries had fixed their currencies to the U.S. dollar, even though most of their trade took place on their own continent. So when the U.S. economy purred on in 1996 and 1997 while the Japanese engine sputtered, the fixed exchange rate regimes in Asia came under severe strain.

The shocking aspect of the crisis was the amounts and scope of U.S. dollar borrowing by Asians—the "free lunch mentality" that created the financial catastrophe and, ultimately, the debt crisis. Asians borrowed dollars because interest rates were lower in the United States than at home, and then converted the dollars into their own currencies, thinking the fixed exchange rate wouldn't be changed. In sum—they thought they were getting something for nothing—borrowing at 8 percent, lending at 13 percent. What a deal.

But a reason existed why interest rates were low in the United States and high in Thailand. Business hummed along in the United States, the economy was overheated in Thailand, and interest rates were targeted to individual national fundamentals.

At the outset, many observers were numbed by events in Asia. How could the "Asian Miracle" not be the pot of gold in which they had believed and heavily invested?

On the surface, Asia did everything by the book—balanced budgets, low inflation, and strong economic growth. So what went wrong? Sometimes it's all about timing, being in the wrong place at the wrong time, or experiencing a financial problem at an inopportune moment. *Some times.* But that's not what happened in Asia.

Former Federal Reserve Bank Chairman Paul Volcker had been right when, in 1999, he wrote:

> *"We have to deal with the simple fact that countries with strong banks, honest and democratic governments, relatively transparent accounting systems, and experienced regulators have not been immune to banking crises. The list is long and it includes the United States."*

The fact was that Asia lacked all of the good qualities Volcker listed. The 1997-98 Asian crises was an example of controlled capitalism going astray, with the use of fixed exchange rates and a lack of transparency throughout the economic and financial system. It was also about panic—investor panic, foreign banks getting out, and domestic banks swamped in foreign debt liabilities with no hope of repayment.

Thailand was the first country to devalue its currency, the baht, on July 2, 1997, locking the stable door, so to speak, after the horse had been stolen. The devaluation triggered the entire disaster that followed.

The *Financial Times* reported:

> *"On June 25, 1997, Asia's economic miracle came to an end. That was the day Thanong Bidya [was] named Thailand's new finance minister . . . and quickly found the numbers he was looking for. He was horrified. With the blessing of his superiors, the central bank's young and inexperienced chief currency trader had locked up most of Thailand's foreign exchange reserves in forward contracts. Thailand's reported foreign reserves of over $30 billion were a myth—in fact they had dwindled to $1.4 billion, equal to just two days of imports. On top of that, the central bank's Financial Institutions Development Fund (FIDF) had lent over Bt200 billion ($8 billion) to struggling financial institutions. Finance One, the country's largest finance company, had alone received over Bt35 billion from the fund in the first quarter of 1997. This lending had effectively drained seven years' worth of the Thai government's fiscal surpluses; the central bank was printing money to make up the rest. The financial system had become a black hole, sucking the government money with no end in sight."[14]*

Asia resembled classic 1994 Mexico, but worse. It consumed an entire region—a continent—and the major financial and economic sponsor for this most populous continent, Japan, was in a deep slump. Mexico in 1994 was confined, and its main trading partner (the U.S.) was in reasonably good shape and could assist.

Asian governments had adopted a pegged currency (when the price of one country's currency is fixed to another). Well and good, but nothing is forever, and a dynamic fluid global economy demands a constant reevaluation of its position. This the Asians did not do. They clung to the pegged currency lifeboat until it sank, weighted down by a massive amount of debt. It might have worked if direct foreign investment into these countries had continued to keep pace with foreign debt obligations.

But the music stopped. Real economic growth slowed along with foreign direct investment and—POW—suddenly foreign investors were fleeing *en masse,* foreign currency reserves eroded, and the threat to the currency peg became reality. Domestic borrowers panicked and tried to cover their hard currency exposure before the peg broke.

A feeding frenzy erupted when investors learned the truth—economic and financial fundamentals were unsound. True information had long remained hidden from the market. When it exploded into the public domain, more investor panic ensued. No one trusted the system.

To protect the fixed exchange rate, interest rates must rise when necessary, and intervention is needed as the tool to maintain currency parities. However, raising interest rates harms economic growth, which worsens the government's fiscal position because tax revenues slow and unemployment lines lengthen.

Adding to Asia's ills was the behavior of the International Monetary Fund. Asian countries were required by the IMF to raise interest rates to onerous levels after the exchange rate peg collapsed, causing further untold economic and financial misery.

When, in 1992-93, the exchange rate mechanism in Europe came under strain, interest rates were raised in an attempt to maintain their currency-pegged values. But, once the mechanism in Europe collapsed, interest rates *fell* in each of the affected countries.

Once a fixed exchange peg falls apart, the best course is to pick up the pieces, let the currency find its own level, and get back to business. Disastrously, the IMF prevented Asian countries from lowering their high rates after the collapse of the fixed exchange system.

No doubt there is enough blame to go around on both sides of the equation. Although it is the Asians who got themselves into the mess, history will show that their system was badly in need of repair, and they ignored the warnings.

A March, 1997, IMF working paper had said:

> *"Rapid growth and ongoing changes in financial markets suggest that policy needs to be guided by a wider set of monetary and real sector indicators of inflationary pressures."*[15]

This was the IMF's way of telling Asian authorities to scrap the fixed exchange rate regime. Another IMF report suggested:

> *". . . a programme to reduce current account deficits in order to reduce the risks that go along with them."*[16]

An important indicator of trouble ahead. Asian countries did not follow traditional Anglo-Saxon market principles regarding transparency and the flow and availability of all relevant information. Instead they hid it, acting more like a super-secret spy agency. Less market information *always* creates investor anxiety.

Still, the Asian macroeconomic landscape entering 1997 should have been no secret, with Japanese economic sluggishness a sure sign of trouble ahead. The writing was on the wall early in 1997, but people didn't read it. If they did, they ignored the obvious.

Finally currency speculators started to notice the imbalances between the business cycles in the U.S. and Asia and the ramifications for the pegged exchange rates. Like a fierce Roman legion, the speculators lined up in May, 1997, mercilessly attacking the Thai baht until the fixed exchange rate collapsed on July 2.

Once the Thai baht fell apart, the rest of Asia followed. Global markets were in total disarray. Hardly maintaining a cool head, George Soros talked about the end of capitalism, while others bemoaned the demise of the "Asian Miracle." Some predicted a global economic recession.

Each Asian country sought ways to create economic growth to get its economy back on track and hold off foreign creditors. But the only policy available at this stage was currency devaluation. Everyone did it and competed for the best terms for trade.

Because of a fax I received from an investment-banking colleague, I felt sure the situation in Asia was headed for a full-blown debt crisis. In a nutshell, Thailand had to agree to certain IMF demands before it received a $15 billion bailout. The six conditions outlined in the fax were stringent (1) raise taxes, (2) clean up the finance industry, (3) balance the budget, (4) end subsidies to state companies and utilities, (5) keep monetary policy tight, and (6) continue the foreign exchange system to preserve currency stability.

The IMF claimed it wanted to reassure foreign investors that the Thai economy was on the mend and to help keep the baht stable. This was nonsense. The IMF package protected only Thailand's creditors. The IMF *should* have allowed Thailand to reduce interest rates, used the power of fiscal policy to write off bad debts, and allowed currency prices to fluctuate.

When the S&L debacle occurred in the U.S., the Federal Reserve Bank *lowered* interest rates. This provided the necessary liquidity to rebuild balance sheets, and the fiscal deficit was expanded to write off bad loans.

Whether in the U.K., Scandinavia, or other European countries, there has *never* been a systemic bank bailout package, which included raising interest rates and taxes, balancing the budget, or maintaining the fixed exchange rate regime. Many of the six conditions imposed on Thailand could not have been worse for the Thai economy. The IMF was strong-arming Asian countries to exact repayment of hard currency debts. Don't forget, it was the fixed exchange rate that got Thailand into trouble.

Depressing economic growth made the economic and financial position of Asian countries much worse, not better. Did the IMF package improve the underlying assets and investment environment? Absolutely not. Even though the Thai baht devalued by 20 percent in July 1997, continuing the fixed exchange rate handed Thai baht investors the opportunity to use the protection of the peg to get out of Thai investments, leaving the Thai taxpayer to pick up the tab.

Unemployment lines grew and social unrest heated up as the Asian people, with standards of living crashing around their feet, demanded political reform. Investors lost, hard currency creditors lost, and the Asian continent lost its "miracle."

Asia has rebound. But they have to learn from their mistakes and play by the new international rules in a competitive global marketplace where investors will not tolerate imprudent policies and will attack anomalies in any system, particularly when it includes a pegged exchange rate. Asia has taught the world that it shouldn't be fixing exchange rates, that transparency is critical, and that the "free lunch" carries a terrible cost.

But just when people thought times couldn't get tougher . . . comes the summer of 1998.

SUMMER OF 1998

In the spring/summer of 1998, the regional Asian economic and financial crisis developed into a global event. As mentioned, the crux of the problem in Asia had to do with the pegged fixed exchange rate and IMF demands, which together created a depression.

The economic slowdown in East Asia decreased trade throughout the world. The original countries affected by the July 1997 devaluation of the Thai baht—Korea, Indonesia, and Malaysia—were joined by Hong Kong, Singapore, the Philippines, and Japan. Then the virus spread to the Indian subcontinent. Any country with a fixed or pegged exchange rate regime and current account deficit found itself in the firing line, including Pakistan, Russia, Brazil, and Venezuela.

By summer, 1998, the financial destruction of asset values in Asia had soared to more than $1.5 *trillion*. The IMF was running out of money. In October 1998, Russia became a casualty, the fall in oil prices being the icing on the cake.

The entire disaster occurred because a relatively few people were trying to scalp a "free lunch" out of a fixed exchange rate system. Because of a belief that the fixed rate exchange would stay in place forever, they borrowed hard currency (the U.S. dollar) at lower U.S. interest rates, and invested the money in higher return projects in Asia. Great, until the local currency devalues, as it must (let's say by 30 percent). Then the cost of repaying the borrowed hard currency becomes crushing.

How serious was the Asia situation? In early September 1998, George Magnus of Warburg Dillon Read announced that unless enlightened monetary and political leadership stepped forward to solve the emerging markets' debt crisis, global economic Armageddon would be next.

In fairness, Michael Camdessus, managing director of IMF, did meet on two occasions in secret with Thai authorities to urge them to unpeg the baht from the U.S. dollar, but the advice was ignored. Korean officials actively misled western bankers about the liquidity of their reserves and the amount of leverage in their banking system.

Stanley Fischer, First Deputy Managing Director of the IMF, said the key factors leading to the Asian crisis were the failures of the countries to dampen economic overheating, apparent by the large current account deficits; rising property prices; and a stock market bubble. Fischer blamed maintenance of the pegged exchange rate, which created the "free lunch" mentality, and a lack of supervision and rules under which financial systems are governed.[17]

The interaction of large capital inflows and weak private and public sector governance no doubt contributed mightily to the problem. Avoiding a crisis requires forward-looking governance, prudent macroeconomic policies, diligent bank supervision, and strong data dissemination.[18]

Now for an even worse disaster.

RUSSIA

When news leaked that George Soros had secretly lent Russia several hundred million dollars to bridge the country's financing gap (until Russia issued $2 billion in eurobonds in 1997), astute investors suspected there would soon be big trouble in store for the former Soviet Union. Russia was, after all, a financial and economic mess.

Martin Wolf, in an August 19, 1998 *Financial Times* article, commented:

> *"Some countries devalue; others default. Few do both the same day. Never inclined to do by halves, the Russians are the exception."*

Russia had mired in an economic swamp since the demise of the Soviet Union, and Western support came because of its nuclear arsenal, more dangerous if the country self-destructed economically. But a nation cannot be helped if it won't help itself. And sometimes by being too helpful, we cause harm. To a degree, this is what happened, creating a debt crisis that led to default by a nuclear superpower.

The Russian debt crisis came about because of large fiscal deficits and the short-term debt instruments issued to finance the deficit spending. The Russian Ministry of Finance peddled a Treasury bill instrument called a GKO and coupon bonds called OFZs, both ruble-denominated instruments.

By 1997, foreign investors owned one-third of all outstanding issued GKOs. Here was a perfect example of what can happen if federal indebtedness becomes too much to handle for foreign investors supporting fiscal deficit spending. Falling oil prices did not help the Russian fiscal revenue picture, nor did the fixed exchange rate. According to IMF sources, as the total debt steadily rose, GKO/OFZ debt redemption payments reached *one billion dollars per week.*

The total nominal gross domestic product in Russia stood at $449 billion in 1997, before crashing to $190 billion in 1999—a catastrophe. Gross external debt as a percentage of GDP rose from 28 percent in 1996 to 114 percent by 1999.[19] The most shocking statistic was the amount of money required to fund the debt servicing to external creditors—a whopping 10 percent of GDP—was $17 billion per annum, the equivalent of the entire federal budget.[20] This meant that *no* public money was available for schools, hospitals, public improvements, public power, and so on. Every penny went to servicing debt.

This is why the debt in the United States should be paid off. Debt is truly the scourge of society—any society. When nations go through difficult times, rainy days become downpours and even biblical storms. Just look at Russia. Fiscal deficits feed on themselves until there is nothing left.

On August 17, 1998, the Ruble was devalued and Russia suspended payments on its debt. It had become unmanageable. Russian budget revenues had fallen 50 percent of the planned revenue amount in the first half of 1998. The problem was finding the money to repay bondholders either their coupon payments or the principal amount invested.

Earlier, on July 8, 1998, repercussions of the budget crisis had been felt in the Russian Treasury bill market as yields on short-term government debt rose in excess of 100 percent on new 45-day Treasury bill issues. Another good news/bad news situation. The good news was that investors had doubled their money. The bad news, they'll never see the money.

Up to this period, the Russian central bank had used hard currency reserves to meet redemption payments on the bonds. Once the central bank used up all these reserves, the lender of last resort became—ta da!—The International Monetary Fund. In other words, you and me.

Should we taxpayers be forced to bail another country out from under massive indebtedness?

In many cases, yes.

But Russia represented, on the face of it, a total waste of taxpayer money. Russia had a pegged exchange rate mechanism in place, which it insisted on keeping. Still, the IMF came in and loaned the Russians $10 billion to meet their dollar-denominated obligations over the next 10 weeks. Big hard currency speculators pounced on the chance to get out of ruble paper and any other associated paper before the $10 billion ran out.

What did the IMF accomplish by helping the Russian people? What did these people gain? Nothing to both questions.

Taxes, (i.e., IMF loans) should not go to finance someone else's capital flight.

In fact, the IMF provided $22.6 billion of financial assistance, which represented Russia's short-term debt exposure. A *Wall Street Journal* editorial (July 15, 1998), posed the question:

> *"We can't help wondering, how did the IMF get into the business of using U.S. taxpayers money to finance capital flight from Russia?"*

What was more insulting, an audit uncovered that the Russian central bank had lied to the IMF about the size of its hard currency reserves in order to receive an IMF loan in 1996 by hiding money in a Channel Islands company.

Russia has a huge economic and financial problem to solve, perhaps greater than any other country in history. Said the *Wall Street Journal* (July 15, 1998):

> *"Under central planning, when the government ran and owned everything, Russians became adept at siphoning off state assets for private uses, that is, for survival. Progress since then has been awkwardly paired with huge property grabs by men in positions of power. There's the notoriously secretive and strange way in which the government chose to 'privatize' in the hands of select cronies effective control of the national gas company, Gazprom, a big hard-currency earner that claims about one-third of the world's known natural gas reserves. In a world that increasingly demands and rewards market transparency, Russia remains global finance's house of horrors."*

The IMF and the U.S. government argue that the IMF loans restored confidence in the Russian markets—yeah, and pigs fly.

It comes as no surprise that the Russian markets did not improve after the IMF loan or as a result of any new economic measures, announcements, pronouncements, initiatives, or any other fancy labeling attached to fiscal policymaking. The Russian government bond market continued to weaken. U.S. dollar-denominated Russian bonds fell in value by more than 9 percent on a single day, July 27, 1998.

Finally, on August 17, 1998, a joint announcement from the Russian government and the central bank shocked the markets, bringing chaos once again. It proclaimed abandonment of the pegged exchange rate system, and unilaterally froze some of the internal and external debt—it defaulted.

The Russians basically had no choice because they could not find anyone willing to buy their bonds. A great deal of talk ensued on how the Russians should stabilize and reform their economy. But until government authorities actually start to collect taxes and put their fiscal house in order, all the talk in the world won't solves the Russian debt crisis.

Adding to market anxieties were political woes created by President Boris Yeltsin's firing his government, headed by Sergei Kiriyenko, and asking Victor Chernomyrdin to form a new one. The Duma rejected the appointment, and Yevgeni Primakov became Prime Minister. The reason Kiriyenko was fired was that Russia's banking and corporate elite believed his policies would bankrupt their companies, allowing foreign creditors to seize their assets.

When the announcement came on August 17, the Russian Ruble traded around the official pegged exchange rate of 6.43 for every one dollar. It immediately tumbled to Ruble 9.1 per one dollar. In addition, Russian government bonds fell by nearly a third in value as yield in relation to U.S. Treasury bonds rose by 5 percent (500 basis points), adding to the cost for servicing debts—this on top of the currency devaluation.

The Russians had few policy options, but then again they had no policies. Perhaps the August 17 announcement was the best of nothing else to do. The financial press was surprisingly kind and understanding toward the Russian decision. The *Wall Street Journal* played down the crisis in global terms in an August 18 editorial, in essence saying that Russia's role in the global economy is extremely minor and therefore the problem is a strictly national one. The *Financial Times* was more constructive, calling the crisis a painful lesson and urging the Russian government to learn from the experience once and for all.

Why was everyone so sympathetic? Perhaps there was hope that after this train wreck Russia would get its act together. Certainly the problems are known—a fiscal policy without the ability to generate tax revenue, wild spending, a floating pegged exchange rate, basically fixed, with a growing current account deficit, and a stupendously corrupt economic and financial system.

Some economists suggest Russia use a currency board. But the problem with an absolute fixed exchange rate is that the economic and financial restructuring has not taken place. Before putting anything into Russia, investors would insist on a system they could trust and understand.

There are reports that the Russian people have stashed more than $40 billion in actual U.S. dollars under their mattresses. If they deposited that money into their banking system, then the Russian government could anchor its domestic money supply with the U.S. dollar and, presto!—a currency board. But there's a very good reason why that money is sitting under the mattress.

The Russian people should not give up U.S. dollars carefully saved until they are extremely confident in the system under which they live.

Russia's problems are very basic, and very difficult to solve because of corruption. It needs to create and enforce elementary rules the world can understand—including reform of fiscal policy, bankruptcy laws, financial regulations, labor laws, reporting and accounting standards, and civil and criminal laws. The gangsters must be purged.

President Yeltsin's administration seemed incapable to sort out the corruption.

In August 1999, President Yeltsin appointed Vladimir Putin his fifth prime minister in 17 months.

Yeltsin subsequently resigned on December 31, 1999, a stunning development that left Putin acting president. Putin then grants Yeltsin immunity from prosecution for corruption and financial mismanagement charges against him and his family members.

As Prime Minister and acting President, Putin put his stamp firmly on the required changes that Russia needed to re-fashion and revive Russia's corrupt and ailing economy.

Acting President Putin called for a presidential election on March 26, 2000. With a 52.64 percent majority of the total votes cast over 11 time zones, President Putin had a daunting task ahead of him and his cabinet. No question that the rising price in the price of a barrel of oil helped the tax revenue for the Russian government, but by 2001 and early 2002 Mr. Putin made tremendous progress in fundamental restructuring of the economy and financial system. Russia has implemented a flat tax of 13 percent on personal income, simplified income tax, and lowered corporate taxes with further tax reductions in the future. His government has reformed the labor code and permits the sale of land. For the first time, Russia is running a budget surplus. Foreign debt is being serviced although foreign direct investment remains pitiful considering that in 2001, China received more in a single year than Russia's total over the past decade.

The civil service needs to be convinced to go out there and collect taxes and that may take some time, but the Russian economic liberalization is under way, and it looks to be a success.

CONCLUSION

The theme of this chapter has been debt, and it should be clear that debt is not a good public sector tool to promote the welfare of nations for long periods of time. Keynes intended it only for short-term disequilibriums occurring within the economic system, not as a policy tool over several decades.

As we've seen, government indebtedness can careen out of control and, in today's world, must be dealt with in a swift, transparent manner. Anything less, and global investors will punish without mercy.

ENDNOTES

[1] Dziobe, C., and C. Pazarbasioglu. "Lessons From Systemic Bank Restructuring." Washington, D.C.: International Monetary Fund, April 1998.
[2] Sources: Merrill Lynch and World Bank.

[3] Porter, M., and H. Takeuchi. "What Went Wrong in Japan." *Foreign Affairs,* May/June 1999, page 68.

[4] Ibid., pages 71 and 72.

[5] "Banking System Outlook—Japan." *Moody's Investor Service,* March 1997, page 6.

[6] "So How has Japan Fallen? Take a Look at These Numbers." *International Herald Tribune,* July 4, 1998.

[7] Ibid.

[8] "How to Waste $250 billion." *The Economist,* January 24, 1998, page 16.

[9] Ibid.

[10] "Home Truths for Japan." *Financial Times,* November 18, 1998.

[11] "Japan Urges U.S. to Buy Its Bonds." *International Herald Tribune,* February 10, 1999.

[12] "Human Cost of Japan's Recession." *Financial Times,* June 13, 1998.

[13] "More Good News for Japan." *Euromoney,* April 1999.

[14] "Asia in Crisis." *Financial Times,* June 12, 1998.

[15] Dekle, R., and M. Pradhan. "Financial Liberalization and Money Demand in Asian Countries: Implications for Monetary Policy." IMF Working Paper, March 1997. Washington, D.C.: International Monetary Fund.

[16] Ostry, J. D. "Current Account Imbalances in Asian Countries: Are They a Problem?" IMF Working Paper, April 1997. Washington, D.C.: International Monetary Fund.

[17] "The Asian Crisis: A View from the IMF." Address by Stanley Fischer at Midwinter Conference of the Bankers' Association for Foreign Trade, January 22, 1998. Washington, D.C.: International Monetary Fund.

[18] Kochhar, K., P. Loungani, and M. Stone. "The East Asia Crisis: Macroeconomic Developments and Policy Lessons," August 1998. Washington, D.C.: International Monetary Fund.

[19] Source: J. P. Morgan.

[20] Source: Creditanstalt Bankverein.

Chapter 12

THE POWER OF GLOBAL CAPITAL:
NEW INTERNATIONAL RULES— NEW GLOBAL RISKS

INTRODUCTION

This book has been an attempt to explain the way in which the global financial and economic system has been converging. In other words, how individual country financial and economic systems are competitively merging into one global system. I believe this convergence process is irreversible because we have a much greater understanding for the science of economics, and that understanding is filtering down to every person—every voter wants his standard of living either protected or improved. Government policymakers will have to deliver—or rather stay out of the way and allow market forces to continue—'the new international rules.'

Economic and financial power has shifted from the public sector to the private sector as individuals throughout the world invest in pension funds, mutual funds, and other private pools of capital. This weight of capital will have the final word over government policy. Central government policymakers must attract, entice, and encourage investment in their countries. To ensure success they must continually compete with other countries in making their economic and financial environment attractive at all times. This process is dynamic, and as competitive as any private sector industry. The freedoms of movement of capital throughout the world, tax levels, both corporate and personal, regulation, and the rule of law are all part of this equation and as discussed throughout this book, the difference between Anglo-Saxon and Centralist capitalist systems play an enormous role or barrier to offering an attractive economic environment.

I truly believe that the reverse crowding-out effect, when the central government runs a budget surplus, injecting the surplus back into hands of the taxpayers and paying down outstanding debt, reverses its demand for money, which puts more money into the private sector, has had a huge and positive financial impact on the U.S. economy over the past six years. By reversing their demand for funding the fiscal deficit, the private sector has been able to stimulate economic growth on an unprecedented scale. I believe this process, and not technology, has been the true stimulus for economic growth. Institutional investors have been able to invest more and more of personal savings into venture capital funds, technology and other private funds, which has stimulated economic growth in the United States. I also believe that it is this process which is creating the new global economy, feeding technology investments.

Investors have greater and increasing choice as government policymakers have less choice in fiscal policies and monetary policy. Central governments can no longer be big brother as populations' age and growth. They must help those who cannot help themselves, and those who can help themselves must become more self-sufficient and responsible for their own well being. Central governments have a responsibility to live within their means, balancing their budgets, reducing gross debt burdens, and to begin the process of reducing the tax burden. Government also has a responsibility to educate and point the way toward individual self-sufficiency, but cannot be everyone's nanny. We can no longer afford it—it is that simple. Public finances must be protected and not abused year after year. There is no right or left, but only right and wrong policy in our new global economy.

The new challenges we face involve our ability and resolve to continue the process of self-sufficiency, maintaining and increasing the attractiveness of our investment environment for both domestic and international investors. If not, the penalty will be extreme, as investors withdraw their funds and invest where it is more attractive. The Japanese story paints this picture and now the opportunity for Japanese policymakers to recover from their mistakes, and their ability to improve their economic and financial system, is limited. Therefore, the Japanese people will be facing a generational struggle to bring their economy right.

Monetary policymaking will also change and evolve. As fiscal policies must be restrained, monetary policymaking must ensure low inflationary economic growth. Monetary policy must become the check and balance for fiscal policies to ensure that low inflationary growth is achieved. The Japanese story also proves that monetary policy alone will not solve national economic and financial problems. Fiscal policymakers and monetary policymakers must work hand in hand, and not on opposing sides. Global competition will intensify and the economic and financial environment each country has to offer will be a big component of the ability of those industries to compete globally. Credibility is a big part of this ability to attract global capital. Keeping the credibility of institutions, their policies, and the individuals themselves to maintain policy will be a big part of the new global economy and the new global risks that we face.

As central government credibility becomes more evident, so too must individual industry standards for doing business with one another. The rule of law governing the way we do business will also have an impact on institutional investments. At the same time, investors must become responsible for their investment decisions, whether bad or good, and central government—the taxpayer—cannot be lenders of last resort when all goes wrong. The rules and laws for those investments must be made crystal clear. I would prefer that my tax monies be used to help those who do not have proper health care, or toward better education, and not for individuals who have abused their corporate powers and have lost huge sums of money making bad loans or investments.

Global relationships and inter-relationships require that we establish global rules of engagement. We can no longer merely react to one crisis or another but implement rules that we can all understand and therefore prosper from. Global risks, such as a currency crisis or debt crises, will not go away. But our ability to understand and receive all available relevant information for each country and its industries is vital. Transparency of information is required throughout the world and is a major part of the credibility factor for all institutional investors. In each case of a currency crisis, information transparency was a key ingredient and the root cause for the crisis. Understanding how the global capital markets operate and what attracts global capital flows has also been a large ingredient as exchange rates are fixed in one fashion or another.

THE U.S. BUDGET SURPLUS

Once upon a time, the United States had a federal budget surplus and there was a debate: "What should the American people do with an annual budget surplus?" The broad assumption that by the year 2011 the total fiscal surplus will approach $4.561 trillion, excluding social security reserves (expected to be $2.174 trillion), could be very misleading and inspire inappropriate fiscal policy in the short-term, resulting in missed opportunities for the longer-term, which could cost the American people a tremendous price in later years.

I have experienced numerous unexpected budget surpluses in other countries, such as the United Kingdom, Australia, Sweden, and Japan in the 1980s, which quickly turned into budget deficits for one reason or another, causing these countries to issue huge amounts of public sector debt within a year or two after their last annual budget surplus. Each of these countries faced boom-bust economic cycles within a period of a few months, causing their budget surpluses to disappear. Their fiscal policies included tax reductions and fiscal expenditure cuts, with promises of further tax reductions as their budget surpluses continued into the future. They miscalculated. Fiscal spending had to rise to help stimulate economic growth, and tax cuts turned into across-the-board tax rises in very short order. The statistics in Table 12.1 speak for themselves.

Table 12.1: General Government Budget Balances (% of GDP)

	1983	1989	1995
Australia	-5.4	0.0	-3.7
Japan	-3.2	+2.4	-5.6
Sweden	-4.8	+5.2	-7.8
United Kingdom	-3.3	+0.9	-6.7

Source: J. P. Morgan.

The budget surplus in the United States and its expectations have gone the same way as the four countries described, particularly after the costs and budget increases since the September 11, 2001 World Trade Center bombing. In fact, the U.S. federal budget has gone into deficit and will remain there for the next few years.

When considering the prospects for a budget surplus on an annual basis, policymakers should focus on what is best for the long term rather than the short term. I am referring to the debate between tax reductions versus paying down the total government indebtedness. I am also referring to the way in which Americans are saving money, or, in this case, not saving money.

Using a budget surplus to pay down our national debt has its rewards, but as that one goes down, corporate and consumer indebtedness is on the rise. The *Wall Street Journal*, (July 5, 2000) reported that U.S. nonfinancial corporations have accumulated a record $4.5 trillion in debt, a rise of 67 percent over the past five years. Consumer debt (household borrowing) has risen by 60 percent, to $6.5 trillion, over the last five years. Another interesting aspect to the rise in corporate debt is the rise in junk bond issues, soaring from $173 billion a decade ago to $529 billion today. The annual personal savings rate as a percentage of disposable income has collapsed since 1970, falling from 8 percent to zero and actually moving into negative as spending is increasing faster than personal income. I believe that fiscal policymakers should focus their attention on this statistic because, instead of cutting taxes, perhaps tax incentives to promote and induce personal savings would better serve the American people.

Our present social security system is a pay-as-you-go scheme, which does not own any assets. In 1940 there were 16 workers for every social security beneficiary in the United States. Today it is 3.3 to 1, and when the baby boomers start retiring this ratio of taxpayers to retirees in the United States will drop to 2.8 to 1 and could fall below 2 to 1. I am certainly not suggesting that our beloved central government should manage our pension fund on our behalf, or that the social security system start accumulating assets and investing those funds into the stock market. I do believe that Americans should become more self-sufficient in the way they save and structure their finances for retirement. I do not believe that these assets should be used to collateralize personal borrowings, but be put into a scheme or vehicle, which will be there when retirement comes. A greater proportion of our gross annual income should be put aside for retirement and not given back to us in tax reductions, because a tax reduction today will be a tax rise tomorrow.

Once policymakers have sorted out the savings ratio, the next step is to pay down the national debt. Over the past three years the U.S. Treasury has paid down $363 billion of the $3.4 trillion publicly held debt. Of all the policies I have witnessed thus far, the U.K. government handled their budget surplus the best. They sterilized the annual surplus each month by paying off maturing debt and actually paying down expensive debt. I would like the U.S. government to do the same—pay down maturing debt each month or calendar quarter, which will provide the fuel for future long-term economic growth through the reverse crowding-out process explained earlier.

The combination of promoting personal savings allowing the American people to put money away for retirement, along with paying down the national debt, is the best policy for the United States today and for future generations. The national government must point the way and provide incentives for Americans to save, and coupled with reducing the national debt, this will continually promote economic growth each year as more private wealth is created. Thus more investment capital will be made available to the private sector. If and when we arrive at the point when the national debt has been paid down enough and the personal savings rate has grown to an appropriate level, which ensures that each working American's retirement has been accomplished, then and only then should we start talking about tax reductions. If working Americans are able to save for and secure their retirement, the burden posed to the national social security system will be greatly reduced. To ensure we accomplish these objectives, policymakers can allow older workers to save more per annum than younger workers, who have more time to save for retirement. There are a number of variations on this theme that can be used to take the burden off the social security system into the future, rather than protecting and building the social security system into something that makes no sense.

Now is the time to act. A little bit here that can be saved, or a little national debt there that can be paid down, would make a huge difference by 2011 when the budget surplus is expected to be in its zenith. Cutting taxes as a means of repaying the budget surplus to tax-payers is not the right solution today, nor was it the correct assumption to project $5 trillion surpluses by 2011 that allow for tax cuts today. I am not the only person warning of this prospect. The Concord Coalition, a non-partisan budget watchdog group, warned that the 10-year surplus projections were unreliable. This coalition includes Paul Volcker who, quoted in the *Financial Times,* stated:

"I don't think we're in a position to confidently project 10 years ahead and in effect enact a permanent tax programme, increasing in scope over a 10-year period, against the uncertainty that's out there."

I sincerely believe we will pay a huge price for this action in the future, particularly as surpluses quickly dwindled as a result of September 11th coupled with a slow economy requiring President George W. Bush to announce economic stimulus packages.

Increasing personal savings and paying down the national debt year after year will ensure that there is plenty of domestic investment fuel for the U.S. economy into the future, creating a self-sustaining economic machine for years to come. And actually the removal of the double tax on stockholder dividends is a long overdue idea which will ensure that the U.S. stock markets will remain attractive to both the domestic and foreign investor.

The tax cuts and increased spending for the defense of the homeland will create a budget deficit of $158 billion in 2002, $225 billion in 2003, and expected to be $525 billion in 2004. An historic sum of money. The budget surplus projected to be $5.6 trillion has shrunk to $1 trillion and the social security surplus will also be substantially less as a result of tax cuts. So much for the budget surplus and the end to issuing 30-year U.S. Treasury bonds!

The actions by President Bush that create a budget deficit will have to go back into surplus before too long.

In addition, The U.S. current account deficit is huge and growing and must be brought down. Raising the savings ratio would help slow overseas imports, reducing the current account deficit. The current account deficit has been breaking record over the past few years and broke another record in 2002 with a deficit of $505 billion, $575 billion in 2003, and expected to rise further to $611 billion in 2004 representing 5.4 percent of the U.S. GDP.

However, think what the U.S. economic options would have been, from the September 11th attacks, had the U.S. been running 1980s-style annual budget deficits! The U.S. economy will recover from the 2001/2002 economic downturn and its uncertainty. The budget surplus and also our ability to allow 'creative destruction,' which allows market forces to prevail, the Enron bankruptcy, the second-largest in U.S. corporate history in 2001, along with the largest bankruptcy, WorldCom, in Spring 2002, will create greater transparency in corporate accounting. One of the better aspects of the Anglo-Saxon system in the United States was when the U.S. government refused to bail-out each company. However, as is often the case, in the midst of despair, the U.S. rose to the occasion, requiring all major companies to announce any restatement of their report and accounts by August 17, 2002, otherwise, recertified corporate accounts hold the senior executives legally accountable. This swift measure is something the Japanese should be practicing. Many innocent people are always hurt by bankruptcies, but I believe that the recertification process was one of America's finest hours in the midst of crashing investor confidence of U.S. companies.

NEW RULES FOR BAD RISK-TAKING

The financial and economic risks and events documented in the previous chapters on currency crises and debt crises, coupled with global risks, outline the potential damage that financial crises can cause. The events that lead to poor fiscal and monetary judgment, such as fixing an exchange rate, can lead to enormous economic hardship, and the inability to create an economically transparent society will deter investors. The use of leverage as an investment tool and an asset class without transparency of all information about that leveraged position can lead to huge financial and economic losses. The Japanese economy, using poor fiscal management, will undergo a generational slide from economic power, and it will now take another 10 years to sort out the financial and economic problems that could have been sorted out in 1991.

The differences between the Anglo-Saxon capitalist system and the Centralist capitalist system are very clear today. Does central government know better than the open marketplace? No, they do not know better, and therefore the way that capital is fed into an economic system is vital to its future economic and financial growth. Corporatist, Rhineland, or Centralist capitalism represents a huge risk to the global financial system, and those countries that have adopted this version of capitalism must think carefully about how to evolve from it.

In many ways, we are moving in the right direction. For example, the new Basle Capital Accords, announced in January 2001, to come into force in 2005 after further revision, will tie the amount of capital banks have to hold in reserve to a closer relationship to the actual risks they face. The new accord will require financial institutions to disclose far more risk management information than they do now. In addition, operational risks may account for 20 percent of a bank's risk. There is controversy regarding the Accords' effects on the European asset-management community—particularly as it relates to their operational risks.

The Economist's 'Leader' reported (January 20, 2001):

> *"The new rules tie banks' capital more closely to the actual risks they are taking. That should create a stronger incentive for banks to adopt better risk management, because they will be rewarded with lower capital requirements. [The original accord fixed banks' capital at 8% of their risk-adjusted assets.] The new rules propose three pillars to keep a check on them: the risk- based capital rules; better and more stringent supervision; and more market discipline, which includes greater transparency. Bad banks are rarely penalized for taking more risks, thanks to government deposit insurance, privileged access to bailout funds from central banks, and a perception that they are too big to fail. The new rules should make risk taking more expensive."*

The Basle Accords are a good start, but much more is needed to help improve and stabilize our global financial system. As this book and this chapter are entitled 'The Power of Global Capital: New International Rules—New Global Risks,' the new risks are in fact global. The financial and economic inter-relationships are so intertwined that, without new rules of global financial engagement, we will continue every few years to face one more currency crisis or debt crisis. If it affects the global system, it will affect the U.S. economic and financial system. The global financial system needs new rules of engagement for events such as sovereign bankruptcy, transparent economic statistics, and acceptable and transparent global accounting standards.

But we also have to be more realistic. Taxpayers can no longer be lenders of last resort, particularly if we want to save more for retirement and pay down our national debt. Shareholders, management, and the individuals who cause the problems must be held more responsible for their actions. In addition, to hold them accountable and to enforce prudent regulation, all available relevant information about their activities must be transparent and open to scrutiny. I am not suggesting that we have a right to second-guess management, but we do have a right to all the relevant information to make informed decisions on who we do business with and what companies we invest in. I strongly believe that the best police force for our global financial system is the market. Market forces will determine who is a good credit or bad credit risk, if all available information is transparent to the marketplace. This includes industrial, developing, and emerging market countries. Banks and countries alike will be better able to manage their financial affairs, knowing what the market thinks and how it values its risk-taking positions and strategies. The market may not necessarily be right, but it is the best check and balance we have on the system as a whole. We cannot rely on good government to police the system.

ECONOMIC REALITIES

The economic realities that we face in the future and the risks that any nation faces is the way global capital flows throughout the world. In very simple terms, capturing global capital flows is vital to any nation, whether industrial, developing, or emerging market countries. The new global risk in this new global economy is the inability of any nation to attract global capital flows or, in the event a nation is attractive today but not tomorrow, capital flight and hardship caused any country, which may someday include the United States. The new global economy is about the way global capital freely flows throughout the world, seeking the best return on investment. The new risk is any country not offering a competitive return on investment.

The new global economy is often used in relation to information technology, but without the freedom of movement of capital, rest assured that information technology or the Internet network would never have developed in the way it has over the past 10 years or so. Every country throughout the world is competing for this global capital. The sums of money are enormous. When looking at the global economic risks, one has only to look at the current account deficit in the United States. As I have said all along about any deficit, the money has to come from somewhere, and the private inflow of capital into the U.S. has financed the U.S. current account deficit thus far. The current account deficit is projected to rise dramatically, doubling, over the next few years, which will cause the demand for overseas investors to rise to $2 billion per day. Without foreign capital inflows, the U.S. economy would be in very serious trouble because of its current account deficit. Thank goodness that the budget deficit eroded and became a surplus over the past few years, because if the United States had maintained its twin deficits, the U.S. economy would look radically different today, albeit more like Japan.

Global investors see the United States as a safe haven for their investment funds. Therefore, any country that seeks to attract global capital flows must compete in relative terms with the United States. I talked about this relative relationship when I discussed real interest rate analysis in an earlier chapter. In contrast, the Euroland countries' portfolio outflows were euro120 billion, with euro146 billion inflows into debt instruments, but euro266 billion in equity outflows. The reason for euro outflows and U.S. dollar inflows is all about the best return on investment, and obviously investors vote with their investment funds and move their monies accordingly.

Economic reality is also all about global trade with Asia, Europe, and Latin America. It is all about the fall of Japan and the rise of China as a major trading partner with the United States. It is about the balance of economic power within the European Union as Eastern and Central European countries join the EU, creating a massive economic power. It is also dividing the power within the Euro area as Northern European countries dominate the Southern European countries. The balance of power in Asia is going through a huge dislocation as Japanese economic power dwindles, and Chinese economic prowess expands regionally and globally.

The economic realities will require policymakers to be more practical and think in new practical terms, rather than economic ideology—those days are in the past. More and more individuals will be investing in mutual funds and stocks, which will have a profound effect on the way policymakers will be allowed to behave. The days of deficit spending are over, the days of high taxes are gone, and as long as the United States is moving in this direction, every other country in the world will have to do the same or be left behind.

If there is one word I would use to describe the hopes for the global economy, it would be "transparency." The need for transparency of economic data, bank balance sheets, global capital flows, the way in which leverage is used, and the amount of risk one institution is undertaking versus another is necessary. The market and the weight of global capital will have the final word on the subject of transparency. I would expect greater investor interest in a country or institution behaving in a more transparent manner versus another.

There is no going back, because of information technology and the Internet network. The global convergence of economic and financial systems is too far advanced to turn back now, even if one wanted to revisit the economic past. Therefore, the new global economy is here to stay, and if decision-makers at all levels of the public and private sector do not face up to this reality, the cost of the new global risks is too great to contemplate.

THE SEPTEMBER 11, 2001 AFTERMATH

In the aftermath of the WTC attacks, what do Islamic nations have to do to stop being angry at the United States?

The Islamic Arabs must throw out their political dictators immediately! The Arab people should not blame the United States for their economic, social, and political woes. It's their leadership that is responsible. By getting rid of their dictatorships, creating a lawful society with full political suffrage, the economic reforms necessary to bring the Islamic people into the modern global society can be accomplished.

The regimes of the Gulf States are controlled by family dynasties resisting all political, economic, and social change. These rulers use Islam as a means to hold onto power. They are nothing more than ruthless thugs holding onto power. These Islamic rulers use old-fashioned economic thought and social repression. They use Islam and rally the Arab world for the destruction of Israel as their foundation for holding onto power. These political dictators and their policies hide the fact that their societies and economies have failed so completely. Look at the economic facts. The United States is only 225 years old with a per capita gross national income of $34,260, (as of 2000), while Israel is just 50 years old and has achieved $19,320. Compare these numbers with the Islamic world (Table 12.2):

Table 12.2: Gross National Income by Country

Country	Gross National Income
Saudi Arabia	$11,050
Tunisia	$6,090
Iran	$5,900
Algeria	$5,040
Lebanon	$4,530
Jordan	$4,040
Egypt	$3,690
Morocco	$3,410
Syria	$3,230
Pakistan	$1,960
Bangladesh	$1,650
Mauritania	$1,650
Yemen	$780

Source: World Bank.

The economic divide between the West and the Islamic world will continue to grow. This is a direct reflection on the leaders running these countries and nothing to do with Islam itself. Also, the economic divide will increase between the Islamic ruling class and their people, no doubt a problem the ruling class will blame on the West and the existence of Israel. An *Economist* editorial (February 19, 2000) stated:

> *"Don't blame Islam for bad behavior—Alas, the Islamic world is not burdened with examples of good government, let alone democracy. But religion is seldom the culprit: look, rather, for cruel autocrats, corrupt feudal systems, overbearing armies or any combination of the above. . . . The Arabs inhabit the least democratic patch on God's earth."*

The United States is also to blame. By protecting our oil supplies, we protect these 50 regimes—we fear the political alternative. The average Arab sees our support for their leaders and our support for a democratic Israel as hypocrisy. We do whatever is necessary to access our oil supplies while preaching democracy throughout the world, offending the Arabs with our support of Israel. Does the United States stand for promoting democracy and freedom or is it to make sure oil supplies are safe? Easier said than done because of the nature of these regimes, but the economic resentment felt by the Arab people is being channeled toward the United States rather than the family dynasties or the individual dictators who repress them. And let's be honest, if these rulers can deflect the anger toward America rather than on them, there is little we can do to persuade the common Arab because these people are prevented from hearing the truth.

Another interesting twist is that the highly-educated and wealthy Arabs are the most ruthless and militant leaders of these terrorist networks. They use the economic disparity between the Arab ruling class and their people as a weapon against the United States. These are bright individuals.

The fact remains that Islamic countries have not kept economic pace with the West—and don't blame the arid desert land—look at Israel. In 1950, Egypt and South Korea had the same standard of living. Today South Korea is nearly five times as high. As the Western world moves forward, near and Middle Eastern countries move backward. The Arabs want to annihilate Israel but ironically Israel is the best thing to happen to this area of the world—they have proven that deserts can be turned into a Garden of Eden. Please remember that one million Israeli citizens are Arabs with a better standard of living than any other Arab country. Also, note that nearly half of Israel's population emigrated from Arab countries.

One of the first steps needed to be taken by the Muslim people is to stop blaming Israel and the West for their economic depravation—the Arabs have themselves to blame, their rulers are to blame for their economic failure and pathetic standards of living. A wonderful summary appeared in an article by Fareed Zakaria first published in *Newsweek* (October 15, 2001). He stated:

> ". . . for all their energy these regimes chose bad ideas and implemented them in the worse ways. Socialism produced bureaucracy and stagnation. Rather than an adjusting to the failures of central planning, the economies never really moved on. The republics calcified into dictatorships. Third World "nonalignment" became pro-Soviet propaganda. Arab unity cracked and crumbled as countries discovered their own national interests and opportunities. Worst of all, Israel humiliated the Arabs in the wars of 1967 and 1973. When Saddam Hussein invaded Kuwait in 1990, he destroyed the last remnants of the Arab idea."

Look at Egypt today. The promise of Nasserism has turned into a quiet nightmare. In the 1950s, Gamel Abdel Nasser ruled Egypt after the end of British colonialism. He believed that Arab society needed modern ideas for self-determination that included socialistic economic policies along with Arab unity throughout the Middle East. Unfortunately, the Egyptian government today is efficient in only one area—squashing dissent and strangling civil society. In the past 30 years Egypt's economy has sputtered along while its population has doubled. Unemployment is at 25 percent, and 90 percent of those searching for jobs hold college diplomas. Once the heart of Arab intellectual life, the country produces just 375 books every year (compared with Israel's 2,000). The article continues:

> "Shockingly, Egypt has fared better than its Arab neighborhoods. Syria has become one of the world's most oppressive police states, a country where

*25,000 people can be rounded up and killed by the regime with no conse-
quences. In 30 years, Iraq has gone from one of the most modern and secular
of Arab countries—with women working, artists thriving, and journalists writing—into a squalid playpen for Saddam Hussein's megalomania. Lebanon, a
diverse, cosmopolitan society with a capital, Beirut, that was once called the
Paris of the Middle East, has become a hellhole of war and terror. In an almost
unthinkable reversal of a global pattern, almost every Arab country today is
less free than it was 30 years ago."*

We think of Africa's dictators as rapacious, but those in the Middle East are just as
greedy. And when contrasted with the success of Israel, Arab failures are even more
humiliating."

Foreign direct investment into this region is less than 1 percent of all global investment flows with intraregional trade representing only 8 percent of all trade in the Middle
East region. They can't even do business with themselves.

A *Financial Times* article (February 3, 2000), "Arab Rulers with a New Agenda,"
wrote:

*". . . many of the young Arab leaders are trying to proceed with economic
reforms in an attempt to curb political reforms. Isn't this something the Soviet
Union tried and failed. There are a number of new and young leaders in the Arab
world; King Mohammad of Morocco (35 years old), King Abdullah of Jordan (39
years old), Bashar al Assad of Syria (35 years old) and Sheikh Hamad Bin Isa Al
Khalifa of Bahrain (48 years old), they are the new generation. After decades of
economic neglect they have their hands full. But how can economic reform work
without democratic reforms? The freedom of expression and thought is the basis
of any modern economy. Middle Eastern countries are centrally controlled and
"despite huge spending on education, schools and universities are churning out
young Arabs who can memorize texts but are not used to thinking freely. Youth
unemployment is adding to the level of joblessness, which averages 15 percent
across the region."*

So let us not confuse Islam with the real culprit for the September 11 catastrophe—
it is the rulers of the near and Middle Eastern countries. The Arab people will live in
squalor resenting the United States for supporting these evil dictators until democracy,
freedom of speech and expression for men and women, and promotion of an economic
environment that perpetuates a better standard of living are allowed. The time has come
for the West to go back to their post World War II and post Soviet policies that helped
build democratic governments. Just look at Central and Eastern Europe, the Asian continent, and Latin America and see what they have accomplished as they have moved away
from dictatorships to democracies, from socialism to capitalism. Economically desperate
people do desperate things. The time has come to bring the near and Middle East into the
modern global economy, but let's start with political reform.

INDEX